Freedom of Speech and Information in Global Perspective

Pekka Hallberg • Janne Virkkunen

Freedom of Speech and Information in Global Perspective

palgrave
macmillan

Pekka Hallberg
Rule of Law Finland—Rolfi
Helsinki, Finland

Janne Virkkunen
Helsinki, Finland

ISBN 978-1-349-94989-2   ISBN 978-1-349-94990-8 (eBook)
DOI 10.1057/978-1-349-94990-8

Library of Congress Control Number: 2016960703

© The Editor(s) (if applicable) and The Author(s) 2017
This work is subject to copyright. All rights are solely and exclusively licensed by the Publisher, whether the whole or part of the material is concerned, specifically the rights of translation, reprinting, reuse of illustrations, recitation, broadcasting, reproduction on microfilms or in any other physical way, and transmission or information storage and retrieval, electronic adaptation, computer software, or by similar or dissimilar methodology now known or hereafter developed.
The use of general descriptive names, registered names, trademarks, service marks, etc. in this publication does not imply, even in the absence of a specific statement, that such names are exempt from the relevant protective laws and regulations and therefore free for general use.
The publisher, the authors and the editors are safe to assume that the advice and information in this book are believed to be true and accurate at the date of publication. Neither the publisher nor the authors or the editors give a warranty, express or implied, with respect to the material contained herein or for any errors or omissions that may have been made. The publisher remains neutral with regard to jurisdictional claims in published maps and institutional affiliations.

Cover design by Samantha Johnson

Printed on acid-free paper

This Palgrave Macmillan imprint is published by Springer Nature
The registered company is Nature America Inc.
The registered company address is: 1 New York Plaza, New York NY 10004, U.S.A.

Preface

In January 2015 "*Je suis Charlie* – I am Charlie" became the catchphrase for freedom of speech after eleven reporters and a police officer were killed in a terrorist attack on the office of *Charlie Hebdo* magazine. Over a million people participated in the march in Paris after the attack. Side by side walked heads of states even from places where freedom of speech is merely a utopia, constantly compromised. As the demonstrations become yesterday's news, what is to become of freedom of speech? In the future, how possible will it be for people to express themselves and access the accuracy of information? How do we make out our conception of the world in this abundance of information?

Freedom of speech usually refers to the right of every person to not only express but also to receive information without interference. In this way freedom of speech becomes a foundation for constructing a free society and a common welfare. Alongside these conceptions the status of social development is reflected in the fulfilment of freedom of speech principles, its guarantees and infringements.

What is the status of the concomitant to freedom of speech, the right to access information? In the constant winds of change fragmented information flow can make it difficult to access accurate information and form a conception of the big picture. Truth and objectivity are always the first victims in the information war. The mass demonstrations of the Arab Spring of 2011 grew with the help of social media and at first actually led to the fall of a few dictators. The new rulers set high hopes but the follow-up was still elusive. How mass movements can be properly channelled towards permanent reform remains to be seen. The same question is now also asked in Ukraine: how are the citizens to make out the accurate conception of the world from the quivering pile of information jelly, when Russia is feeding them Russian news about the chain of events and, most importantly, of the interests that lie beneath?

It is important to understand history in order to assess the future. The ideology of freedom of speech is the result of long historical development, the roots of which can be found back in antiquity and even further. However, the more specific groundwork only gained strength as late as the eighteenth century, during the Enlightenment period in Europe. The Free Press Act, ratified at Sweden's Assembly of the Estates in Stockholm in 1766, was the first breakthrough for freedom of speech. It is here that the judicial development of the principles of freedom of press and freedom of information began, making Nordic countries the top performers in the world when measuring social openness.

Nowadays freedom of speech is known as a fundamental right both in the constitutions of most countries and in several international treaties. Among the most important are the United Nations (UN) Universal Declaration of Human Rights dating from 1948, the International Covenant on Civil and Political Rights from 1966 and the European Convention on Human Rights from 1952. In this conception freedom of speech is a unitary, universal ideal. It has been defended as a leading principle of democracy and social development. But the other side of the coin is how these judicial values have been fulfilled. What is the reality of freedom of speech?

International monitoring systems, especially the annual Press Freedom Index (which ranks 179 countries), open up a worldwide perspective on freedom of speech. Many international organisations, for example the International Press Institute (IPI), are also observing such trends with concern. Criminal laws and the risk of penalty, the despotism of central governments, widespread corruption, withholding of information and pressure stemming from the power of money obstruct communication and journalists' work in many countries.

Freedom of speech is always linked with duties and responsibilities; it will not function in a vacuum. This side is often forgotten. The language of print and pictures always has an impact, and thus also has consequences. Freedom of speech has its boundaries. It is not meant for assaulting, provoking hate speech or as a tool for criminal activity. Thus, when using one's right to free speech as a societal fundamental right, and this goes for social media too, responsibility and sense of balance are required.

According to international treaties, however, freedom of speech can be restricted only when necessary in a democratic society. This is another concept that emphasises freedom of speech as a fundamental political right and foundation for democratic development. Yet the world is still full of gross violations of freedom of speech that infringe the very principles that were forged together.

The crudest violations of freedom of speech—liquidation of journalists and activists, undue arrests and censorship, prevention of demonstrations, blocking of communication channels and manipulation through ownership accumulation—are common examples of sensational episodes that catch the public eye. Data from 2015 tell a grim story of the dozens of reporters that have been murdered, the more than one hundred that are missing. The mood of the communication media environment is getting tense.

The world of communication media is going through an enormous change, comparable to Gutenberg's invention of the printing press. Modern technology and digitalisation have completely changed the media environment. With modern technology, anyone can become a distributor.

The digital age offers its users an abundance of possibilities to provide people with information and search for original sources. The internet user is like a shopper at a bazaar—the multitude of products is confusing, but for an experienced customer it is a magnificent world. Does the digital world mean greater freedom? Or will it bring about more surveillance? Are there limits to communication media, information leaks, surveillance systems and source confidentiality? And who establishes these limits?

Freedom of speech may change its form, but arguments for freedom of speech remain the same, even in the new age. The American Frederick Douglass, born a plantation slave and later to become an anti-slavery activist, wrote in 1860:

> Liberty is meaningless where the right to utter one's thoughts and opinions has ceased to exist. That, of all rights, is the dread of tyrants. It is the right which they first of all strike down. They know its power. Equally clear is the right to hear. To suppress free speech is a double wrong. It violates the rights of the hearer as well as those of the speaker.[1]

In this book we reflect on freedom of speech, civil society and rule-of-law development as solid foundations of a democratic society. If even one pillar collapses, people are not free in their actions. The book describes the evolution of freedom of speech, but concentrates on the significance of information in an environment that is constantly being reshaped by new technology. Traditional communication media is going through a radical transformation.

In a scientific sense it is increasingly important to reflect on those interests that underlie restrictions on freedom of speech, or which justify the very reason freedom of speech must be protected. This leads us to contemplate the central questions of our social environment: the tensions between freedom of the individual and the system; preconditions for access to information and participation; the legitimacy of public power; and tackling corruption and building general trust, or social capital. Thus in this book we will analyse freedom of speech from several perspectives, looking for a cross-disciplinary vision, the long arc of freedom of speech development.

Why have we embarked on this worldwide writing project from Finland, known as a safe haven for freedom of speech? There are many reasons, one of which being that the first free speech Act started here, from a motion proposed by Riksdag's (Estates) member Anders Chydenius in the eastern half of Sweden. Another reason is Finland's top ranking in the Press Freedom Index, and its position as one of the least corrupt countries in the world. Against the background of these accomplishments we can find the historical principles of transparent governance.

These records do not mean that the Nordic countries could pose as an example, or that we could deal out instructions to other countries. On the contrary, for small countries it is especially important to pay close attention to signs of developments in freedom of speech, and try to adapt to tightening competition in the global market in order to preserve the preconditions for the welfare state.

For this book we have sought and received the valuable comments of many internationally renowned judges, researchers and journalists. There is a list of these experts in the acknowledgements section of this book. These influential actors from different fields of society—Justice of the US Supreme Court Sandra Day O'Connor and the Emeritus President of the European Court of Human Rights Jean-Paul Costa, as well as the world renowned reporters, Steven Ellis, who reports on Russia, Claude E. Erbsen of the USA, from South Africa Raymond Louw and from Great Britain Peter Preston, along with leading experts from Finland, late Ambassador Ilkka Heiskanen, Professor Paavo Hohti, Former Advocate General of the Court of Justice of the European Union and Member of the Supreme Administrative Court of Finland, Dr. Niilo Jääskinen, former

Assistant Director of the city of Helsinki Dr. Pekka Korpinen, Member of the Supreme Administrative Court and former Judge of the European Court of Human Rights Dr. Matti Pellonpää, Ambassador Mikko Pyhälä and Minister Counsellor Ingmar Ström—have recounted their own experiences and helped our book to cover the meaning of freedom of speech in a truly global sense. They have opened windows onto the development of their own countries, and helped us to understand the meaning of freedom of speech generally as a basis for social development. Additionally, we have chosen some relevant statements from the internet. We would like to extend our profound thanks to all our associates in this project.

This book is closely associated with the work of the Rule of Law Finland (ROLFI) research unit, which has in the recent years been funded by the Jenny and Antti Wihuri Foundation, to which we would like to express our gratitude. We especially thank the assistant editor of our book, Sanna Leisti, MA (international relations), the office manager of ROLFI, who has compiled reports of her observations on the internet. Petra Jääskeläinen, MA (social sciences), whose comments were a great help, also joined us as a research assistant during the final phase. David Scott, MA (international law and legal studies) worked as a critical reader. His contribution was also valuable.

Finally we would like to thank Sanoma Company, the leading Finnish media company, for the financial support that enabled the publication of this research. For printing we thank the Palgrave Macmillan publishing company and international politics editor Sara Doskow, whose comments during our conversations and the review work have contributed to our final writing phase.

Writing about freedom of speech will not offer permanent solutions or universally applicable opinions in our quickly changing environment. Our objective is to strengthen the concepts of guarantees and infringements of free speech as well as the significance of the free transmission of information, and to this end we have compiled material from all over the world.

Finally it is important to remember that even freedom of speech is only a tool for everyone to, where possible, access the accuracy of information and try to create a perception of what kind of a world we live in. The actual objectives will be found in the development of social and human welfare, the preconditions for a good life. This is what we wish to promote.

The freedom to make a statement and to think, to speak and write, and to announce one's case in public, must never lose its meaning. The freedom to live rests on these freedoms. The author Salman Rushdie has expressed this as follows: "Free speech is everything, the whole ball game. Free speech is life itself."[2] Helsinki, June 2016.

Notes

1. A Plea for Free Speech in Boston 1860 by Frederick Douglass, available at http://www.thisnation.com/library/douglassplea.html, accessed 28 August 2016.
2. Available at https://www.nytimes.com/books/99/04/18/specials/rushdie-address.html, accessed 28 August 2016.

Rule of Law Finland—Rolfi   Pekka Hallberg
Helsinki, Finland

Helsinki, Finland   Janne Virkkunen

Acknowledgements

The following experts, at our request, sent their previously unpublished comments for our book.

Costa, Jean-Paul (Chap. 6), Emeritus President of the European Court of Human Rights, President of the International Institute of Human rights.

Ellis, Steven (Chap. 5), IPI Director of Advocacy and Communication, reported the prospects in Russia.

Erbsen, Claude E. (Chap. 5), Vice president and director, World Services, The Associated Press (retired).

Heiskanen, Ilkka (Chap. 5), late former Finnish Ambassador to Chile.

Hohti, Paavo (Chaps. 4 and 7), Professor, expert on ancient literature.

Jääskinen, Niilo, Dr. (Chap. 6), Former Advocate General of the Court of Justice of the European Union and Member of the Supreme Administrative Court of Finland.

Korpinen, Pekka, Dr. (Chaps. 4 and 5), former Assistant Director of the city of Helsinki, published a book on Berlusconi's Italy.

Louw, Raymond (Chap. 5), Deputy Chairperson of the Media Institute of Southern Africa (MISA).

O´Connor, Sandra Day (Chap. 5), Justice of the US Supreme Court, served on the board of trustees of the National Constitution Center in Philadelphia, Pennsylvania.

Pellonpää, Matti, Dr. (Chap. 6), Member of the Supreme Administrative Court of Finland, former Judge of the European Court of Human Rights.

Preston, Peter (Chap. 5), British journalist and author, former Editor of the *Guardian*, Chairman of the International Press Institute 1995–1997.

Pyhälä, Mikko (Chap. 7), former Finnish Ambassador to Venezuela and East Caribbean region.

Ström, Ingmar (Chaps. 3 and 5), Minister Counsellor, who has worked in Finnish embassies in China and South America.

We would like once more to offer our sincerest appreciation for their important comments.[1]

Note

1. The comments by the experts listed here were specifically written for this book, have not been edited and are published with their permission by Palgrave Macmillan.

CONTENTS

1 Introduction and Overview 1

2 First Notes 9

3 The State of Freedom of Speech in the World 15
The criteria of the Reporters Without Borders' annual index 18
Developments in Some Countries 27
Dark Clouds Over the Flow of Information 31
Free Speech—In the Core of Judicial Development 39
How to Monitor Development? 53

4 From the Origins of Freedom of Speech to the Modern Information Society 61
First Steps Towards Free Speech in the Ancient World 61
The Idea of Free Speech during the Age of European Enlightenment 65
The First Freedom of the Press Act 67
Free Speech as a Fundamental and Human Right 71
In Search of the Reality of Free Speech 74

5 Freedom of Speech in Books and in Action 79
Development of Freedom of Speech in Finland 79
Free Speech in Other Nordic Countries 83
Foundations of Free Speech elsewhere in Europe 86

xiii

No Free Speech in Russia?	102
How is Freedom of Speech in North America?	109
Is Free Speech a Utopian Idea in Latin America?	118
Searching for Freedom of Speech on the African Continent	125
Freedom of Speech Under Pressure by the Asian Great Powers	133
Along the Silk Road in Central Asia	141
Light and Shadows in the Southeast Asian Countries	145
Australia, the Final Destination of our World Tour	150
Theory and Reality	151

6 **Human Rights Obligations: From Ideas to Reality?** 159
The European Convention on Human Rights (ECHR) 159
How Does the European Union (EU) Protect Freedom of Speech? 172
Freedom of Speech in the United Nations (UN) Treaties 178
Freedom of Speech and Other Organisations for International Co-operation 184

7 **Violations and Threat Scenarios** 191
Extremes—Terrorism and Oppression of Media 191
Different Ways to Restrict Media 195
The Conflict Between Security Interests and Privacy of Free Information 202
Corruption Destroys Trust and Free Speech 207
New Dark Clouds Rising 211

8 **Freedom of Speech in the Turbulence of the Changing World** 223
Globalisation 223
Digital Era and Social Media Shaping the World 234
The Arab Spring—Disruption or Development in Egypt? 240
Challenges of Rule of Law in the Digital Era 246
The Role of Media in a Radically Changing Environment 250

9	**Final Chords**	255
	On a Path Towards Freedom or Restrictions?	255
	For Freedom of Speech!	257
	Images and Imaginings	258

Rule of Law Finland—Rolfi   263

Bibliography   265

Index   283

List of Figures

Fig. 3.1	World map categorising countries according to their level of freedom of speech	17
Fig. 3.2	List of top 10 countries and bottom 10 countries	27
Fig. 3.3	Freedom of speech and society	40
Fig. 3.4	Rule of law on the basis of four variables	42
Fig. 3.5	Regulatory system quality and policy	43
Fig. 3.6	Organs of the state: Separation of powers	46
Fig. 3.7	Status of the people	48
Fig. 3.8	Functioning of the rule of law	49
Fig. 3.9	Durability of the rule of law	50
Fig. 7.1	Transparency International Corruption Perceptions Index 2015	208

List of Tables

Table 3.1	Reporters Without Borders World Press Freedom Index, 2015	19
Table 3.2	Comparison of country ranking based on the 2015 freedom of speech indices of Freedom House (FH) and Reporters Without Borders (RSF)	24
Table 3.3	Reporters Without Borders indices for selected countries, 2002–2015	25
Table 7.1	Corruption perceptions index criteria	210
Table 8.1	Top 25 countries ranked by smartphone users, 2013–2018 (Millions)	239

CHAPTER 1

Introduction and Overview

Exploring Freedom of Speech The theme of the book is an intriguing exploration of the core of societal development. The principle of freedom of speech means the right to express, publish and receive information, opinions and other communication without interference from any source. The purpose of freedom of speech is to guarantee the preconditions for societal development—freedom of opinion, open public discussion, free development of mass media and pluralism, and the opportunity to publicly criticise the powers that be. Thus, freedom of speech sustains societal freedom of action, and is a right that belongs to everyone.

A wider concept often used alongside freedom of speech is that of freedom of expression. In addition to describing the meaning of freedom of speech, this principle generally protects forms of creative action and self-expression. Freedom of expression and freedom of information are complementary—hence the main title of this book! Freedom of speech is thus both multifaceted and interactive. The two freedoms can be seen as two sides of a coin, so closely intertwined that one (freedom of information) is a counterpart of the other (freedom of expression).

As a point of departure, freedom of speech is broadly understood as a fundamental principle that is reflected in the development of entire societies. Freedom of expression and transparency are both essential aspects of a healthy democracy. Freedom of expression can be defined as the liberty to express opinions, regardless of their truth or falsity, and transparency as the enforceable right of access to documented facts. Be that as it may, true information is often lacking. Francis Bacon's (1561–1626) famous phrase "knowledge itself is power"[1] aptly describes both the battle between correct and false information and the market competition of today's information jungle.

How Can We Research Freedom of Speech? The execution of this research project has involved the combination of different scholarships: historical research; a new perspective on the various stages of development of freedom of speech; use of modern indicators to analyse the reality of freedom of speech in the world under different legal regimes; an evaluation of the obligations of international treaties; and consideration of the effects on media of the globalising and digitalising environment. The purpose of the book is to depict the development of freedom of speech as a long arc stretching from early settings of the right to speak in ancient times and evolving into modern freedom of speech guaranteed by fundamental and human rights, its future in the haze of the digitalised world yet to be predicted.

Freedom of speech is inextricably linked with the premises of the rule of law and democracy. Thus the research methods and materials of legal and political sciences are central to the development, substance and significance of freedom of speech research. A German proverb pithily expresses the link between these principles: "Where power is right, justice has no power." Thus, justice that is subservient to power is not strong. In the same vein, shackling free speech hinders the development of a free society. This is why one of the central themes of the book is that the fulfilment of and threats to the right to freedom of speech are associated with the general development of the rule of law.

Freedom of Speech as an Element of Rule of Law Development The origin of the principle of freedom of speech is associated with the consolidation of the principle of the rule of law and the formation of the liberal state. In Europe this happened mainly during the eighteenth-century Age of Enlightenment, although we can trace the historical roots of freedom of speech to a much earlier age. The strengthening of the democratic state ruled by law has clarified the nature of freedom of speech as a basic political right. The same applies to access to information, as well as to free elections and the freedom to participate in them. On the other hand, in a social context free speech is associated with more everyday matters: freedom of opinion, creativity, social environment and the importance of mental well-being.

The book analyses legality and principles of the rule of law, the separation of powers and the relationships between institutions, guarantees of fundamental rights and obligations of the people, and the prospects for the development of legal systems in relation to the realisation of the right to freedom of speech. This broad view of freedom of speech as an element of societal development provides the opportunity to analyse both legal guarantees securing freedom of speech and the violations and threats it faces. The book also looks at the development of contemporary indicators, analyses their usefulness and looks at how we can measure the future of freedom of speech.

The Present State of Freedom of Speech Based on Indicators One of the most important chapters of the book, Chap. 5, looks at freedom of speech in theory and in action. The present state of freedom of speech in different countries is comprehensively covered. Many organisations produce classifications of freedom of speech. The most well known are Freedom House in the USA and Reporters without Borders, which originated in France. The International Press Institute (IPI), based in Vienna, Austria, is also an important organisation. Other prominent organisations engaged in the valuable work of promoting free speech are the Committee to Protect Journalists (CPJ), the Commonwealth Press Union (CPU), the Inter American Press Association (IAPA), the World Association of Newspapers (WAN) and the World Press Freedom Committee (WPFC). Different indicators and comparative materials make it possible for us to evaluate the state of freedom of speech across the world. In many countries, however, dark clouds are overshadowing development. The fact that freedom of speech is a right enjoyed only by a small minority of the world's population puts a strain on idealism. Of the 7.2 billion people in the world, less than a billion live in societies where the right to free speech is, at least to some extent, a reality. Even though the chapter describing national legal cultures, 'Law in Theory and in Action' is mostly descriptive, we hope that, taking into account the numerous comments of renowned experts that are included, it provides a diversified picture of development. These comments include not only legal reviews but also more general observations by leading journalists on the development prospects for freedom of speech. The idea of asking for actual comments was to initiate a kind of a contemporary expert dialogue.

Legal Guarantees of Freedom of Speech? Next we analyse legal guarantees of the freedom of speech from these realistic starting points. Nowadays, as a result of historical developments, most countries' constitutions protect freedom of speech as a fundamental right. Free speech as a universal principle is an integral part of international human rights treaties, the first of which was the United Nations Declaration of Human Rights of 1948. Consequently, legal regulations, national fundamental rights and human rights treaties are essential studies for scholars concerned with the content and guarantees of freedom of speech.

Human Rights Obligations Freedom of expression is recognised as a human right in international and regional treaties and human rights laws. On the international level this human right is enshrined in Article 19 of the International Covenant on Civil and Political Rights (ICCPR), Article 19 of the Universal Declaration of Human Rights, Article 13 of the American Convention on Human Rights, Article 9 of the African Charter on Human and People's Rights and, of course, in Article 10 of the European Convention on Human Rights (ECHR)—one of the most widely cited and used sources of human rights law.

The ECHR is generally regarded as the most efficient international human rights monitoring system, as it allows for individual applications as well as states with complaints against each other. The European Court of Human Rights (ECtHR) provides legal opinions on judicial questions. In practice, private appeals are the most important monitoring mechanism. Therefore it has been necessary to analyse how freedom of speech has developed, especially as regards the decisions and interpretations of the ECtHR. In this respect the authors have had the advantage of a number of analytical articles as contributions to this book from leading judges of the ECtHR and the European Union (EU).

Meanwhile, it has been apparent that, apart from those of the ECHR, human rights obligations do not include any binding monitoring mechanism, although advisory opinions associated with abiding by the treaties do affect practice. Thus the decisions of the Human Rights Committee that monitors adherence to the ICCPR differs from the legally binding decisions of the ECtHR. The Optional Protocol of the ICCPR does not include any notion that the decisions of the Committee are binding. In practice, this has meant that the Committee usually contemplates, in a free format, the different ways in which violations may be compensated. These decisions, however, do have a general influence as statements of an expert body on how the Protocol should be interpreted.

Can Freedom of Speech Development Be Controlled? Based on the material and conclusions presented in the book, we can say that, at international level, as yet no tools are sufficiently effective to ensure the fulfilment of the right to freedom of speech or to act on violations. Therefore the focus of legal guarantees of freedom of speech is clearly on the national level, relying on the government systems of nation states. Meanwhile, societal and cultural differences lead to differences in the realisation of freedom of speech and information. Despite the differences, the cosmopolitan models of a homogeneous world order or "global government" are, in our opinion, utopia. This does not eliminate the need to strengthen international cooperation, to look for common rule-of-law principles and guarantees of the realisation of freedom of speech. Therefore, this book also seeks to promote international dialogue in favour of freedom of speech and flames of resistance against violations of freedom of speech and undemocratic restrictions.

What Are the Safeguards of Freedom of Speech on the National Level? Our tour around the world takes us to many nations and continents. The objective is to find out how freedom of speech is guaranteed in the constitutions and other legislative provisions of different countries. The regulatory practices concerning freedom of speech and the criteria for restricting it are especially interesting. The book also includes compilations of recent events and online commentaries on attitudes towards freedom of speech and its development.

The journey begins in the Nordic countries, where it is evident that freedom of speech includes the right both to express and to receive forms of communication. Historically, the Swedish Freedom of the Press Act of 1766 was the world's first freedom of information legislation. This historically significant breakthrough was followed by Denmark and Norway in 1770, the declaration of human rights adopted in the spirit of the French revolution of 1789 and the often quoted US Constitution's First Amendment from 1791. It is worth noting that it was nearly 200 more years before the first Act bearing upon the access to information, the Freedom of Information Act 1966, was adopted in the USA.

The journey continues to other countries of Europe, Russia, both continents of America, then to Africa and Asia as well as finally to Australia. It is essential to clarify the substance of constitutions in the chosen destination countries as well as other regulations concerning freedom of speech in their cultural and societal context. Freedom of speech does not exist in a vacuum: there is always a question of the social environment too. What we are looking for here is a connection to sociological research, because so-called social capital, or societal trust capital, is key to the fulfilment of the right to freedom of speech.

Social capital is considered both an important condition for economic growth and a stabiliser of liberal democracy. The importance of social capital and its increase has been discussed as a second-generation model of economic reform. At the same time, the rule of law and freedom of speech, its fundamental elements, are considered in a social context. This forms one of the most important methodological innovations of the book as we try to combine the traditions of legal and political science with sociological analysis, aiming not only at a broader vision of the operation of civil society but also at the big picture of the future development of freedom of speech in the digitalising environment.

As regards the future, the information market and the struggle for information will be at the heart of development. In this respect an interesting observation is that it was only during the last century that the expression 'freedom of information'—considered rather imprecise and unhelpful—entered into use. The expression, in general, conveys that there is a right to access information, notably government information, and that this is freely available rather than closely restricted. This side of freedom of speech, the transparency of the use of power and everybody's right to access information, has progressed slowly.

Violations and Threat Scenarios? From the reader's point of view, one of the most interesting chapters in our book (Chap. 7) is perhaps the overview of violations of freedom of speech and threat scenarios. Among recent acts of terror, it is probably the crude and bloody terrorist attack on the office of the French magazine *Charlie Hebdo* on 7 January 2015 that has gathered most attention. One of the most current analyses discusses the Arab Spring, especially recent events in Egypt. Changes of leader, widespread demonstrations, five elections and constitutional reforms have still not been enough to calm this Northern African nation where tanks still appear on the streets every now and then. For now, we can only speculate on what direction future development will take.

One of the examples of particular interest to researchers comes from Asia. Events in Hong Kong in early July 2014 remind us of the tough everyday life of media in another, maybe more traditional way. We have also included in Chap. 7 case categories of threat scenarios collected by the International Press Institute (IPI). This categorisation indicates how many different categories of violations there are in practice.

New dark clouds are rising, for example in Venezuela and Turkey, where the governments have attempted in different ways to intervene in communication channels and close down Twitter and Facebook. In Hungary the Prime Minister and his party have used their parliamentary supermajority to pass numerous mutually reinforcing laws tightening government control over broadcast media and extending regulation to print and online media.

What if limitations on freedom of speech are a follow-up to the continuing struggle for power, the aspiration of government powers to restrict the flow of information? Or are market forces behind the manipulation of information? In these situations an individual citizen is quite powerless. Information that the United States and British intelligence services had stolen keys from the biggest manufacturer of sim cards, the Gemalto Company, was a shocking example of how things work in our digital era. At worst, this may have led to around 450 big operators and 1.5 billion people's mobile phones coming under official surveillance.

Challenges in the Digital Era? This is just one aspect of the new threats to freedom of speech. Our modern high-tech society is vulnerable in other ways, for example when we consider malfunctions and risks of accidents concerning data traffic, urban technologies and food supply. Even though modern risk analysis is used as a basis for large-scale strategic decisions, preparing for violations and malfunctions is difficult. Therefore we should be asking 'how' rather than 'what' to prepare for. Can a citizen in any way prepare for these types of threat, when governments are crossing the line? These questions also concern development of the rule of law.

The development and societal significance of freedom of speech is best explored from many different angles. It is important to look out for tensions between the ideas of free speech and flow of information, and the restrictions, threats and constraints imposed on them. Through the ages, there have been cross-violations of freedom of speech, suppression of the right to opinion, censorship and misrepresentations. However, freedom of speech always entails duties and responsibilities, too. As the British proverb says, "the pen is mightier than the sword". This universal wisdom is expressed in the Philippines as "slander stings more than lashes".

Freedom of Speech and Information in Global Perspective—*Quo Vadis?* The path of freedom of speech from the ancient to the modern information society was lit in the beginning by the torches of the right to speak; then came the invention of the free press, the burning of piles of books, and in the modern day, the enormous possibilities of free information and managing it in the digital world. The traveller, seeing on his path the eternal contest between light and shadows may well be perplexed at the reality of societal development.

Therefore freedom of speech is of great significance not only to its beneficiaries but also indirectly to the atmosphere of society in general. Although at times we have problems understanding the different social conditions and hierarchical structures related to different cultures, we should look for a common perspective when it comes to communication between people, information exchange and hence the development of free speech in today's globalising world. "*Quo vadis?*" We must not lose hope!

Note

1. The now-famous equation, "knowledge is power" (*scientia potestas est*), was coined by Francis Bacon in 1597. Since then it has been rephrased in a wide variety of contexts from Thomas Hobbes to Michel Foucault. In recent years, this elusive topos has in fact proved essential to the poststructuralist critique of the humanist subject. See José Maria Rodriguez Garcia, Scientia Potestas Est – Knowledge is Power: Francis Bacon to Michel Foucoult, *Neohelicon* 2001:28 p. 109.

CHAPTER 2

First Notes

Starting Points The exploration of freedom of speech opens a window on the development of democracy, the economy and well-being in the world. Technological development, from Gutenberg's 1436 invention of the printing press to modern real-time communication through the internet, provides a brand new framework for freedom of speech—a dialogue between freedom and surveillance. Attempts to obstruct social media channels such as Twitter and Facebook are a reality in many countries.

In our review of the development and significance of freedom of speech, we draw on internet references to current news, providing the reader with links to supplementary reading and the opportunity of forming their own opinions. The book also includes specially commissioned statements by leading judges, researchers and journalists, which form the type of contemporary expert dialogue by qualified professionals that has in recent years been a particular feature of works of political science. There is also a bibliography of our main sources at the end of the book.

History Provides Perspective The quest for the source of the modern concept of freedom of speech has generally led to the eighteenth-century Age of Enlightenment on the European continent. One of the most famous maxims is attributed to Voltaire: "I disapprove of what you say, but I will defend to the death your right to say it".[1] However, the roots of freedom of speech go deeper historically and spread wider geographically.

Even in Europe, the idea of free speech stems from much earlier times: we must look as far back as Ancient Greek and Roman models of society.

A glance at history is essential for the understanding of the development of freedom of speech; it must be kept in mind, however, that circumstances were different then. The original ideal of the ancient Greek city-states was a relatively small-scale society in which the citizens—in practice, however, only the free men—could take part in common decision making. According to Plato, city-states of 5040 inhabitants were best suited for "social contracts and co-operation, and all sorts of divisions".[2]

In the Roman Empire freedom of speech steadily gained more significance as a tool for political participation and representative democracy, expressed in the concepts of *Libertas* and *Res Publica*. The concentration of power in state and Church gradually led to the emergence of ways of obstructing criticism and the spread of information that was deemed awkward or unpleasant by the powers that be. Examples from history include book burning by the Church, the condemnation of dissidents, and Galileo Galilei, who changed the then existing worldview and died as a martyr.

In the long run of history, Magna Carta of 1215 must not be forgotten. Eight hundred years have passed since the signing of this important document. In Magna Carta the feudal barons of England forced King John to agree, in writing, to accept limitations of his power over them, establishing the principle that the king was not above the law. Later on, this document paved the way for the first steps towards the common man gaining a partial voice in a legislative parliament. But this was not yet real freedom of speech.

Breakthrough of the Idea of Freedom of Speech The Enlightenment philosophers were the counterforce to censorship in eighteenth-century Europe. Freedom of opinion was, for them, at the forefront of liberal development. The first legal regulation that tackled censorship, the Freedom of the Press Act adopted in Stockholm in 1766, dates from this historical climate. It incorporated both access to information and freedom to express one's opinion in a single article: "(e)very Swedish citizen shall be entitled to have free access to official documents, in order to encourage the free exchange of opinion and the availability of comprehensive information".[3]

Can Free Speech Be Protected by Law? Normative examination *de jure* is insufficient. Justice is not merely about the law but also about the quest for reality, the "norm in action". The realisation of freedom of speech is dependent upon *de facto* access to information and the limitations thereof—the actual state of the society. Crucial aspects include people's need for information, their level of education, the functioning of the authorities, court cases, power structures, international principles and recommendations, violations of freedom of speech, and the manipulation and oversight of the flow of information. From a wider perspective, we may juxtapose individual rights and liberties with the prevalent informational values and infrastructure in a society.

True Reality of Free Speech? The World Press Freedom Index is an indicator of the worldwide condition of free speech, and positions countries and continents on a freedom of speech scale. It is produced by Reporters Without Borders, who promote and defend the freedom to be informed and to inform others throughout the world. Based in Paris, the organisation has ten international offices and more than 150 correspondents in all five continents. Through its wide network, it looks for factors that explain changes to the state of freedom of expression, and it has consultant status at both the United Nations and UNESCO.

The Press Freedom Index does not take a stand in favour of any kind of political system, but it is clear that democracies provide better protection for the freedom to produce and circulate accurate news and information than countries where human rights are flouted. The freedom to produce and circulate news and information needs to be evaluated at the global as well as the national level.[4]

Significance of Free Speech to Societal Development? There are many different ways of evaluating societal development globally, including transparency in governance, electoral freedom, fulfilment of human rights obligations and levels of corruption. One of the best-known research institutes in this field is Freedom House, which has ten offices and conducts programmes in over two dozen countries in all regions of the world. Freedom House's latest research publication, *Freedom on the Net* (2013), examines development in 60 countries. When revelations made by former National Security Agency subcontractor Edward Snowden about the US government's secret surveillance activities took centre stage in the international media in June 2013, 34 of the 60 countries assessed had experienced a negative development trajectory since May 2012.

Multiple journals and internet sites promote freedom of expression, internationally as well as nationally, and several organisations campaign for their rights to freedom of expression. Freedom of expression has a pre-eminent role to play in the fight against corruption in countries all over the world.

The World Bank set out its guidelines in the 2006 World Bank Governance and Anti-corruption Strategy. It explores the need to expand the supply and demand side of governance by further strengthening transparency and accountability mechanisms. The guidelines support access to information laws and highlight the media as its centrepiece. The NGO *Transparency International,* which campaigns for greater transparency on a global level, believes, just like the World Bank, in the mechanism of freedom of information as a way of reducing poverty. Transparency International believes that an open information environment is necessary for building skills among journalists and other stakeholders to foster effective coverage of transparency and governance issues. Positioning these issues on the public agenda can reduce poverty.

Because freedom of speech plays an essential role in all development, free speech must be considered in its societal context. Restricting ourselves to indices of freedom of speech is not enough. To construct a holistic picture, it is necessary to compile several current societal development monitoring systems. The aim is to create a more reliable snapshot of the state of freedom of speech than individual indices can produce. The purpose of this book is to present such a perspective.

Struggle For and Against Freedom of Speech The exploration of freedom of speech opens a window on the development of democracy, the economy and well-being in the world. The discussion should delve below the surface to provide an analysis of the interests for which free speech should be defended and those for which free speech is curtailed and the flow of information constrained.

Questions arise about freedom of speech not only as a safeguard against power but also with regard to the interests of political and economic power in restricting and controlling access to information. Has the importance of freedom of speech to societal development been sufficiently understood? Are narrow territorial disputes, power struggles between systems and politics, information wars between superpowers, the concentration of media house ownerships, technological development and digitalisation at the forefront of today's world?

Is the Role of Free Speech Changing? An investigation into the development of freedom of speech must first take into account processes of globalisation. It is often asked, cynically, why we should ponder the future when the past is so much more easily understood. The answer is that the world is no longer what it used to be.

Globalisation is not a new phenomenon, even if systematic research on the reasons and effects only intensified in the 1990s. The term is used in many ways, but the principal underlying idea of globalisation is the progressive integration of economies and societies. It is driven by new technologies, new economic relationships, and the national and international policies of a wide range of actors, including governments, international organisations, business, labour and civil society.

Technological development, from Gutenberg's 1436 invention of the printing press to modern real-time communication through the internet, provides free speech with a brand new framework—a dialogue between freedom and surveillance. Attempts to obstruct social media channels (Twitter and Facebook) are a reality in many countries.

Are There Any Answers? When examining the different dimensions of freedom of speech, we find ourselves facing fundamental questions: What opportunities are there to access information, to forward information and opinions, to influence and participate in the development of free societies? In other words, are there opportunities for participation in the structuring of collective well-being and a good life? Herein lies the idea of freedom of speech. How did we get here and what is going to happen in the future? We are on a quest to find out.

British author George Orwell (Eric Blair 1903–1950) became famous as the portrayer of those fears and emotions that controlled the Western world after the Second World War. His famous novel *Nineteen Eighty-Four* (1949) is a satire on the tendencies and methods of totalitarian countries, a prophecy of the future. The main character in the imaginary world of Oceania, Winston Smith, submits to the system to love Big Brother. Orwell predicted that the artificial Newspeak language of the closed Oceanian society would start becoming a reality in the first decades of the twenty-first century.

The book leads us to ask who or what is today's Big Brother. Is the surrendered Winston Smith still among us? We will return to his destiny later. Is there something to learn from the repressive Oceanian system? Could something similar happen in reality? Which way is the development of freedom of speech and society going? In this book also, we contemplate these questions and search for answers.

Notes

1. Voltaire, real name Francois-Marie Arouet (1694–1778), was a French author and Enlightenment philosopher. This famous maxim apparently dates from Evelyn Beatrice Hall in the year 1906.
2. Plato (427–347 BCE) mentions in his book *Laws*, believed to have been published around 350 BCE, that 5040 is a convenient number to use for dividing many things (including both the citizens and the land of a state) into lesser parts. He remarks that this number can be divided by all the (natural) numbers from 1 to 12 with the single exception of 11. See Plato, *Teokset VI* published in Finnish 1999 and *Laws*, at Project Gutenberg; retrieved 7 July 2009.
3. See Freedom of the Press Act of 1766 passed by the Swedish Riksdag (parliament) as "His Majesty's Gracious Ordinance Relating to Freedom of Writing and of the Press" [*Konglige Majestäts Nådige Förordning, Angående Skrif- och Tryck-friheten*]. Gifwen Stockholm i Råd-Cammaren then 2. Decembr, 1766.
4. For the RSF's methodology, see https://rsf.org/en/detailed-methodology, last accessed 27 May 2016.

CHAPTER 3

The State of Freedom of Speech in the World

Freedom of Speech Indices

Informative Rankings The map of the world colour-coded according to levels of freedom of speech and expression shows very few countries in the top category: only Finland, Sweden, Denmark, Iceland, Holland, Belgium, Luxemburg, Andorra and Switzerland. Depending on the criteria, Germany, Czech Republic, Slovakia, Canada and New Zealand also make the cut. Namibia is the only country representing the African continent.

The rankings vary somewhat according to author. But even if the criteria are slightly relaxed, the reality is that less than a billion of the world's 7.2 billion inhabitants, or 14 per cent according to a 2015 Freedom House estimate, live in countries where freedom of speech can even be mentioned. We have become used to thinking that free speech is a universal right. It is not, although our set of values might tell us otherwise. This will be discussed further in the section on human rights.

Many organisations produce classifications of freedom of speech. The most well-known are Freedom House in the USA and Reporters Without Borders, originating in France.

Freedom House (FH) was founded in 1941 and has dedicated itself to promoting free institutions worldwide. Its mission states: "Freedom is possible only in democratic political environments where governments are accountable to their own people; the rule of law prevails; and freedom

© The Author(s) 2017
P. Hallberg, J. Virkkunen, *Freedom of Speech and Information in Global Perspective*, DOI 10.1057/978-1-349-94990-8_3

of expression, association and belief as well as respect for the rights of minorities and women are guaranteed. Freedom ultimately depends on the actions of committed and courageous men and women. We support non-violent civic initiatives in societies where freedom is denied or under threat and promote the right of all people to be free."[1]

Reporters Without Borders (RSF) was founded by four journalists in France in 1985. It has since become a global organisation. RSF seeks to:

- continuously monitor attacks on freedom of information worldwide;
- denounce any such attacks in the media;
- act in co-operation with governments to fight censorship and laws aimed at restricting freedom of information;
- morally and financially assist persecuted journalists, as well as their families;
- offer material assistance to war correspondents in order to enhance their safety.

The International Press Institute (IPI), based in Vienna, Austria, is another organisation promoting freedom of speech. It was founded in New York in 1950 and its members include editors, leading journalists and media researchers from around the world. IPI defines itself as follows:

"The International Press Institute is a global network of editors, media executives and leading journalists. We are dedicated to the furtherance and safeguarding of press freedom, the protection of freedom of opinion and expression, the promotion of the free flow of news and information and the improvement of the practices of journalism."[2]

There are several other organisations engaged in the valuable work of promoting free speech in the world. The most prominent are the Committee to Protect Journalists (CPJ), the Commonwealth Press Union (CPU), the Inter American Press Association (IAPA), the World Association of Newspapers (WAN) and the World Press Freedom Committee (WPFC).

The purpose of these organisations is to protect freedom of the press wherever it is under threat and to defend citizens' right to information. This is a task that will never be completed. There will always be dictators and other political leaders who want to do away with freedom, because for them, governing is easier if the rights of the citizens are restricted.

Which way is development heading? In recent years there has been little progress, as more and more dark clouds have gathered over freedom of expression. Alison Bethel McKenzie, who stepped down from her post as Director of IPI at the end of 2014, wrote:

THE STATE OF FREEDOM OF SPEECH IN THE WORLD   17

But at no other time than the past two years have we seen such a disturbing decline in the principles of press freedom worldwide – from developing countries and new democracies, to the United States, where the right to freedom of speech and the press are enshrined in the Constitution's First Amendment.

For the moment, there appears to be no light at the end of the tunnel. Journalists continue to systematically lose their lives to conflict, militants, paid thugs, governments, drug dealers, corrupt politicians, unscrupulous security officers and others. Or they are viciously assaulted, tortured, terrorised, locked up after arbitraryarrests and unfair trials, monitored, harassed, intimidated and proverbially suffocated.[3].

McKenzie's bleak assessment is confirmed by the fact that close to 100 journalists were killed and more than 150 imprisoned in the line of duty in 2014. A world map of the state of freedom of speech has been compiled by Reporters Without Borders (RSF) (Fig. 3.1).

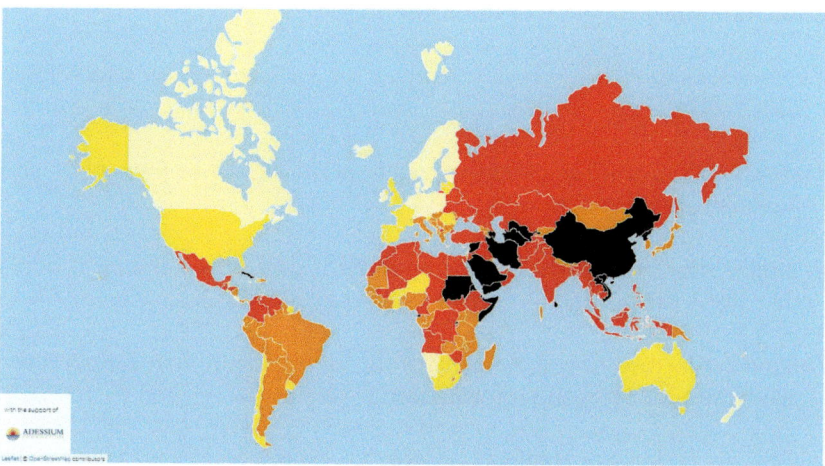

Fig. 3.1 World map categorising countries according to their level of freedom of speech (*Source*: © OpenStreetMap contributors, Reporters Without Borders, https://rsf.org/en/ranking/2015 . The black areas indicate a very serious situation for freedom of speech, red a difficult situation, orange noticeable problems, yellow a satisfactory situation and white good situation)

The sorry state of free speech in the world is clearly visible. The situation is good in only a few countries, mainly in Europe. Canada and New Zealand are also at the forefront. Placed 22nd on the index, South-west Africa's Namibia is the one positive exception on the African continent.

The criteria of the Reporters Without Borders' annual index

The countries are scored based on questions that consider six general criteria. Using a system of weighting for each possible response, countries are given a score between 0 and 100 for each of the six overall criteria. These scores are then used to calculate each country's final score.

Pluralism measures the degree to which opinions are represented in the media.

Media independence measures the degree to which the media are able to function independently of the authorities.

Environment and self-censorship analyses the environment in which journalists work.

Legislative framework analyses the quality of the legislative framework and measures its effectiveness.

Transparency measures the transparency of the institutions and procedures that affect the production of news and information.

Infrastructure measures the quality of the infrastructure that supports the production of news and information.

RSF also calculates the level of violence against journalists during the period considered, on a score of 0–100. The score is based on the monitoring carried out by RSF's own staff.

Table 3.1 ranks countries in order for 2015. After the country's name is an indication of whether its position has risen or fallen in relation to its score in 2014. The complete table including the scores (abuses score,

Table 3.1 Reporters Without Borders World Press Freedom Index, 2015

Rank 2015	Country	Diff. 2014 rank
1	Finland	0
2	Norway	+1
3	Denmark	+4
4	Netherlands	−2
5	Sweden	+5
6	New Zealand	+3
7	Austria	+5
8	Canada	+10
9	Jamaica	+8
10	Estonia	+1
11	Ireland	+5
12	Germany	+2
13	Czech Republic	0
14	Slovakia	+6
15	Belgium	+8
16	Costa Rica	+5
17	Namibia	+5
18	Poland	+1
19	Luxembourg	−15
20	Switzerland	−5
21	Iceland	−13
22	Ghana	+5
23	Uruguay	+3
24	Cyprus	+1
25	Australia	+3
26	Portugal	+4
27	Liechtenstein	−21
28	Latvia	+9
29	Suriname	+2
30	Belize	−1
31	Lithuania	+1
32	Andorra	−27
33	Spain	+2
34	United Kingdom	−1
35	Slovenia	−1
36	Cape Verde	−12
37	Eastern Caribbean	−1
38	France	+1
39	South Africa	+3
40	Samoa	0

(*continued*)

Table 3.1 (continued)

Rank 2015	Country	Diff. 2014 rank
41	Trinidad and Tobago	+2
42	Botswana	−1
43	Chile	+15
44	Tonga	+19
45	El Salvador	−7
46	Burkina Faso	+6
47	Niger	+1
48	Malta	+3
49	United States	−3
50	Comoros	+3
51	Taiwan	−1
52	Romania	−7
53	Haiti	−6
54	Mongolia	+34
55	Mauritania	+5
56	Papua New Guinea	−12
57	Argentina	−2
58	Croatia	+7
59	Malawi	+14
60	Republic of Korea	−3
61	Japan	−2
62	Guyana	+5
63	Dominican Republic	+5
64	Madagascar	+17
65	Hungary	−1
66	Bosnia and Herzegovina	0
67	Serbia	−13
68	Mauritius	+2
69	Georgia	+15
70	Hong Kong	−9
71	Senegal	−9
72	Republic of Moldova	−16
73	Italy	−24
74	Nicaragua	−3
75	United Republic of Tanzania	−6
76	Cyprus North	+7
77	Lesotho	−3
78	Armenia	0
79	Sierra Leone	−7
80	Togo	−4
81	Guinea Bissau	+5

(*continued*)

Table 3.1 (continued)

Rank 2015	Country	Diff. 2014 rank
82	Albania	+3
83	Panama	+4
84	Benin	−9
85	Mozambique	−6
86	Côte d'Ivoire	+15
87	Kosovo	−7
88	Kyrgyzstan	+9
89	Liberia	0
90	Kuwait	+1
91	Greece	+8
92	Peru	+12
93	Fiji	+14
94	Bolivia	0
95	Gabon	+3
96	Seychelles	+7
97	Uganda	+13
98	Lebanon	+8
99	Brazil	+12
100	Kenya	−10
101	Israel	−5
102	Guinea	0
103	Timor-Leste	−26
104	Bhutan	−12
105	Nepal	+15
106	Bulgaria	−6
107	Republic of the Congo	−25
108	Ecuador	−13
109	Paraguay	−4
110	Central African Republic	−1
111	Nigeria	+1
112	Maldives	−4
113	Zambia	−20
114	Montenegro	0
115	Qatar	−2
116	Tajikistan	−1
117	Macedonia	+6
118	Mali	+4
119	Algeria	+2
120	United Arab Emirates	−2

(*continued*)

Table 3.1 (continued)

Rank 2015	Country	Diff. 2014 rank
121	Brunei Darussalam	−4
122	Afghanistan	+6
123	Angola	+1
124	Guatemala	+1
125	South Sudan	−6
126	Tunisia	+7
127	Oman	+7
128	Colombia	−2
129	Ukraine	−2
130	Morocco	+6
131	Zimbabwe	+4
132	Honduras	−3
133	Cameroon	−2
134	Thailand	−4
135	Chad	+4
136	India	+4
137	Venezuela	−21
138	Indonesia	−6
139	Cambodia	+5
140	Palestine	−2
141	Philippines	+8
142	Ethiopia	+1
143	Jordan	−2
144	Myanmar	+1
145	Burundi	−3
146	Bangladesh	0
147	Malaysia	0
148	Mexico	+4
149	Turkey	+5
150	Democratic Republic of the Congo	+1
151	Gambia	+4
152	Russian Federation	−4
153	Singapore	−3
154	Libya	−17
155	Swaziland	+1
156	Iraq	−3
157	Belarus	0
158	Egypt	+1
159	Pakistan	−1

(*continued*)

Table 3.1 (continued)

Rank 2015	Country	Diff. 2014 rank
160	Kazakhstan	+1
161	Rwanda	+1
162	Azerbaijan	−2
163	Bahrain	0
164	Saudi Arabia	0
165	Sri Lanka	0
166	Uzbekistan	0
167	Equatorial Guinea	+1
168	Yemen	−1
169	Cuba	+1
170	Djibouti	−1
171	Lao People's Democratic Republic	0
172	Somalia	+4
173	Islamic Republic of Iran	0
174	Sudan	−2
175	Vietnam	−1
176	China	−1
177	Syrian Arab Republic	0
178	Turkmenistan	0
179	Democratic People's Republic of Korea	0
180	Eritrea	0

Source: Reporters Without borders, https://rsf.org/en/ranking_table, last accessed 27 May 2016

underlying situation score, overall score and difference from the 2015 score) can be found on the RSF website.[4]

While a single survey does not provide a definitive account of the prevailing situation, the yearly index does illustrate trends. It is no co-incidence that the countries that foster freedom of the press and expression are also well positioned in other indices that depict levels of corruption or social stability, for example. We will tackle the struggle against corruption later on in the book.

In pursuit of a more reliable picture several sources must be considered. What follows is a comparison of the 2015 indices of both Freedom House and Reporters Without Borders. The sample includes 29 countries that are considered ideal-typical. This kind of comparison is necessary because

Table 3.2 Comparison of country ranking based on the 2015 freedom of speech indices of Freedom House (FH) and Reporters Without Borders (RSF)

Country	Rank 2015/RSF	Rank 2015/FH
Finland	1	3
Norway	2	1
Denmark	3	6
Netherlands	4	3
Sweden	5	1
Estonia	10	14
Germany	12	22
Namibia	17	67
Luxembourg	19	6
Iceland	21	14
Ghana	22	52
Australia	25	31
Andorra	32	8
Spain	33	52
United Kingdom	34	38
France	38	35
United States	49	31
Mongolia	54	71
Italy	73	64
Ukraine	129	125
India	136	80
Venezuela	137	176
Turkey	149	142
Russian Federation	152	180
Egypt	158	161
China	176	186
Syrian Arab Republic	177	190
Democratic People's Republic of Korea	179	199
Eritrea	180	195

the indices of the two organisations have different scoring systems. A comparison thus increases the validity of the general assessments (Table 3.2). Another way to compose a more reliable picture is to analyse statistics over several years. Table 3.3 shows the Reporters Without Borders indices of the past 13 years. Despite its generality, the table demonstrates developmental trends in various countries.

THE STATE OF FREEDOM OF SPEECH IN THE WORLD   25

Table 3.3 Reporters Without Borders indices for selected countries, 2002–2015

Country	2015	2014	2013	2011–2012	2010	2009	2008	2007	2006	2005	2004	2003	2002
Finland	1	1	1	1	1	1	4	5	1	1	1	1	1
Netherlands	4	2	2	3	1	7	16	12	1	1	1	1	1
Norway	2	3	3	1	1	1	1	1	6	1	1	1	1
Luxembourg	19	4	4	6	14	20	1	N/A	N/A	N/A	N/A	N/A	N/A
Andorra	32	5	5	N/A	N/A	N/A	N/A	N/A	N/A	N/A	N/A	N/A	N/A
Denmark	3	7	6	10	11	1	14	8	19	1	1	1	10
Iceland	21	8	9	6	1	9	1	1	1	1	1	1	1
Sweden	5	10	10	12	1	1	7	5	14	12	11	9	7
Estonia	10	11	11	3	9	6	4	3	6	11	11	12	N/A
Germany	12	14	17	16	17	18	20	20	23	18	11	8	7
Namibia	17	22	19	20	21	35	23	25	26	25	42	56	31
Ghana	22	27	30	41	26	27	31	29	34	66	57	48	67
Australia	25	28	26	30	18	16	28	28	35	31	41	50	12
UK	34	33	29	28	19	20	23	24	27	24	28	27	21
Spain	33	35	36	39	39	44	36	33	41	40	39	42	29
France	38	39	37	38	44	43	35	31	35	30	19	26	11
United States[a]	49	46	32	47	20	20	36	48	53	44	22	31	17
Italy	73	49	57	61	49	49	44	35	40	42	39	53	40
Japan	61	59	53	22	11	17	29	37	51	37	42	44	26
Hong Kong	70	61	58	54	34	48	51	61	58	39	34	56	18
Ukraine	129	127	126	116	131	89	87	92	105	112	138	132	112
India	136	140	140	131	122	105	118	120	105	106	120	128	80
Russian Federation	152	148	148	142	140	153	141	144	147	138	140	148	121
Turkey	149	154	154	148	138	122	102	101	98	98	113	115	99

(continued)

Table 3.3 (continued)

Country	2015	2014	2013	2011–2012	2010	2009	2008	2007	2006	2005	2004	2003	2002
Egypt	158	159	158	166	127	143	146	146	133	143	128	110	101
China	176	175	173	174	171	168	167	163	163	159	162	161	138
Syrian Arab Republic	177	177	176	176	173	165	159	154	153	145	155	155	126
Democratic People's Republic of Korea	179	179	178	178	177	174	172	168	168	167	167	166	139

[a]Does not include extraterritorial areas until 2013. For a more comprehensive list of countries, see the list at Wikipedia (http://en.wikipedia.org/wiki/Press_Freedom_Index, last accessed 27 May 2016)

Developments in Some Countries

The USA's fall in the indices is explained by President Barack Obama's administration's harsh actions on national security issues, which have clearly impacted freedom of speech. Britain's fall is the result of the remarkably stringent measures implemented by the authorities against the *Guardian* newspaper. The situations in these two countries are investigated later in this book by two experienced journalists, Claude E. Erbsen from the USA and Peter Preston from Britain.

The Press Freedom Index demonstrates the negative correlation between military conflicts and freedom of information. When the situation in a country is destabilised, the role of the media is accentuated and forms a threat to the interests of those groupings who want to suppress the supply of news and other information.

Reporters Without Borders observes that even in countries where law and order prevail, security threats are falsely invoked to limit the free flow of information. Britain and the USA are not the only recent examples of this. Free speech is only a memory under the present leadership in Turkey. Turkey is ranked 154th and seems to be steadily falling.

After decades of dictatorship, the Arab Spring of 2011 was loaded with many positive expectations that the rule of law and democratic development would take root. These hopes were in vain. Many Arab countries

Fig. 3.2 List of top 10 countries and bottom 10 countries

rank below 100th. Two kingdoms not involved in the Arab Spring, Jordan and Morocco, still rank poorly despite their good reputations as tourist destinations (Fig. 3.2).

For the purpose of comparison, let's take a look at Freedom House's rankings of the worst and the best performing countries.[5]

The rankings indisputably indicate that the principle of the rule of law also applies to freedom of speech. Freedom of speech cannot exist without the rule of law and democratic institutions, and vice versa: there is no rule of law or democracy without freedom of speech and expression.

Declaration of Table Mountain

Through the lens of freedom of speech, Sub-Saharan Africa appears gloomy. At a meeting in Cape Town in June 2007 on abolishing "insult laws" in Africa and moving free press up the agenda, the World Association of Newspapers and the World Editors Forum adopted the Declaration of Table Mountain and agreed on the following points:

> "That in country after country, the African press is crippled by a panoply of repressive measures, from the jailing and persecution of journalists to the widespread scourge of "insult laws" and criminal defamation which are used, ruthlessly, by governments to prevent critical appraisal of their performance and to deprive the public from information about their misdemeanours and Africa urgently needs a strong, free and independent press to act as a watchdog over public institutions.

Press freedom remains a key to the establishment of good governance and durable economic, political, social and cultural development, prosperity and peace in Africa, and to the fight against corruption, famine, poverty, violent conflict, disease and lack of education.

The parties of the declarations, as global representative organisations of the owners, publishers and editors of the world's press are to conduct "aggressive and persistent campaigning against press freedom violations and restrictions" and are committed to freedom of the press as a basic human right as well as an indispensable constituent of democracy in every country, including those in Africa.

The parties recall that Article 19 of the Universal Declaration of Human Rights guarantees freedom of expression as a fundamental right, and emphasise that freedom of expression is essential to the realization of other rights set forth in international human rights instruments and recall that those principles have been restated and endorsed in the 2002 Declaration on Principles of Freedom of Expression in Africa, adopted by the African Commission on Human and Peoples' Rights and the African Union, thus requiring member states of the African Union to uphold and maintain press freedom.

The parties also recall the 1991 Windhoek Declaration on Promoting an Independent and Pluralistic African Press, and observe that despite numerous opportunities for a free press to emerge from national independence, fully fledged press freedom still does not exist in many African countries and that murder, imprisonment, torture, banning, censorship and legislative edict are the norm in many countries, and recognise that these crude forms of repression are bolstered by the deliberate exclusion of certain newspapers from state advertising placement, the burden of high import taxes on equipment and newsprint and unfair competition from state-owned media.

The declaration notes that despite the adoption of press freedom protocols and the repression of that freedom on a wide scale in Africa, the African Union in instituting its African Peer Review Mechanism under the NEPAD (New Partnership for Africa's Development) programme has excluded the fostering of a free and independent press as a key requirement in the assessment of good governance in the countries of the continent.

It identifies as the greatest scourge of press freedom on the continent the continued implementation of "insult laws," which outlaw criticism of politicians and those in authority, and criminal defamation legislation, both of which are used indiscriminately in the vast majority of African states that maintain them and which have as their prime motive the "locking up of information".

Declare that African states must recognise the indivisibility of press freedom and their responsibility to respect their commitments to African and international protocols upholding the freedom, independence and safety of the press, and to further that aim by, as a matter of urgency, abolishing "insult" and criminal defamation laws which in the five months of this year have caused the harassment, arrest and/or imprisonment of 103 editors, reporters, broadcasters and online journalists in 26 African countries (as outlined in the annexure to this declaration).

Call on African governments as a matter of urgency to review and abolish all other laws that restrict press freedom. Call on African governments that have jailed journalists for their professional activities to free them immediately and to allow the return to their countries of journalists who have been forced into exile.

Condemn all forms of repression of African media that allows for banning of newspapers and the use of other devices such as levying import duties on newsprint and printing materials and withholding advertising.

Call on African states to promote the highest standards of press freedom in furtherance of the principles proclaimed in Article 19 of the Universal Declaration of Human Rights and other protocols and to provide constitutional guarantees of freedom of the press.

Call on the African Union immediately to include in the criteria for "good governance" in the African Peer Review Mechanism the vital requirement that a country promotes free and independent media.

Call on international institutions to promote progress in press freedom in Africa in the next decade, through such steps as assisting newspapers in the areas of legal defence, skills development and access to capital and equipment.

Welcome moves towards a global fund for African media development and recommends that such an initiative gives priority attention to media legal reform and in particular the campaign to rid the continent of "insult" and criminal defamation laws.

Commit WAN and WEF to expand their existing activities in regard to press freedom and development in Africa in the coming decade. WAN and WEF make this declaration from Table Mountain at the southern tip of Africa as an earnest appeal to all Africans to recognise that the political and economic progress they seek flourishes in a climate of freedom and where the press is free and independent of governmental, political or economic control.

This Declaration shall be presented to: The Secretary General of the United Nations with the request that it be presented to the UN General Assembly; to the UNESCO Director General with the request that it be placed before the General Conference of UNESCO; and to the Chairperson of the African Union Commission with the request that it be distributed to all members of the African Union so that it can be endorsed by the AU at its next summit meeting of heads of state.

Cape Town, 3 June 2007.

The Declaration of Table Mountain gathered dust on the shelf and it was not until four years later, in 2011, that President Mahamadou Issoufou of Niger became the first African head of state to sign it. The second signatory was the Liberian Nobel Laureate and president Ellen Johnson-Sirleaf."⁶

Dark Clouds Over the Flow of Information

Hard-Pressed Journalists Journalists are being increasingly persecuted nowadays. They are being killed and imprisoned in record numbers. Online surveillance is gaining strength and the right to privacy is being constantly eroded as technology develops. There is already evidence of attempts to shut down the internet or take it under the control of the authorities.

Journalism's ecosystem of liberty is no longer stable. In addition to authoritarian officials, other threats include militant movements, criminals and terrorists, who aim to influence journalists by pressuring or threatening them.

Sub-Saharan Africa is bad terrain for journalists, which explains the unpopularity of the Declaration of Table Mountain amongst governments. The Declaration should be very easy to adopt as it reiterates the general principles of Western democracy and the proclamations commonly used in efforts to establish and anchor freedom of speech in different countries.

It is not possible to systematically discuss all countries of the world in this book. The ranking of any particular country can be checked in Table 3.1. To mention but one, Somalia is one of the worst countries on the African continent, and ranks amongst the bottom countries worldwide. Together with Syria, Pakistan and India, Somalia heads the statistics on assassinations of journalists.

Timothy Spence writes in the IPI Annual Report (2013): "Killings aside, journalists in many Sub-Saharan countries face a daily dose of legal obstacles, threats, intimidation and assaults that often go unpunished". "We are afraid to write anything, anything bad about our government because when we do, we are accused of treason or of undermining the state", one Ethiopian journalist who asked not to be named for fear of reprisal, said ahead of a press freedom mission to the country, carried out by IPI and WAN in November 2013. "There is no press freedom in

Ethiopia – we never did have, but things are only worse under the ruling EPRDF (Ethiopian People's Revolutionary Democratic Front)."[7]

In 2011 two Swedish journalists, Johan Persson and Martin Schibbye, were sentenced to 11 years in prison on charges of supporting terrorism and illegal entry into Ethiopia. As a result of diplomatic efforts Sweden managed to negotiate their freedom after 438 days of imprisonment.

Violations against freedom of the press are common throughout Sub-Saharan Africa. IPI has noted serious violations in, amongst others, Angola, Sierra Leone, Liberia, Gambia, Uganda, Eritrea, Ethiopia, Somalia and most recently Mali and Kenya. Mali was making progress when it was set back by a military coup. Kenya has passed a new Security Laws Act that seriously impedes freedom of the press and increases the authorities' powers to keep citizens under observation and to interfere in their privacy.

IPI Recommendations for Sub-Saharan Africa

- African leaders should follow their counterparts in Niger and Liberia and endorse action to abolish criminal defamation.
- The successor document to the UN Millennium Development Goals, due to expire in 2015, must contain a strong commitment to freedom of speech and the press.
- National leaders—including those in Kenya, Nigeria, Somalia and South Africa—must reverse efforts to impose state influence over media laws and independent media councils.
- Major development donors, such as the European Union and United States, need to use their influence to press for progressive media environments in major beneficiary countries like Ethiopia, where independent journalists face constant obstacles.

Asia and the Pacific In IPI's latest Annual Report, Barbara Trionfi, IPI's new interim executive director from the beginning of 2015, stated that the most dangerous place to practise journalism is Asia: in particular Pakistan, India and the Philippines. The most common reason is that journalists are investigating organised crime and the corruption associated with it. In the autumn of 2014, four journalists were killed in Pakistan. Crucially, the perpetrators are very seldom brought to justice, while the journalists end up in the graveyard.

The situation in the Philippines is very similar to that in Pakistan. Over 200 journalists have been killed since 1986, and only eleven perpetrators have been convicted in court. Freedom of the press organisations have unsuccessfully demanded that the Philippine government investigate these crimes. Instead, questionable legislation has been invoked to stifle any attempts to report on issues that are awkward for the authorities.

India, the great giant of Asia, is also on the wrong path. Violence and threats against journalists are on the increase. Eight journalists were assassinated in 2013. Criminal organisations, security forces and demonstrators all pose a threat to working journalists.

Myanmar's (formerly Burma) development has been positive, but is now stalling as authorities have begun to be wary of the consequences of increased freedoms in society. On the positive side, Myanmar's government and parliament have stopped advance censorship and have issued permits to independent newspapers. On the other hand, promises of more liberal legislation remain unfulfilled. Myanmar's spring may suffer the same fate as the Arab Spring: plenty of promises and few results. But, to quote an old saying, the future remains to be seen, and we should not give up hope. We will return to Myanmar later on.

China is discussed elsewhere in the book, so at present it is sufficient to mention that, despite constitutional guarantees, freedom of speech is brazenly oppressed in China. Dissidents end up in prison for long periods of time. Furthermore, the Chinese authorities are effective in their monitoring of the internet.

The new General Secretary of the Communist Party and the current President of China, Xi Jinping, said in November 2012: "Friends from the press, China needs to learn more about the world, and the world also needs to learn more about China. I hope you will continue to make more efforts and contributions to deepening the mutual understanding between China and the countries of the world."[8] It seems that Xi's intention was to invite journalists to observe party propaganda, which is indeed the experience that many journalists have had from their conversations with Chinese authorities. Since Xi's speech the official line has been tightened up, and there is no change in sight.

Vietnam's experience is similar to China's. Censorship is effective, and the use of social media to spread news is severely restricted.

Central Asian countries Turkmenistan, Uzbekistan, Kazakhstan, Tajikistan and Kyrgyzstan are territories where development is moving in the wrong direction. We will return to them later.

IPI's Recommendations for Central Asian Countries

- Governments should implement dedicated mechanisms to ensure thorough investigation of crimes committed against journalists.
- All imprisoned journalists and bloggers should be released immediately.
- Governments must immediately halt efforts to limit access to information circulated over the internet or to prevent people from posting news and opinions.
- Libel laws should serve the sole purpose of protecting the right to reputation and should not be abused to limit criticism of those in power. Criminal defamation and *lèse-majesté* laws must be abolished as they violate international standards in the area of freedom of expression.

Quo vadis, Turkey? If Russia, Ukraine and Belarus are excluded, two states in Europe are a particular cause for concern: Hungary and Turkey. A great many things separate these countries from each other, but they also have something in common: Hungary is a member of the EU, and Turkey is negotiating membership. Both are members of NATO.

There are many obstacles on Turkey's road towards the rule of law, not least of which is its leading position amongst countries that detain and imprison journalists. In December 2014 there were nearly 70 journalists in detention. Furthermore, Turkey has developed a system that can force detainees to wait an indefinite time for trial. Journalists often don't even have the right to a trial.

If the EU is unsuccessful in its efforts to put pressure on Turkey to move towards free speech, the end is nigh. If the Turkish state turns away from Europe, the EU's ability to put pressure on Turkey is greatly reduced. Consequently, freedom of speech becomes an ever more unattainable goal for the Turkish people, and the present self-censorship will intensify, especially on TV channels.

At the moment while the dust settles on the attempted *coup d'état* of July 2016, the future of Turkey is unclear. Was the coup a real surprise to the government, as the media and flow of information in Turkey are under strict surveillance? At least the instant systematic clean-up of the officers and the judiciary that began immediately afterwards, is a giveaway showing that the coup had been prepared for. The grip of President Erdoğan of Turkey appears to be tightening, which also affects the international affairs of the country. Islamic nationalism is rising rapidly. The losers of the game will be Turkey's population of 80 million. We will return to developments in Turkey further on in the book.

Hungary Hungary's transformation into the EU's "bad boy" started in 2010, when the nationalist and conservative Fidesz party gained a majority in the parliamentary elections for the first time. After the victory Fidesz began to reform Hungarian society in a self-serving way. Their tactical approach worked, and Fidesz remained in power with a two-thirds majority in the following election. The result was effectively a *carte blanche* to rule.

Since then the path has been clear. First, the Constitutional Court's mandate to monitor the constitutionality of laws was curtailed. The retirement age for judges was then lowered to hasten their replacement with Fidesz supporters. Furthermore, a change in the law allowed for sensitive corruption cases to be transferred to courts with no experience in handling complicated cases.

For the purposes of this book the most fundamental change has been the new media law. It stipulates that any media content must be fair, relevant to the Hungarian people and respectful of human dignity. The parliament appointed a political Media Council to make sure that the media functions as the ruling party expects. The protection of journalistic sources was also weakened. Several executives and hundreds of workers were fired from the state-run media. Political advertising on commercial media was banned, and a 40 per cent tax on any advertising imposed to boot. Non-governmental organisations that received funding from abroad were placed under observation. The excuse given was that these organisations had channelled money for party-political purposes.

Due to pressure from the EU, some restrictions on freedom of speech have been eased, but the basic problem remains, and because of these measures, Fidesz's removal from power is very difficult. We will examine these threats to free speech in greater detail later in the book.

IPI Recommendations for Hungary

- Oppose impunity for attacks on journalists.
- Decriminalise defamation and limit civil defamation awards in proportion to harm caused.
- Ensure that public broadcasters operate independently of political pressure.
- Increase transparency of private media ownership and ensure that private media are not economically or politically dependent on government connections for survival.

- End state regulation of media and encourage media self-regulation.
- Ensure that laws providing widespread access to government information of public interest are both enacted and fully implemented.
- Create mechanisms to ensure that states that enter into economic or political agreements with the European Union and other European intergovernmental organisations continue to adhere to democratic principles following such agreements.

In **South America** there are only a few countries where the state of freedom of speech is satisfactory: Uruguay, Surinam and French Guiana. Nowhere is the situation good. The situation in Venezuela and Columbia is difficult. In Central America there is free speech only in Costa Rica. Obviously, the continent's worst country for free speech is communist **Cuba**—also ranked amongst the lowest countries in freedom of speech indices.

Despite some faltering efforts **Mexico** has in recent years become one of the most insecure countries for quality investigative journalism. The state governments in Mexico have been unwilling to get involved due to the corrupt political culture within the various regional authorities. The police are often in league with local criminal organisations. The climate of fear is an effective constraint on independent journalism, fostering self-censorship that is always detrimental to the media.

IPI Country-Specific Recommendations for South America

- **Mexico:** Ensure the Federal Special Prosecutor for Crimes Against Freedom uses its newly obtained legal powers to the fullest extent possible to challenge impunity for crimes committed against the media and that the Security Mechanism is meeting the needs of journalists in danger.
- **Brazil:** Enact a measure to make crimes against journalists a federal offence.
- **Ecuador:** Amend the Law on Communications to bring it in line with international standards on media regulation. End verbal and legal attacks on the press.
- **Grenada:** Amend the Electronic Crimes legislation so as to protect free expression and prevent a recriminalisation of defamation.
- **Dominican Republic:** Complete the draft of a replacement press law that includes the removal of all criminal penalties for defamation.

- **Trinidad and Tobago:** Pass a bill, currently pending before Parliament, that would partially decriminalise defamation.
- **Guyana:** Ensure that the National Broadcasting Authority acts independently in allocating licences and that all pending applications are reviewed and fairly decided.
- **Honduras:** Follow through on commitments to establish a journalist safety programme and to abolish criminal defamation.
- **Venezuela:** Respect the freedom of the media to criticise and to produce independent, investigative reporting in the interest of the Venezuelan people.

United States The USA's ranking in freedom of speech indices has fallen following the Obama administration's increasingly harsh treatment of the media. Karin Deutsch Karlekar and Jennifer Dunham of American Freedom House write (see also Claude E. Erbsen's contribution in Chap. 5):

> The United States remains one of the stronger performers in the index, but it suffered a significant negative shift for 2013, from 18 to 21 points, due to several factors. The limited willingness of high level government officials to provide access and information to members of the press, already noted in 2012, remained a concern, and additional methods of restricting the flow of information became apparent during the year. For example, there was an increase in the number of Freedom of Information Act requests that were denied or censored on national security grounds. Journalists who endeavoured to cover national security issues faced continued efforts by the federal judiciary to compel them to testify or to hand over materials that would reveal their sources in a number of cases – the James Risen being the most prominent ongoing dispute.
>
> Finally, the practices disclosed by Edward Snowden, a former NSA contractor, regarding mass surveillance and the storage of metadata and digital content by the NSA, coupled with the targeted surveillance of the phones of dozens of Associated Press journalists, raised questions regarding the ability of journalists to protect their sources and cast a pall over free speech protections in the United States. Ongoing challenges include the threat to media diversity stemming from poor economic conditions for the news industry, as well as the lack of protection-of-sources legislation at the federal level.[9]

IPI Recommendations for the USA

- Pass a federal shield law protecting the confidentiality of journalists' sources; end the use of the Espionage Act to target whistleblowers.

- Reject legislative proposals that overreact to disclosures of classified information; further efforts to erode information access laws and efforts to criminalise reporting, especially so-called "Ag-gag" provisions; oppose digital snooping against journalists.
- Ensure that public servants, particularly law enforcement officers, understand and respect the media's necessary role and the added scrutiny that public trust demands.
- Create a federal anti-SLAPP (strategic lawsuits against public participation) statute authorising news media to bring a special motion to dismiss lawsuits against them that arise out of protected speech on public issues.

Conclusion The above overview of the state and development of freedom of speech in the world tells us that journalists are in dire straits in many countries and the situation seems bleak. The overview is limited in scope and many other countries deserve to be discussed.

A good example is oil-rich Azerbaijan in Central Asia, a dictatorship where the Alijev family rules. Freedom House researchers Karlekar and Dunham also single out Libya, South Sudan, Ukraine and Zambia. Furthermore, significant deterioration can be seen in the Central African Republic, Egypt, Greece, Jordan, Kenya, Montenegro, Mozambique, Tanzania and Uganda.

Karlekar and Dunham summarise the state of affairs thus: "Meanwhile as a result of declines in democratic settings over the past several years, the share of the world's population that enjoys a free press remained at 14 percent, meaning only one in seven people live in countries where coverage of political news is robust, the safety of journalists is guaranteed, state intrusion in media affairs is minimal, and the press is not subject to onerous legal or economic pressures." Nothing needs to be added to this conclusion.

This overview illustrates the need for deeper analysis. To start with, it's easy to see that freedom of speech is inextricably linked to the general atmosphere of a society, and in particular to the development of the rule of law. On the other hand, it's important to remember that the war against terrorism has been detrimental to free speech even in traditionally stable democracies like Britain and the United States. No country should be exempt from taking a look in the mirror. Let us start with an evaluation of the development of the rule of law in general, where many perspectives open up from the history of justice through the modern multi-layered judicial system to the interplay between national and international law.

Free Speech—In the Core of Judicial Development

Freedom of Speech and Social Development Greek philosopher Diogenes (412–323 BCE), who declared himself the first citizen of the world, declared from his tub that "the most beautiful thing in the world is freedom of speech". He also said "it is impossible for society to exist without law. But if the law is bad, people are unhappier and more evil in society than in nature".[10] These classic quotes attest to the close bond between freedom of speech and the rule of law. Thus it is essential to examine free speech alongside the principles of law and justice.

Although we are familiar with the principle of the rule of law, it is not easy to define the concept. The rule of law should not be defined too narrowly, merely by reference to different sectors of public power—its legislative, administrative and judicial branches—or other specific activities such as security, administration, welfare, markets and competition. Instead of merely defining the concept it is necessary to come up with a practical method of analysing its development. At the same time it is essential to see information and its communication as principles that permeate throughout society. A more balanced approach to the concept is needed that takes into account the different stages of the development of the rule of law.

Stages of Development The connections between free speech and the development of the rule of law are easy to identify. Conclusions cannot simply be drawn from the developmental stages of the rule of law, but the following tripartition demonstrates in all its simplicity the many connections between free speech and the development of laws. Thus, it is also possible to understand the connections between justice, democracy, economic development and social well-being—with information and free speech as the common thread.

Three stages may be distinguished in the development of the theory of the rule of law: (1) the classical rule of law, which refers to the emergence of the principles; (2) the democratic rule of law, which underlines the role of participation and common laws; and (3) the rule of law in a social context, which concerns the social functioning of law. It is not, however, theories that we need, but an efficient legal system (see Hallberg 2013, p. 29).

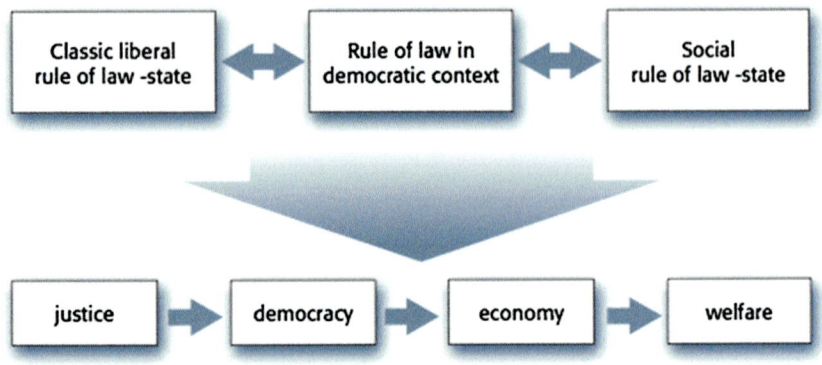

Fig. 3.3 Freedom of speech and society

The birth of the principle of freedom of speech is associated with the consolidation of the principle of the rule of law and the formation of the liberal state. In Europe this happened principally during the eighteenth-century Age of Enlightenment, although we can trace the historical roots of freedom of speech to a much earlier age. The strengthening of the democratic state ruled by law has clarified the nature of freedom of speech as a basic political right. The same applies to access to information, as well as to free elections and the freedom to participate in them. On the other hand, in a social context free speech is associated with more everyday matters: freedom of opinion, creativity, the social environment and the importance of mental well-being (Fig. 3.3).

Among the great works of Enlightenment political philosophy that grew out of the humanist intellectual sensibilities of the seventeenth-century Scientific Revolution are John Locke's (1632–1704) *The Second Treatise of Government* (1690), Jean-Jacques Rousseau's (1712–1778) *The Social Contract* and Thomas Paine's (1737–1809) *Rights of Man*. Paine in particular makes the revolutionary spirit and the ideas of the most elevated Enlightenment authors accessible to the average reader. Paine also distinguishes between "society" and "government" (see *Keystones of Democracy*, 2005 New York). The differences in the thinking of Locke and Rousseau are reflected in the doctrine of basic rights. Similarly, some of Montesquieu's (1669–1755) opinions differ from those of his predecessor Locke. We will return to these later.

Worldwide Differences in Legal Cultures Legal culture is tied to its national, historical and cultural background, and there are significant differences in legal thinking between different regions of the world. The influence of religious and social circumstances is of great importance. We can also see differences between the Nordic pragmatic, American federal liberal, British parliament-oriented, Continental Europe normative constitutional, Eastern European post-socialist formal, Russian "democratic federal-governed", Chinese hierarchical and African poverty- and instability-related systems. All power structures and traditions have left their mark on the prerequisites for free speech, as we shall see.

These rough descriptions also reflect differences in attitude towards the concept of the rule of law. One worldwide change can be seen in attitudes towards terrorism. In some countries recent legal reforms aimed at supporting the fight against terrorism have switched the focus of legal thinking from the traditional ideology of liberty and citizens' rights towards a security-oriented approach. This explains the restrictive attitudes of central government in several countries towards the free flow of communication, even leading to new surveillance systems. New types of restrictions on the flow of information are specifically related to the internet (see *Freedom on the Net*, Freedom House 2013). Can we comprehend, let alone accept, this kind of development?

But beyond the concept of the rule of law, the requirements of definite laws, good administration and access to justice must be a reality. The ability for people to access information and to influence the decisions that affect them are given emphasis. These are the objectives of democratic decision making. In practical terms it also means the right to be heard and to appeal. Indeed, modern constitutional law and political science already highlight the significance of human rights and fundamental rights, as well as obligations.

The Four Cornerstones of the Rule of Law Construction Let us try to create a concrete picture of the development of the rule of law. Simple metaphors often aid understanding. The modern legal system could be presented as a multi-layered pyramid: changing legal norms at the top, supporting principles in the middle and common values at the bottom. The principle of legality has been considered a distinctive mark of the rule of law. A symbolic functional model of the rule of law could be "a house built on solid ground" (Hallberg, *Rule of Law. Prospects in Central Asia*

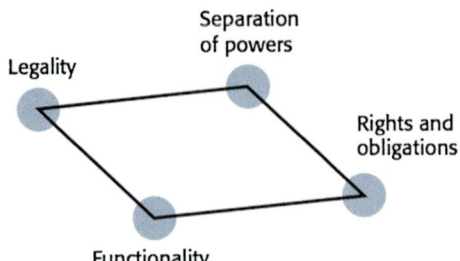

The four corners are:
- the principle of legality
- the balanced separation of powers
- the fundamental and human rights
- the functionality of "the rule of law house"

Rule of law on the basis of four variables – "A house built on solid ground"

Fig. 3.4 Rule of law on the basis of four variables

2013 p. 129). This metaphor doesn't signify a new concept; rather, it is a simpler way to analyse its development.

Where does freedom of speech fit into the development of the rule of law ? To answer this question, we need to examine development at a practical level, rather than through theoretical concepts. A symbolic functional model, a "rule of law house", can be analysed on the basis of four variables—the four corners of the house: (1) the principle of legality; (2) the balanced separation of powers; (3) the implementation of fundamental and human rights; and (4) the functionality of the house from the point of view of its "residents". Freedom of speech is central to the atmosphere in the house and, as we shall see, to the strengthening of the cornerstones and thus the whole society (Fig. 3.4).

The state, power structures and institutions are relevant tools for the purpose of constructing a balanced and functional legal system. It is essential to look at things from the people's perspective, not from that of the institutions. Modern constitutional law and political science highlight the significance of human and fundamental rights, and obligations. The symbolism of a house with its four corners provides a good basis for the analysis of the legal development of society, as well as a lasting foundation for different kinds of development programmes.

Legality and Legal Principles The principle of legality has been considered a hallmark of the rule of law. According to this principle, all public authority has to be based on law. Legislation plays a key role in the development of the rule of law. As legislation develops, the rule of law gains substance. The development of judicial systems and internationalisation can be viewed as a type of reciprocal action in which national and international levels constantly interact; this is, in fact, the usual interpretation of the entire concept. This is why it is in the interests of citizens for legislation to be unambiguous. Unclear norms leave the nature of rights and duties nebulous.

In this regard, the rule of law is a dynamic principle. Law should therefore be seen as a means, not an outcome. The law of today is not, however, unambiguous building material. Legislation has become more fragmented and somewhat indirect. Instead of rights and duties, more and more regulatory instruments relate to the interests of limited groups of persons and to the duties of authorities. This is not only a problem for civil law systems—the same is true under common law.

The law always entails "an element of ought to"—the setting of norms. Scottish philosopher and historian David Hume (1711–1776) developed the so-called "Hume's guillotine", the separation between what is and what ought to be. Without delving deeper into this theory, one must ask how "what ought to be" can be adapted to "what is" in a manner that is as truthful, understandable and balanced as possible.

At this point we may dig deeper into the hierarchy of norms, a theory developed by Hans Kelsen in the 1920s and refer to the following picture depicting the modern multistage system from constitutions to ever more complicated international treaty arrangements and recommendations.

Fig. 3.5 Regulatory system quality and policy

As regards development of theories on judicial systems, grouping into hard law and soft law is more interesting. Instead of competing against each other, these two systems have often been considered complementary (see Luo 2013).

Generally speaking, the problem of legislation and different norms lies in its distance from reality. One of the most eminent Nordic thinkers, Georg Henrik von Wright (1916–2003), crushed "the myth of separate normative reality, the realm of ought to", as he expressed it in his essay.[11] He described how "the removal of norms from the world of facts is tantamount to their removal from the world of truth". Herein lies great wisdom for freedom of speech. In a free society, those who set the norms, those who apply them and those subjected to them face the same reality. In this spirit we will examine, later on our journey around the world, whether the laws and norms on free speech are reality or empty promises (Fig. 3.5).

Despite these principled viewpoints modern legislation encounters many problems, mainly due to insufficient knowledge and the complexity of the issues to be regulated. One of the greatest problems in legal policy today seems to be that laws are too often prepared short-sightedly and by individual administrative sectors. Is legislation thus turning into "defective legislation" that merely addresses current acute problems instead of constructively guiding long-term development? Laws that "feel" real are also easy to understand.

The OECD (2001) differentiated "regulatory transparency" from "information transparency". However, transparency of information is also a crucial component of regulatory transparency. In order for the public to make an accurate assessment of their obligations and their rights, they must have not only regulatory information, but also statistical information and information on ongoing policy discussions within the government. Furthermore, information should be accurate, up to date, timely and easy to access.[12]

When emphasising the social and democratic nature of the principle of legality, the protection accorded to citizens by the law deserves attention. Demands for the protection of individuals and their property vis-à-vis public authorities, and for access to justice to ensure the lawfulness of official acts, were part of the historical development of rule-of-law thinking. Formally, the state was bound by law produced by the state itself. However, if we understand the rule of law only as a principle of legality, we forget the requirement of equity.

Historical discussion suggests that the requirement that the authorities' measures should be lawful as a principle for protecting citizens is broadly understood. This is reminiscent of the traditional Roman system that also strengthened freedom of speech. The same idea relates, as pointed out above, to the British rule-of-law concept as a principle of equity and equal legal practice. Thus, to guarantee legality and justice, the principle of legality should always be studied from the citizen's point of view. Consequently, discussion of societal development should not be limited to a norm-centred reading of the law.

Interesting tendencies can be observed in the development of a legal culture's characteristics. Federal-level legislation is clearly increasing in common-law countries, especially in the United States. The system is thus in this respect coming closer to a system of statutory law. It could also be argued that the legal system of the EU is changing into a more casuistic common-law system as the European Court of Justice increasingly relies on its earlier case law, and the legislative solutions to the implementation of directives differ between Member States.

Centralisation of power or balanced power? Criticism of autocratic development was already present among classical Greek philosophers. Demosthenes (384–322 BCE), for example, defended freedom of opinion and stated that "there is one safeguard known generally to the wise, which is an advantage and security to all, but especially to democracies as against despots—suspicion".

The Press Freedom Index 2013 published by Reporters Without Borders does not take direct account of types of political system, but it is clear that democracies provide better protection for the freedom to produce and circulate accurate news and information than countries where human rights are flouted, says Reporters Without Borders Director General Christophe Deloire.

The separation of powers is the second cornerstone of the rule of law and freedom in society. The doctrine of separation of powers is a result of historical developments. Generally, historical doctrines do not have exact equivalents at present. The origin of the doctrine of separation of powers easily leads, therefore, to a dogmatic approach to the analysis of the duties and functions of state organs. The doctrine is usually associated with the French Enlightenment philosophy of the eighteenth century and Montesquieu's (1689–1755) writings. Montesquieu's principal work *De l'Esprit des Lois* [*Spirit of the Laws*] was published in 1748. There had already been practical applications of the separation of powers in earlier times. The principles were first applied in Roman times. The first presentation of functionally separated powers was not, however, published until *Oceania* (1656) by Englishman James Harrington. Furthermore, the English philosopher John Locke (1632–1704) presented, before Montesquieu, practical suggestions concerning the restriction of executive and legislative powers.

There are some interesting differences of opinion between Locke and Montesquieu. John Locke did not seek a balanced separation of powers, merely the restriction of legislative and executive powers. He saw federative power, or the power to decide on war and peace, as a separate authority. He did not consider judicial power to be on a par with the other functions of the state. As long ago as 1701, special provision had granted independent status to judicial power. The right of judges to stay in office was also established at that time.

In contrast, Montesquieu did not support special status for judicial powers. According to him, permanent courts should not be formed, but the members of the court should be appointed for short periods only. In this way, the judges would not form an estate of their own. Montesquieu held that the administration of justice was a passive by-product of the will of the legislator. His principal idea was the prevention of the accumulation of power, not its consistent distribution.

In practice, Montesquieu's doctrines were first manifested in the United States. In contrast, development in England did not strictly follow the doctrine, although Parliament did possess supreme power. A parlia-

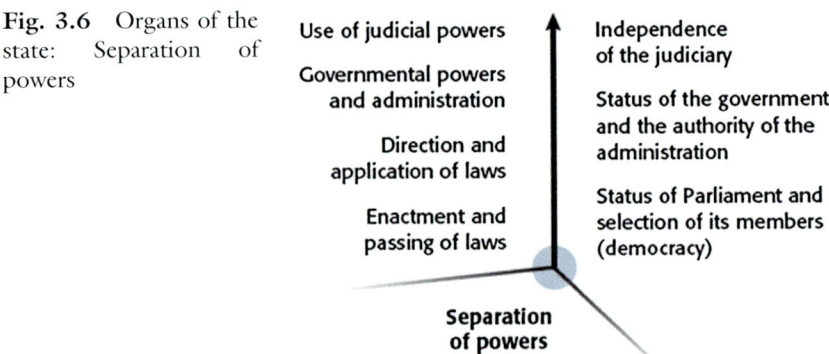

Fig. 3.6 Organs of the state: Separation of powers

mentary system was developed between legislative powers and administrative authorities, but the traditional independence of judicial power was preserved. In France, republican constitutions have been shaped in turn by the doctrines of separation of powers and sovereignty.

Figure 3.6 shows the basic elements of the separation of powers. The reality of the relationship between institutions and general social development is considerably more complicated and is also shaped by transparency.

Since models of the separation of powers doctrine have developed in various ways in different countries, according to their culture, it is important to consider the balance of power as well as the relationships between institutions and the functionality of the system when it comes to freedom of speech. The French state system, for example, can be characterised as hierarchical and underlining the powers of officials. The French tradition has been influential in the development of the administrative culture of the EU.

In Great Britain, the state is conceived in a more informal manner. State traditions, customary law, the liberty of the individual and the sovereignty of Parliament have greater weight. This has created a kind of liberal-democratic administrative organisation. The thinking of Locke is clearly visible: the powers of subsequent parliaments cannot be restricted. Other characteristics of the British system are the absence of a written constitution and—typical of common-law countries—a greater importance given to precedent in the administration of justice.

The separation of powers doctrine is viewed from a different perspective in federalist thinking, according to which society constructs itself as a co-ordination between entities rather than a hierarchy. Thus neither the constituent state nor the federal state is subordinate, the objective being to balance unity and diversity in state development. Nevertheless, in most federations, the constituent states are weaker than the federal state—both politically and economically—and there are several other tensions present.

We asked Ingmar Ström, who served as a ministerial counsellor in several Finnish embassies in South America and Asia, to comment on this arrangement. Ström quoted a newspaper article by Mexican writer Jorge Zepeda which analysed the thinking around the separation of powers in the US television drama series *House of Cards* which began in 2003:

> In a recent episode US President Francis Underwood suggests that people respect power, not honesty. Zepeda commented that this is exactly what most national leaders think, even in democracies. Another fictional character

in the series, the equivalent of Russia's Putin, goes further: The law is everything; the purpose of laws is not to give guarantees to citizens but to ensure that the leaders stay in power. This best proves the claims that people would rather prefer a strong than an honest leader.

Ecuador's cantankerous and populist president Rafael Correa is more popular than Chile's Bachelet or Brazil's Rousseff, Zepeda observed. Barack Obama's approval rating is just above 40%, which doesn't differ much from that of his Mexican colleague Enrique Peña Nieto.

It is perhaps understandable that rulers don't always take pleasure in democratic procedures. What is more worrying, however, is that the citizens approve of such assertions as President Underwood's. We can get rid of the *House of Cards* series by switching off the TV set but we can't escape reality, Zepeda concluded his column.[13]

The problem with the lack of separation of powers is that it usually leads to the centralisation of government systems and corruption, electoral systems that distort the composition of parliament, electoral fraud and deficiencies in the safeguarding of the impartiality of the courts, as well as in secrecy and the hidden exercise of power. In many transitional countries, for example in Central Asia, these questions on the separation of powers are timely. The independence of the judiciary is indeed at the forefront of discussions about guaranteeing freedom of speech. Tools to intervene in

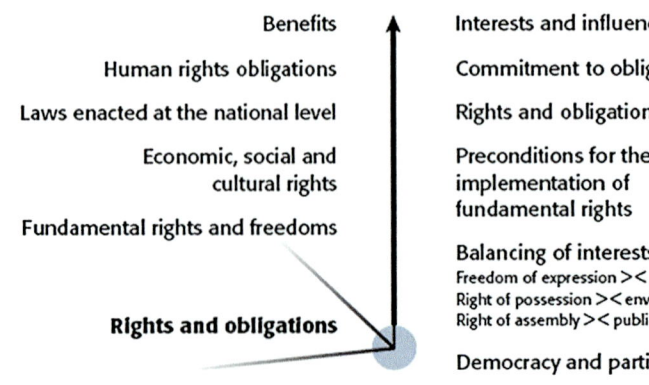

Fig. 3.7 Status of the people

violations of the right to free speech are naturally decided on the national level, which explains the considerable differences between countries that we shall note later on in this book.

Status of the People From the people's point of view, rights and obligations should be viewed as a single entity, and—in accordance with modern fundamental rights law—as the pursuit of a balance between conflicting rights. When it comes to news media it is, for instance, difficult to strike a balance between freedom of expression on the one hand and the protection of privacy on the other. As a political right, freedom of expression naturally constitutes a cornerstone of society, and should therefore not be infringed unless there are extremely well-founded reasons to do so. From the same perspective, the impartiality of the judicial system is essential for the realisation of freedom of speech. At the same time, it is worth bearing in mind that there are often conflicting interests at play (Fig. 3.7).

Using one's own mother tongue is crucial for access to information. In many countries minorities are forced to struggle for their language rights and freedom of expression. We must not forget the realities of linguistic circumstances. The world is a veritable Tower of Babel. The European map of languages alone has 23 official languages, 60 regional languages and 175 other languages. Even in a small country like Finland, there are 148 mother tongues spoken: in addition to the national Finnish and Swedish

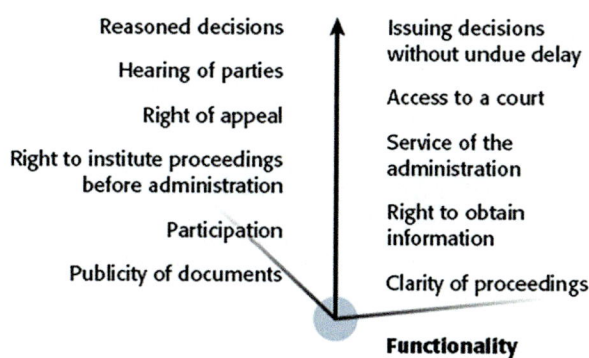

Fig. 3.8 Functioning of the rule of law

languages, there are indigenous Sami languages, Romani language, sign language, Tatar language, and so on. The biggest minority languages are Russian, Estonian and Somali. Linguistic rights are governed by many international agreements.

Functionality of the Rule-of-Law House The fourth corner of the house is the functionality of the system. Acts should be comprehensible, bureaucracy should be reduced, decisions should be taken promptly and access to justice should be simple. From the citizen's point of view the prerequisites for a functioning system include the public availability of documents, the right to obtain information, administrative services, the right to have one's case heard, reasoned decisions and the right of appeal, which together amount to transparent use of public power. Figure 3.8 shows socially transparent problem solving, decision making and solution seeking.

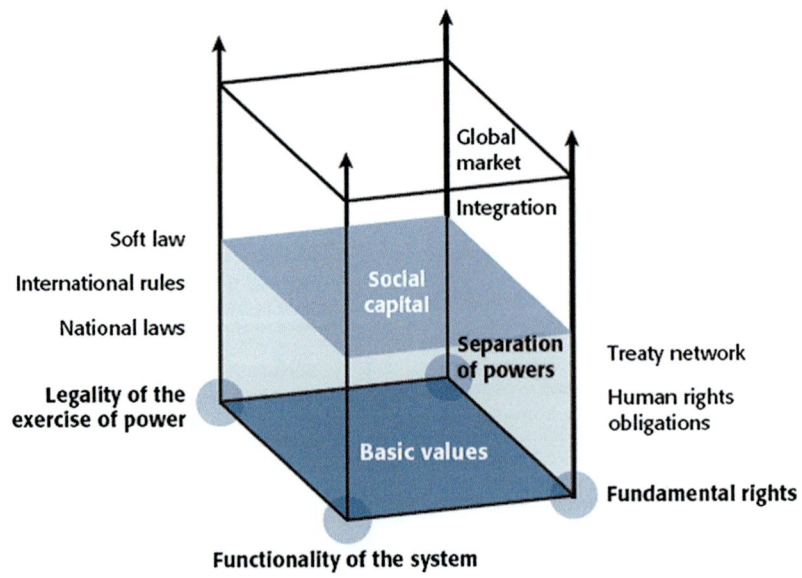

Fig. 3.9 Durability of the rule of law

Durability of Rule-of-Law Principles Our four-cornered structure lays a firm foundation for the observation of legal development. Continuing with this imagery, the different corners of the house need interlocking support structures to sustain the rule of law. Without these support structures the construction would sway in the wind and becometilted. This in turn highlights the importance of social capital—a concept studied in political science and sociology—as a factor contributing to the durability of the rule of law.

The foundations of the house require strong values. By measuring the height of the building one can estimate the level of economic development in a country (Fig. 3.9).

The construction of skyscrapers—competitive economies—also requires solid support structures and confidence in the durability of the system. The importance of human resources and their interaction, in other words, of social capital, should be discussed with regard not only to economic growth, but also to social welfare more generally.

The notion of the rule of law as a skyscraper, as global government, remains a utopian idea. The sustainable way to manage development is to envisage global governance as a world village of rule-of-law houses. It is essential to network from the bottom up, not from the top down.

The Human Rights Ombudsperson for the Organisation for Security and Co-operation in Europe, Gret Haller, provides a moving account of work separated from real life in her memoirs, entitled *Die Grenzen der Solidarität. Europa und die USA im Umgang mit Staat, Nation und Religion* (2002). She discusses her stint as Human Rights Ombudsperson in Bosnia and Herzegovina in 1996–2000, where her work was delineated by the conditions laid down in the Dayton Peace Agreement of 1995, and she thus felt she was working in a vacuum, in isolation from local people.

In a functioning house the doors open and close; windows let in light and provide visibility; lifts ease movement from one floor to another. However, global development is not like a skyscraper: not "global government", but more like a global village—a "global governance"—that has houses of different shapes and sizes. In order to ensure the well-being of inhabitants, the same rights to free movement, transparency and social mobility must be granted to all.

Social capital and trust play a key role. Social capital is considered both an important condition for economic growth and a stabiliser of liberal democracy. The importance of social capital and its increase has been discussed as a second-generation model of economic reform. At the same time, the rule of law is considered in a social context. A question thus arises: How can we increase the stock of social capital? As social capital is essentially a resource of civil society, state action has a limited part to play. There is always a fear that someone is misappropriating, that decision makers are manipulating and conspiring against us. The question here is about ideological influence, tempting us to be a "part of the team": take, for example, socialism and its aftermath.

The Soviet heritage is an example of what can result from lack of societal trust. When it comes to Russians not having trust in their system and their government institutions, to simply claim that they lack trust is not the whole truth. The trust is there: at least when it comes to friends, family and relatives. A low level of trust in other people, and the fact that they have learned not to trust political organisations, is at the heart of the problem. Democracy requires trust in political institutions, but the simple question is: why should people trust institutions?[14] The latest news from Russia still mentions firm trust. Is it real, or the result of an efficient media?

What is the core substance of this key concept of social capital? Essentially, it is a certain kind of communality that is not bound to explicit norms, but is based on feelings of solidarity and trust between people. Fukuyama[15] suggests a short practical definition: "social capital is an instantiated informal norm that promotes co-operation between two or more individuals". Putnam[16] argues that a special feature of social capital, trust, norms and networks, is that it is ordinarily a public good. Social capital, unlike other forms of capital, must be produced as a by-product of other social activities.

From a historical perspective it is interesting to observe in the field of political research that social capital is often associated explicitly with the democratic concepts of Alexis de Tocqueville—that is, communality as experienced by the people. More generally, drawing from the Italian experience, Putnam argues that social capital supports the functioning of both the market and the state: "Social capital, as embodied in horizontal networks of civic engagement, bolsters the performance of the polity and the economy, rather than reverse: Strong society, strong economy; strong society, strong state". Moreover, "for political stability, for government effectiveness, and even for economic progress social capital may be even more important than physical or human capital".

It is important to analyse the essence of social capital and its promotion from the perspective of civil society, of the people. In the context of the legal system the focus of reforms should be on the practical development of fundamental rights and freedoms, not on definitions of institutional competence. Furthermore, the connections between the legal system and the broader social system should be considered in order to reach the next, even more important, step of analysis. Without open and genuine knowledge of the state of affairs in society, it is impossible for social capital and trust to grow. Consequently, freedom of speech and the free flow of information are crucial.

How to Monitor Development?

Dimensions and Indicators Above we have attempted to prove that freedom of information and the development of the rule of law are fundamental principles of a free functioning society. However, these basic values have not been formulated in such a way as to facilitate monitoring and evaluation. Moreover, the lack of conceptual clarity has been exacerbated by the introduction of related values and principles into legal and political frameworks—freedom of speech, equality and respect for fundamental rights, efficient justice systems and access to justice.

A relevant question is asked in a concept paper, "Monitoring and Evaluation of the Rule of Law and Justice in the EU: Status Quo and the Way Ahead?", prepared by The Hague Institute for the Internationalisation of Law's (HiiL) Innovating Justice Forum. HiiL is an independent research and advisory institute devoted to promoting a deeper understanding and more transparent and effective implementation of justice and rule of law worldwide.[17]

HiiL has done excellent work in monitoring and evaluating rule-of-law development in EU countries. These analyses could be useful worldwide. The question is: can we find indicators to evaluate rule-of-law development? The rule of law has been defined as a multidimensional concept consisting of the following eight facets:

Rule-of-Law Dimensions[18]

- *Accountability* to the law refers to the processes, norms and structures that hold the population, organisations and public officials legally responsible for their actions and imposes sanctions if they violate the law.

- *Access to information* refers to the ability of citizens and organisations to request, receive and process public information.
- *Independent judiciary* Judges and other dispute resolution professionals are not subject to external pressure, notably from the executive and legislative branches of government, and resolve disputes according to the law.
- *Effective judicial system* (criminal, civil and administrative) provides mechanisms for recognising, protecting and enforcing rights and legitimate interests. The emphasis of this dimension is on the effectiveness of the legal system, which means that the disputes are resolved in a predictable, timely and cost-effective manner.
- *Respect for the fundamental rights* as foreseen in the Charter on Fundamental Rights and European Convention on Human Rights. Respect for fundamental rights means that there are accessible mechanisms for remedying violations of fundamental rights and the citizens have equal opportunities to use these mechanisms to seek redress.
- *Effective implementation* of laws refers to the extent to which laws, regulations and case law are implemented in an equal and fair manner.
- *Access to justice* refers to the equal availability of dispute resolution mechanisms which lead to fair outcomes in all areas of lawcivil, family, criminal, administrative etc. Access to fair dispute resolution mechanisms and outcomes should not be contingent on wealth, social or political power, ethnicity, gender, religion or any other characteristic of the person. Geographical location, access to technologies and legal awareness should also not be factors that impede access to justice.
- *Absence of corruption* Corruption is the abuse of public powers for private gains. Public and private officials who are entrusted with powers have to use this power for achieving legitimate outcomes. Use of entrusted power for attainment of illegitimate private gains is corruption.

There is also a need to operationalise justice. Some starting points are very important: (1) Justice as fairness (see John Rawls' famous work *A Theory of Justice*, 1971, 2nd ed. 2005). Fairness refers to having equal rights to basic liberties and ensuring that inequalities are remedied to the greatest benefit of the least advantaged members of society. (2) Empirical justice research. The research has to be identified with many specific factors that make a procedure or an outcome fair as experienced by the people involved. (3) Bottom-up justice, interests and needs of citizens. Dimensions of bottom-up justice are accessibility to dispute resolution (low costs of access to justice), fair dispute resolution processes (procedural, interpersonal and informational justice) and fair outcomes (functionality, transparency etc.).

From these starting points, we might be able to develop indicators to measure rule-of-law experiences by gathering material based on the judicial experiences of citizens and making use of existing sources. However, there are some problems in drawing conclusions from these indicators, such as: who may carry out these calculations?; are they too largely based on interview material?; and what kind of monitoring and follow-up operations would it be possible to carry out when results turn out negative?

Different Indicators Moreover, research organisations and international institutions are currently creating indicators for the evaluation of justice and the economy, as well as human rights. Many of these analyses are very limited in scope, and a broader dialogue for rule-of-law monitoring in Europe is necessary. In this context, here is a list of some contemporary rule-of-law datasets. [19] There are several references to the materials online.[20] Many of the indicators at the same time measure the degree of freedom of speech and social climate.

1. **The World Justice Project** (66 countries) is a multinational and multidisciplinary initiative which aims to monitor the rule of law throughout the world. The model is based on four universal principles of rule of law, which are defined as: (1) accountable government; (2) published and stable laws that protect fundamental rights; (3) an accessible, fair and efficient process; and (4) access to justice.
2. **The Freedom of the World Index** (194 countries) provides an annual evaluation of the state of global freedom. Experts assess the extent to which a set of ten political rights and fifteen civil liberties are implemented in real life.
3. **Doing Business** (183 countries) is a World Bank-associated project which assesses annually the impact of legal regulations and administrative practices on the business environment.

4. **The Global Competitiveness Report** of the World Economic Forum (GCR, 42 countries) studies various factors underpinning national competitiveness. Twelve pillars of competitiveness are identified and studied mostly with data from the World Economic Forum's annual Executive Opinion Survey.
5. **The Index of Economic Freedom of the Heritage Foundation** (183 countries) analyses ten components of economic freedom which are grouped into four domains: rule of law, limited government, regulatory efficiency and open markets.
6. **The Democracy Index** (167 countries) is compiled annually by the Economist Intelligence Unit. According to their assigned scores countries are categorised into full democracies, flawed democracies, hybrid regimes and authoritarian regimes.
7. **The Sustainable Governance Indicators** (SGI, 31 countries) evaluate aspects of governance in the member states of the Organisation for Economic Co-operation and Development. Data are collected from official statistical sources and expert opinions.
8. **The Civicus Civil Society Index** (56 countries) assesses the state of civil society at national level. Civil society has been conceptualised as "the arena, outside of the family, the state, and the market where people associate to advance common interest".
9. **The United Nations Surveys on Crime Trends and the Operations of Criminal Justice Systems** (100 countries) collect data on the incidence of reported crime and the operations of criminal justice systems with a view to improving the analysis and dissemination of that information globally.
10. **The International Crime Victim Survey** (ICVS) (37 nationwide, 78 cities) is a programme of standardised sample surveys that look at householders' experience of crime, policing, crime prevention and feelings of insecurity in a large number of countries.
11. **The Global Integrity Index** (GII, 38 countries) annually assesses more than 300 indicators of the existence, effectiveness and citizens' access to key national-level anti-corruption mechanisms (accountability of the law, access to information, absence of corruption, independent judiciary, effective judicial system and access to justice).
12. **The Cingranelli-Richard Human Rights Dataset** (CIRI) contains longitudinal quantitative information (195 countries) about the level of respect that national governments provide for fifteen

human rights, as recognised internationally. The index covers the concept of respect for fundamental rights. These rights include both physical integrity such as the right to not be tortured and civil liberties such as freedom of speech and freedom of religion.

13. **The Bertelsmann Transformation Index** (BTI) assesses and evaluates the progress, development and transformation of 128 countries in transition. Specifically, BTI focuses on progress in democracy, market economy and governance.
14. **The bi-annual report of the European Commission for the Effectiveness of Justice** (CEPEJ, 45 countries) describes and compares the judicial systems of the Council of Europe member states. The statistics describe national systems but do not evaluate them.
15. Transparency International defines corruption as "the abuse of entrusted power for private gain". **The Corruption Perceptions Index** (CPI) ranks countries according to the degree to which corruption is perceived to exist among public officials and politicians. Perception-based data (178 countries) is collected from different sources "produced by reputable organisations and data-gathering organisations".
16. **Worldwide Governance Indicators** (WGI) (212 countries) is a project of the World Bank mostly known from the popular Governance Matters series of papers authored by Daniel Kauffman and others.
17. **The Global Peace Index** (153 countries) is composed of 23 indicators, ranging from a nation's level of military expenditure to its relations with neighbouring countries and the level of respect for human rights. Included in the index are indicators such as violent crime, access to weapons, prison population, displaced people, homicides, security officers and terrorist acts.
18. **The Human Rights Index** (195 countries) measures the degree of lack of protection or noncompliance with their obligations of states in regard to human rights and international humanitarian law. Similar to the CIRI and GPI, the main focus is on respect for human rights.
19. **The Failed States Index** (177 countries), prepared by the Fund for Peace and published by Foreign Policy, is based on their levels of stability and pressures they face. It includes 12 indicators includ-

ing human rights, delegitimisation of the state, demographic pressure, and so on.
20. **The Ibrahim Index of African Governance** is a composite index (48 countries) constructed by combining underlying indicators in a standardised way to provide a statistical measure of governance performance in all African countries. The three categories are independent judiciary, absence of corruption and respect for fundamental rights.
21. **The Political Terror Scale** (PTS, 190 countries) measures levels of political violence and terror, using a 5-point indicator.
22. **The Human Security Index** (HSI) (232 countries) is intended to represent the recent-to-current situation. It includes the Economic Fabric Index, the Environmental Fabric Index and the Social Fabric Index (most important to justice-related issues), indicators of freedom from corruption, environmental protection, peace, protection of diversity and information empowerment.
23. **The Social Institutions and Gender Index** (SIGI) (102 countries) draws on twelve social institutions' variables from the OECD Gender, Institutions and Development (GID) Database that have been grouped into five categories or sub-indexes: Family Code, Physical Integrity, Son Preference, Civil Liberties and Ownership Rights. The SIGI looks at discriminatory social institutions.

These databases contain an enormous amount of information that can be combined in different ways to monitor judicial, economic and social development. Even though most of the indicators are based on interviews, and therefore opinions, they are clearly significant as guide-posts of development. This may, however, narrow down the perspective of analyses to mere evaluation of first-hand experiences, resulting in more general issues related to power structures and the functioning of legislative policy and public authority being left in the background.

Research shows that there is a correlation between the strength of the rule of law and economic growth. Favourable rule-of-law development promotes economic growth.[21] However, the exact cause-and-effect relationship is difficult to determine due to the quality of data and the complexity of the phenomenon. Be that as it may, it is obvious that a functioning rule of law is a central prerequisite for a stable and predictable economic climate. Similarly, the fostering of ecological sustainability requires new research and several of the hallmarks of the rule of law. The transition towards more sustainable technologies and modes of production will not succeed without viable judicial systems.

The relationship between the rule of law and the social dimension of development is even more straightforward. Social equality suffers if there are deficiencies in the implementation of human and basic rights, especially freedom of speech. Corrupt systems are predisposed to exclude citizens from public services. In particular, safeguarding of the equal provision of education and health services depends both on functioning legislation and on sufficient access to information. "The rate of economic growth turns out to respond more to education at the secondary and higher levels", writes Barro.[22]

We can conclude that the mainstay of sustainable societal development and social well-being is the protection of free speech and sufficient access to information. Not enough attention has been given to this fundamental aspect of the development of the rule of law. This is partly due to the limited scope of many of the indices discussed above and their tendency to measure development from differing perspectives. In order to construct a more comprehensive picture it could be of use to compile matrices of the survey data—unfortunately beyond the scope of this book. Later on we will outline the societal significance of freedom of speech and information in a different way.

Notes

1. Available at Freedom House homepage at: https://freedomhouse.org/content/request-proposals-seeking-annual-audit-tax-services-9, last accessed 28 August 2016.
2. The IPI homepage, available at: http://ipi.freemedia.at/about-us.html, last accessed 28 August 2016.
3. IPI World Press Freedom Review 2012–2013, p 6, available at https://www.academia.edu/7800829/IPI_World_Press_Freedom_Review_2012_2013, last accessed 28 August 2016).
4. https://rsf.org/en/ranking_table, last accessed 27 May 2016.
5. Available at https://freedomhouse.org/report/freedom-press/freedom-press-2015#.Vk8DDHbhCUl, last accessed 27 May 2016.
6. See The Declaration of Table Mountain, World Association of Newspapers and News Publishers, 4 June 2007. Available at http://www.wan-ifra.org/articles/2011/02/16/the-declaration-of-table-mountain, last accessed 28 August 2016.
7. The World Press Freedom Review 2012–2013, available at http://ipi.freemedia.at/fileadmin/resources/application/IPI_World_Press_Freedom_Review_2013_single_pages.pdf, last accessed 30 August 2016.

8. See www.bbc.com/news/world-asia-china-20338586, accessed 8 September 2016.
9. Press Freedom in 2013: Media Freedom Hits Decade Low, by Karin Deutsch Karlekar and Jennifer Dunham, available at https://freedomhouse.org/report/freedom-press-2014/overview-essay, accessed 29 August 2016.
10. See *Classical Rhetorics and Rhetorians. The Lives and Opinions of Eminent Philosophers, Diogenes Laertius (VI)*, Literally translated Br. C.D. Yonge, London MDCCCLIII.
11. See von Wright, *Philosophical writings, Part I: Practical Reason*, 1983 and *Part II: Philosophical Logic*, 1983.
12. See Jin-Guk Kim (Konyang University), Tae-Yun Kim (Hanyang University) and Junsok Yang (KIEP), Regulatory Transparency: What We Learned in Korea.
13. Jorge Zepeda Paterson, *House of Cards* a la Mexicana, *Los esfuerzos de Peña Nieto para hacer frente a la corrupción son tibios y desangelados*, published in *El País* (Madrid) 4 March 2015.
14. Haarala-Nystén (2001, p. 51) summarises: "the way out of corrupt politics is not centralism ... a strong authoritarian presidency weakens the parliament and the parties".
15. 1995: The Primacy of Culture and Social Capital, Civil Society and Development, *Third World Quarterly*, 2001, pp. 7–20.
16. Bowling Alone: America's Declining Social Capital, 1995, *Journal of Democracy*, 6: pp. 65–78.
17. See more at HiiL homepage: www.hiil.org, last accessed 27 May 2016.
18. See more at HiiL homepage: http://www.hiil.org/data/sitemanagement/media/Concept_Paper%20EU%20monitoring.pdf, last accessed 30 August 2016.
19. The list was compiled by Pekka Hallberg's research assistant *Mika Sainio* in 2013, based on the references of footnote 19 and analyzing the substance of each reference. This list was first published in *Hallberg, Pekka*, Rule of Law. Prospects in Central Asia. 2013 p. 124–127.
20. See http://www.americanbar.org/advocacy/rule_of_law.html; http://un.org/en/ruleoflaw/index.shtml; http://www.unrol.org; http://www.venice.coe.int/site/main/Central_Asia/default_E.asp; http://www.icj.org/; www.hiil.org.
21. See *Barro, R*: Democracy, Law and Order, and Economic Growth, Chapter 3, in 2013 Index of Economic Freedom, http://www.heritage.org/index/book/chapter-3, last accessed 27 May 2016.
22. See *Robert J. Barro*, Nothing is Sacred: Economic Ideas for the New Millennium, Cambridge 2002, 104.

CHAPTER 4

From the Origins of Freedom of Speech to the Modern Information Society

First Steps Towards Free Speech in the Ancient World

The Idea of Freedom of Opinion in Ancient Greece In the direct democracy of ancient Athens, citizens had the right to participate in common decision making. Of the total population of some 300,000 there were only 30,000 "citizens", meaning political participation and the right to speak was available to just 10 per cent of the population. The highest authority was vested in the assembly, in which any free adult male citizen could take part. The assembly would gather 10 times each year. Government power was in the hands of the council of 500 citizens selected by lottery a term at a time. This ensured wide participation in the use of public power. Aristotle described the system as "ruling and being ruled in turn" and insisted "that man is a political animal".[1]

We have asked Professor Paavo Hohti,[2] well known for his scholarship in classical Greek language and culture, to comment on freedom of speech in ancient Athens. He comments:

> The assemblies of Ancient Athens were opened with the question "who wants to talk?" This question clearly expresses how all citizens who had the right to participate in the assemblies also had an equal right to talk to all citizens

© The Author(s) 2017
P. Hallberg, J. Virkkunen, *Freedom of Speech and Information in Global Perspective*, DOI 10.1057/978-1-349-94990-8_4

Equality before the Law (isonomia), once it came to encompass all citizens in the 5th and 4th century BC, implied the same as democracy. Historian Herodotus says that the people (demos) can only be free it they govern themselves. The equal right to speak (isegoria), the first prerequisite for freedom of speech, was deemed inherent in the principle of equality before the Law. The right to speak essentially entails the freedom to voice one's thoughts and opinions frankly, candidly and without shame (parrhesia).

Ancient Greece's principle of freedom of speech is difficult to transfer to a different historical context, because the people, who used their right to speak, governed themselves. There was no power hierarchy that would have had to be keenly watched or against whom it would have been appropriate to apply free speech.

Were democracy and free speech smoothly compatible in Ancient Athens? Thucydides attributes these words to the statesman Pericles: "… what restrains us from lawlessness in public life is reverential fear, since we obey authorities and laws … albeit unwritten, the infringement of which will lead to everyone's joint contempt".

According to Pericles, freedom of speech was regulated by unwritten laws that were associated with the "shared idea of shame" (aiskhyne). Unwritten laws consisted of historical knowledge and customs that directed one to act in line with traditional values. These formed an ethical code that regulated social life with the aid of the sense of shame. This is where freedom of speech met its limits; what was at issue was where the limit was at any particular time. On the other hand, it was possible to break with the past, old values and customs by speaking out frankly, to free oneself from their burden; to thus devolve the task of argumentation and decision-making to the current generation.

It is easy to understand the cross-pressure between freedom of speech as expressed in the ideals of Athenian democracy and the ethical code that set limits to free speech. The limits were reinforced by a law against libel and hybris. The law provided strong protection against mental and physical abuse. In reality, the limits to freedom of speech were continually tested by the libel and vilification of political opponents. Had this not been the case, it would hardly have been possible to talk about free and frank speech. It was in the nature of freedom of speech that it was under constant scrutiny to see what was allowed and tolerated. The fate of Socrates provides an example of this.

We can conclude that the freedom to speak was enjoyed by those involved in the system of governance. Rather than a legally protected right, it was an acknowledged freedom from hierarchy, awe, reverence and shame. That freedom was challenged by the consequences of the rejection of shame (*aidos*), which had served as a cohesive force within the polity. Herodotus was justified in writing that the Greeks were a free people; he meant that they were not slaves under foreign conquest or domination.³

Readings of Socrates' trial, Greek tragedy and comedy, Thucydides's *History* and Plato's *Protagoras* show the paradoxical connections between free speech, democracy, shame, and Socratic philosophy and Thucydidean history.

The fate of Socrates was a great tragedy.

> In 399 BC an Athenian jury convicted Socrates, then aged 70, on two counts: rejecting the gods of the city and corrupting the young. Both of these charges involved solely things he had said, not any physical actions. In history's first democracy, renowned for freedom of speech, Socrates was convicted and executed for its exercise.

This historical event is well summarised by James Owens (1998):

> Was the Athenian free-speech tradition abandoned by a jury enraged at atrocities they had suffered just months ago, all linked directly to the ideas Socrates had taught for years? These questions have been argued by scholars for centuries. We have no actual writings of Socrates, only the Socrates of his devoted student Plato (*Dialogues*), reports from contemporary historians (Thucydides and Xenophon, both friends and admirers of Socrates) and a few mentions in the comedies of Aristophanes.
>
> We know, especially from the Republic, that Plato had only contempt for Athens' democratic and raucous law-making assembly, and idealized the social order and stability of Sparta. So did Socrates, according to Plato. Socrates is characterized in Aristophanes' 414-BC hit comedy play *The Birds* as the "idol of pro-Spartan malcontents and 'socratified' aristocratic bullies. The abundant literature of Athens verifies its wide-open democratic assemblies and its virtually unlimited freedom of speech.⁴

The solid beginnings of democracy and freedom of speech are clearly etched in the earliest literature of Athens. Serious philosophical questioning appears as early as Thales (circa 600 BCE), followed by schools of philosophy and unrestricted debate. Nowhere was free speech more hearty and open than on the Athenian stage. The classic plays of Sophocles and Aeschylus brim with candid public talk before the Athenian audiences, as do the later plays of Euripides. The satirist Aristophanes, in his play *Clouds* (423 BCE), delights the Athenians by freely poking fun at the gods, local politicians, the foibles and follies of Athenian daily morals, and at town atheist Socrates as a Sophist egghead.

There can be no doubt that freedom of speech was prized and uninhibited in ancient Athens. Indeed, while we need three words ("freedom of speech") to express the concept, the Athenians used only one: *isegoria*. "Whether or not the Athenians abandoned isegoria in their trial of Socrates, within fifty years of his death all genuine democracy was ended in Athens and throughout Greece. Free speech, isegoria, as in all past history, was silenced for the next 2,000 years".[5]

Freedom of Expression Becomes a Right in the Roman Empire Freedom of religion and opinion were especially valued at the beginning of the Roman Empire.[6] However, direct participation in decision making was not as common as in ancient Athens. Gradually, the system of government came to consist of political parties and interest groups. At the same time freedom of speech lost part of its character as a citizens' right, but was adopted into the political system through two central concepts: *Libertas* and *Res Publica*. The former referred to freedom from tyranny, although specifically in later Roman governance it meant the centralised use of power. The latter signified political rights. Roman citizens felt that they were part of a *Res Publica*, and enjoyed the freedom to express opinions granted by the political system.

This development is interesting in comparison to the culture of Ancient Greece, where freedom of expression was regarded as an individual's right to freedom from hierarchies. In Rome freedoms were simultaneously seen also as a duty that all citizens were to be treated equally under the law (see Zakaria, p. 32). The steps of rule-of-law development are identifiable in this duty vested in public power. The system guaranteed an individual's right to express opinions. This was manifested in different sectors: not only in electoral speeches and in senators' conduct in the Senate, but also in citizens' speeches in the Forum, in artistic works, poems and plays. However, during Caesar's time the exercise of freedom of speech started to become risky. Cicero, for example, risked it in his speeches, was finally forced to flee for his life, but was caught as he fled and executed.

The Roman Empire collapsed around 400 CE and was replaced by the Holy Roman Empire of autocratic popes, sharing totalitarian power with the kings of Europe. It is correct to observe that the most concrete legacy of Rome is the Roman Catholic Church—the culture of Rome became the culture of Catholicism (see Zakaria, p. 33). "Genuine freedom of speech throughout these many centuries (from 300 BC to the late Renaissance period in the 1600s) was ruthlessly suppressed as heresy or treason. 'Heretics' and 'traitors' were executed routinely by the many thousands.

All writings which veered from approved Church doctrine were banned or burned", writes Owens.[7]

Censorship Rears its Head Before Gutenberg's invention of the printing press in 1436, books and writings had to be laboriously copied by hand. In practice, this happened mostly in monasteries and other religions institutions. It was not necessary to check texts or to have carefully monitored censorship. Printing techniques and the distribution of several copies of the same text changed the situation. The first statute forbidding any unlicensed printing was issued by Pope Alexander VI in 1501.

Thereafter, in 1559 the Catholic Church published an index of "evil books". The aim was to hold responsible the distributors of anti-church dogma and thoughts. This famous list, the *Index Expurgatoris*, was compiled by the Roman Inquisition, but was in fact put into effect by local authorities who combed through over 300 publications.

Many famous writers later ended up on the Church's blacklist: René Descartes, Giordano Bruno, Galileo Galilei, David Hume, John Locke, Jean-Jacques Rousseau and Voltaire, to name but a few (see Anastasio Castillo, 2010, *Banned Book. Censorship in Eighteenth-Century England*). On the European scale, large-scale censorship ensued. As early as the Renaissance, however, censorship had been countered by the so-called Humanistic Movement that protested against the Church's attempts to curtail freedom of opinion.

A true counterforce emerged when the enlightened liberal philosophers challenged the tight shackles brought about by printing licences and censorship. The first to achieve fame was John Milton, who published the essay 'Areopagitica'—without prior licence—in which he opposed the licensing system that had been passed in Parliament. Milton's statement "Give me the liberty to know, to utter, and to argue freely according to conscience, above all liberties"[8] became a byword for freedom of speech and the coming Age of Enlightenment in Britain.

The Idea of Free Speech during the Age of European Enlightenment

Against Censorship At the forefront of freedom of speech in Britain were John Milton (1608–74) and John Locke, who cultivated the principle of separation of powers, even though some groups, such as atheists, were excluded from his principle of free speech (see Jonathan Israel, 2002, *Radical Enlightenment*, pp. 265–267). Later in the eighteenth century, many continental European philosophers continued developing liberal ideologies and broadened the concept of free speech to a universal principle. The most noteworthy of these thinkers were Baruch Spinoza, Denis Diderot and Claude Adrian Helvétius (see Jonathan Israel, p. 155, 781 ff.). An illustrative summary of the writings of John Locke, Jean-Jacques Rousseau and Thomas Paine is given in the anthology *Keystones of Democracy* (New York 2005).

One of the most famous liberals in history was John Stuart Mill (1806–1873), whose work *On Liberty* (1859) is considered a classic in its defence of free speech and its importance (see Karen Sanders, p. 66). Mill argued that without human freedom there can be no progress in science, law or politics, which according to Mill required free expression of opinion.

Having got its revolution out of the way early, England was able to proceed more smoothly and gradually along the road to democracy, but English liberty was dynamite when transported to France, where Church and state put up fierce resistance to the end. The result was, ironically, that Britain remained saturated with class privilege and relatively pious, while France was to become, after its own revolution, the most egalitarian and anticlerical state in Europe, at least in its ideals. Voltaire opposed tyranny and dogma, but had no notion of reinventing that discredited Athenian folly of democracy.

Not all Enlightenment thinkers were like Voltaire. His chief adversary, Jean-Jacques Rousseau, distrusted aristocrats not out of a thirst for change but because he believed they were betraying decent traditional values. He opposed the theatre, which was Voltaire's lifeblood, shunned the aristocracy, which Voltaire courted, and argued for something dangerously like democratic revolution.[9]

The differences in opinion between the Enlightenment philosophers are also reflected in modern notions of basic rights. Increasingly specific determination of rights and duties of the individual and, in particular, the protection of the individual's status in relation to public authorities has been an overarching trend. With regard to the history of ideas, it seems that in the Anglo-American world the inspiration of Locke is more prevalent: human rights are essentially taken to mean freedom from the state. Rousseau as a source of inspiration is more common on the European continent: human rights are more than a mere freedom from the state. Thus, the latter tradition has a more positive attitude towards the state as an instrument of common welfare.

Freedom of speech was not always the all-encompassing right it is today. When Sir William Blackstone wrote his famous *Commentaries on the Laws of England* in the mid-eighteenth century, he defined freedom of speech as the lack of prior restraint. By that he meant that the government could not stop someone from saying or publishing what they believed, but once a person had uttered those remarks, they could be punished if the type of speech was forbidden.

The English, like the Ancient Greeks, had established legal restrictions on three types of speech—sedition (criticism of the government), defamation (criticism of individuals), and blasphemy (criticism of religion)—each of which they called "libels". Of these three, the one that is most important in terms of political liberty is seditious libel, because ruling elites in Blackstone's era believed that any criticism of government or of its officials, even if true, subverted public order by undermining confidence in the government. While the government could not stop someone from criticising the government, it could punish them once they had done so.

During the seventeenth and eighteenth centuries, the British Crown prosecuted hundreds of cases of seditious libel, often imposing draconian penalties. When William Twyn declared that the people had the right to rebel against a government, he was arrested and convicted of sedition and of imagining the death of the King. The court sentenced him to be hanged, emasculated, disembowelled, quartered, and then beheaded. William Twyn was hanged in 1664 because he would not reveal the name of the author of the book titled *A Treatise of the Execution of Justice*. Given the possibility of such punishment after publication, the lack of prior restraint meant little.

The English settlers who came to North America brought English law with them, but early on a discrepancy arose between theory and practice, between the law as written and the law as applied.[10]

THE FIRST FREEDOM OF THE PRESS ACT

Legal Breakthrough The Enlightenment ideology also gained strong ground in Nordic countries. The most prominent Finnish Enlightenment ideologue was Anders Chydenius, whose thesis *"Den nationala winsten"* of 1765 laid down the leading principles of economic liberalism even earlier than Adam Smith. His idea of societal development in free nations underlined the need for a broad knowledge base.

It is thought that the Swedish Freedom of the Press Act of 1766 drew on the earlier writings of Peter Forsskål. Chydenius was a vehement advocate of the Act but its intellectual father was at least partially Forsskål (1732–1763). Forsskål had completed his doctorate at the University of Göttingen in Germany and his book *Thoughts on Civil Liberties* was originally his doctoral dissertation "De libertate civile". The Swedish-language version, published in 1759, was initially banned, but Sweden's then other main party, "the Caps", favoured Forsskål's ideas and protected him. Pekka Korpinen[11] has studied these historical events and also the background of.

Peter Forsskål, who, he says:

> hailed from the eastern part of the kingdom of Sweden, then already called Finland. He was, in Lund, the student of Carl von Linné, the best known botanist of the time and also a botanist himself. Linné named a plant after Forsskål. Linné's taxonomies pre-empted Darwin's theory of evolution. The liberal ideas of the 18th century might have emanated from social Darwinism, from the belief in progress. Much later in history traces of Darwinism can also be detected in the thinking of Marx.
>
> The end of the 18th century, the time following Sweden's position as a major power, was sort of an intellectual age of liberalism. This is only now beginning to be understood around Europe. Adam Smith's predecessor Chydenius was known in England as a great thinker. Forsskål is about to be similarly recognised in philosophy. In 1997 he was officially acknowledged as his face appeared on a Finnish stamp.

Let us return to the political thinking of Chydenius, the advocate of the Freedom of the Press Act. Characterised by Enlightenment individualism and influenced by John Locke's analysis of state power and separation of powers, Chydenius regarded coercive power as necessary in pursuit of the common good. However, it was not to be used in the particular interests of the powers that be, but rather for the securing of peace, security and private property for all. Drawing on the ideas of liberty and justice, Chydenius particularly emphasised the importance of freedom and the principles of economic liberalism (see also Nils Erik Villstrand, *Riksdelen*, 2009, p.95).

From Chydenius' point of view personal freedom meant everybody's right to freely utter, write and print whatever they liked. It was, however, incumbent on the citizen to be legally responsible for the abuse of intellectual freedom. Thus, Chydenius pursued a reasonable freedom of expression and the press on which a free system of governance could lean. In the absence of such freedom those who exercised power would not have sufficient knowledge to enact good laws or supervise the executive and the implementation of laws; nor would the people have sufficient knowledge to act according to the laws. The modern tension between public power and the citizen is apparent here too.

Freedom did not mean that the estates in the assembly could act in a high-handed manner. Instead, freedom presupposed that an enlightened citizenry would restrain them and prevent them from acting autocratically. This was precisely why the freedom to write and freedom of the press were important. Chydenius stressed the duty of the highest authority to particularly safeguard this side of freedom. At the initiative of Chydenius, the Freedom of the Press Act was adopted in the assembly of the representatives of the estates in 1766. It was a far-reaching reform, given that public critique against the political system was very rare during the first half of the eighteenth century. The first Freedom of the Press Act was not just the result of favourable political conditions—"the Caps' triumph over the Hats"—but its principles derived from a longer societal development process and the breakthrough of Enlightenment philosophy.

As was to be expected, various complications followed, but the law proved to be a success in Scandinavia. It is partly due to this Act that the European North, which previously had a very different image, became the world's least corrupt area and, concurrently, exceptionally socially responsible, with strong commitment to democratic principles. The Swedish name for the Freedom of the Press Act is *offentlighetsprincipen*, the principle of publicity. It is in Sweden that the Freedom of the Press Act was first put into practice, gaining a place in the country's constitution. The story of its origin should be better known.[12]

In its original formulation the Swedish Freedom of the Press Act was short-lived—a mere six years—but its effect on the general consciousness regarding rights was indelible. Recurring in new forms and developing in various ways, the way of thinking expressed by the Freedom of the Press Act of the Swedish Realm has today become a cornerstone of the worldwide struggle for freedom of information. Freedom of information is conceived as a prerequisite for freedom of expression, widely seen as a human right, and it is just a matter of time before it will finally be acknowledged as an integral part of them.

Legalistic Idea of Free Speech Gains Currency In 1770 the idea of freedom of the press was legally consolidated in another Nordic country, Denmark-Norway, under the leadership of Johann Friedric Struensen—although in the following years he pushed for certain restrictions to the law.[13]

The next legal milestone for free speech is to be found in the United States. Freedom of speech was established in the First Amendment of the United States Constitution in 1791, along with freedom of religion, freedom of the press and "the right of the people peaceably to assemble and to petition the government for a redress of grievances".[14] It is the first article in the Bill of Rights. This constitutes the basic norm for free speech and we will return to it later. Below is a brief look at its development.

From the time that the states ratified the First Amendment ("Congress shall make no law abridging the freedom of speech, or of the press") in 1791, until World War I, Congress passed but one law restricting speech, the Sedition Act of 1798. This was an ill-conceived statute that grew out of the quasi-war with France and expired three years later. Yet although this Act has been widely and properly condemned, it should be noted that it contained truth as a defence. During the American Civil War of 1861–1865, there were also a few minor regulations aimed at sedition, but not until the Espionage Act of 1917 and the Sedition Act of 1918 did the real debate over the meaning of the First Amendment Speech Clause begin. That debate has been public and has involved the American people, Congress and the President, but above all it has been played out in the courts.

The first cases to reach the Supreme Court grew out of these wartime measures aimed against disruption of the military as well as criticism of the government, and the Court initially approved them. The justices seemed to say that while freedom of speech is the rule, it is not absolute, and at certain periods—especially in wartime—speech may be restricted for the public good.[15]

Nowadays the principle of freedom of information has been approved as part of the legislation of around 70 countries—at its strongest within constitutions. Of the states approving freedom of information acts, 35 did so following the unprecedented worldwide revolution in openness in the 1990s. The number is growing every year; yet even today there are barriers to freedom of information in individual countries.

It is noteworthy that the Nordic countries were the precursors to the legal recognition of the idea of free speech. Today they remain among the top countries in the Press Freedom Index, and are highly ranked in competitiveness indices of the World Economic Forum. The same conclusions apply to the low level of corruption in Nordic countries.

The availability of documents guarantees that the actions of authorities can be followed and monitored. The importance of freedom of speech and specifically the meaning of free media as the watchdog of the use of power is evident. In principle, all citizens have the right to receive information about any documents from any civil service department. The availability of administrative documents is an old tradition. Even the taxation data of private citizens is public. It is obvious that government transparency and the availability of official documents are the foundations for low levels of corruption.

Free Speech as a Fundamental and Human Right

What Is a Fundamental Right? As a result of historical development, freedom of speech is nowadays recognised in the constitutions of most countries and in many international agreements as a fundamental right that belongs to every human being. On a national level the key role is a vested adherence to the constitutional articles relating to free speech and access to information. It is therefore appropriate to start our legal consideration by taking a look at constitutional development.

Fundamental rights are regarded as individual rights enacted in national constitutions. The definition of a fundamental right is often paired with substantive content in addition to its formal constitutionality. Only fundamental, especially important rights can be regarded as basic fundamental rights. These rights must be common and, in principle, apply equally to all. Consequently, special group rights, for example earlier privileges accorded to the upper class, have not been fundamental rights.

Despite differences in various countries' social systems they share many common features when it comes to individual rights that have been enshrined and protected in their legal systems. The code of fundamental rights is inherent in national constitutions. By contrast, the term "human right" refers to basic rights guaranteed to individuals under the auspices of international agreements. Although the formal bases of fundamental and human rights are different, their content pertains largely to the same rights; there is significant interplay between them.

Fundamental rights are characterised by stability and a legalistic nature due to their constitutional status. A constitution's position as the bedrock of the state and its judicial institutions also signifies a reluctance to make changes to its content. Additionally, it is important that the constitution is a true reflection of any system of state power and the basis of an individual's legal status.

Enhanced formal legal validity is typical of fundamental rights. Fundamental rights can be changed or deviated from only through country-specific special legislative procedures. Thus, freedom of speech is more securely protected by the constitution than by ordinary laws or statutes. Fundamental rights are higher in the legal hierarchy than ordinary laws, and thus hold significance as the value base of the whole legal system. The nature of fundamental rights as basic norms conveying the content of justice is well-described by American Professor A.E. Dick Howard (see The Indeterminacy of Constitutions, *Wake Forest Law Review* 1996, pp. 383–410).

Fundamental rights are an integral feature of the rule of law. These features include the requirement for the constitutional safeguarding of civil liberties and legal protection. In Finland, fundamental rights were previously considered individual freedoms from state action. Nowadays individual freedoms and rights have come to mean both the centrality of the system of fundamental rights in the judicial system and an individual's right to self-determination. Fundamental rights set active responsibilities to state power. A return to the source ideals of Ancient Greece and Rome is identifiable.

Background to the Documentation of Fundamental Rights Fundamental rights were included in a written constitution for the first time in the settlements of North America at the end of the eighteenth century. One of the central documents of the French Revolution had been the Declaration of the Rights of Man and of the Citizen of 1789, which was referred to later on in the preamble of 1791 Constitution of the United States. The declaration's import to the development of constitutional and fundamental rights in Europe has also been crucial.

These days most countries' constitutions include some form of fundamental rights. The most important exception is the United Kingdom, which has neither a written constitution nor a constitutional listing of individual rights. However, Magna Carta of 1215 and the Bill of Rights of 1688 have often been interpreted as the early equivalents of constitutional fundamental rights.

Comparison Between Different Fundamental Rights Traditions The constitutions of European countries have traditionally guaranteed particularly civil liberties (e.g., freedom of speech, freedom of religion and right of ownership) and equality, following the model of the French Revolution. The inclusion of economic, social and cultural rights is characteristic of post-World War II constitutions. In the past few decades, Sweden (1974, 1976, 1979), Canada (1982) and the Netherlands (1983) have reformed their fundamental rights norms. The whole system of fundamental rights was remodelled by the 1995 reform in Finland. In addition, reforms have long been under way in Switzerland and Austria.

In legal comparisons, we must not restrict ourselves to comparisons of Western constitutions, however, as most fundamental rights were also guaranteed in, for example, the 1977 Constitution of the Soviet Union, at least formally. In addition, the development of increasingly detailed legislation on fundamental rights and a shift towards the principles of socialist market economy and better comparability with Western constitutions can be seen in Chinese constitutional reform since 1982. Generally, it may be observed that the focus of constitutions is gradually switching towards fundamental rights legislation.

Yet there are clear differences in the emphases, and in the precision of legislation, between civil liberties on the one hand and economic, social and cultural rights on the other. The question is, of course, also about the existence of economic resources for the implementation of different fundamental rights.

Increasingly specific determination of the rights and duties of the individual and, in particular, the protection of the individual's status in relation to public authorities has been an overarching trend. With regard to the history of ideas, it seems that in the Anglo-American world the inspiration of Locke is more prevalent: human rights are essentially viewed as freedom from the state. Rousseau is a more common source of inspiration on the European continent: human rights are more than a mere freedom from the state. Thus, the latter tradition has a more positive attitude towards the state as an instrument of common welfare. Herein lies, in our view, the most significant difference in traditions, which also explains aspects of the relationship between freedom of speech and the use of power. In the Anglo-American tradition freedom of speech is regarded an individual right, whereas in the European tradition the public power's duty to safeguard societal openness is also at issue.

In the process of globalisation, international human rights obligations play an important role. However, international human rights obligations are not a sufficient measure of fundamental rights. If there are financial and realistic possibilities to do so, further steps should be taken to safeguard everyone's rights and obligations. On the other hand, it is important that fundamental rights should be realistic.

In Search of the Reality of Free Speech

Quo Vadis? The map collection of the Nordic explorer Nordenskiöld provides a fascinating insight into the world of the olden days. At the turn of the millennium there was an exhibition of these maps called *Terra Cognita* in Helsinki. The exhibition showed concretely how the old worldview was culture bound and, in addition to knowledge, dependent on beliefs. There is good reason to wonder whether our modern maps are any more accurate or real.

Today, we talk about the information society. The information revolution, with the importance of networks and the demolition of old hierarchies, has resulted in knowledge being placed at the core of the economy. Flowing networks promote globalisation but are also sources for international civic societies and subversive movements.

The information society's atmosphere has been aptly described by the discipline's guru Manuel Castells. He observes that of essential importance is the tension between global technological and economic networks and local identities. Identities are formed both among one's local reference groups and among far-off like-minded people with whom one connects through networks. It is predicted that the next generation will chase after such experiences.

However, it remains a question as to whether we are forgetting the vast societal and cultural differences of the world while reviewing the development of information technology. Maybe development is not after all so simple and unidirectional. We must go about on our travels with our eyes open!

Let us resort to a proper map as we embark upon a journey to investigate the safeguards and reality of free speech and the principle of publicity. Our basic material consists of the principles concerning freedom of speech, fundamental rights and laws, as well as the exceptions to the rule in various countries and continents. We will discover common principles, but also differences due to traditions, societal realities and systems of power. Consequently, the viewpoint "law in books" does not adequately depict the safeguards of free speech. Instead, we must somehow get a deeper picture of the reality, of the "law in action".

Let us start with the authors' region, the Nordic countries. As has been discussed above, the Nordic countries have a strong tradition of free speech. We can illustrate that rule-of-law development is largely based on the historical and social circumstances of the countries concerned, and that the question here is more about embarking on a dialogue and a new dynamic process than about delivering a finished product. Nordic rule-of-law thinking is practical in nature. It underlines the importance of traditional conformity to law, separation of powers, free participation and representative democracy, and today an increasing focus on fundamental and human rights as standard features of the rule of law.

Writing in 2012 about the media landscape in Scandinavian countries, which are consistently ranked highest in the world for both freedom of the press and participatory democracy, Lauren Kirchner asks: what are these countries doing right? She points to two reasons. First, she praises press self-regulation. She also notes it is unusual to see a US journalist favouring press regulation of any kind. Here is Kirchner's view:

> Self-regulation works, as long as everyone's on board. Scandinavia's press councils are independent organisations, staffed and (for the most part) funded by the journalism industry, that were established to give readers a place to bring grievances against news outlets. Each one is like a combination ombudsman and courtroom: the reader with the complaint and the news organisation in question have their say, and then a group of journalists, editors, and members of the public decide whether to uphold or deny the complaint.
>
> If they decide that the news organisation has broken the journalistic code of ethics, the organisation must pay penance by printing or broadcasting a notice saying so. Involvement in the press council system is voluntary, but pretty much every news organisation in each country belongs; audiences recognise the outlets' signing up for such scrutiny as a kind of stamp of accountability.[16]

Next we will head to the European continent, visit Great Britain and Ireland and then sail across the Atlantic to North America. Our journey will continue via the Caribbean to South America and then to Africa. The huge, populous Asian continent provides the explorer with countless experiences, traditions and opposites of modernity, as well as illusions of and restrictions to free speech. Our last stop is Australia.

As travellers we will attempt to illustrate the legal foundations and different realities of free speech in various countries and continents. The main material consists of countries' constitutions and other regulations relating to freedom of speech, the most interesting court cases and current news on the state of free speech. As the reader will soon notice, it is challenging to avoid a rather dry mode of presentation when the material is so extensive.

In case the reader believes we are overstating the limitations and threats to free speech are overly pronounced, we invoke the Polish thinker Stanislaw Krzeminski (published 1 May 2009 as a cultural act Zarysy Literackie (1895) as a facsimile reprint and with a comment): "Were it not for a book that protests against today's injustices, humankind would not progress".

NOTES

1. See Richard Kraut, Steven Skultety, *Aristotle's Politics: Critical Essays*. Rowman & Littlefield, 2005, p. 174.
2. This comment was written by Paavo Hohti specifically for this book and is published, unedited, with his permission. It has not been previously published.
3. See also Fareed Zakaria, *The Future of Freedom*, 2003, p. 32.
4. Socrates, Freedom of Speech and Hate Crime by James Owens, PhD. (December 1998), p. 3., available at http://www.solargeneral.org/wp-content/uploads/library/Free-Speech/socrates-freedom-of-speech-and-hate-crime.pdf, last accessed 27 May 2016.
5. Socrates, Freedom of Speech and Hate Crime by James Owens, Ph.D. (December 1998), p. 5., available at http://www.solargeneral.org/wp-content/uploads/library/Free-Speech/socrates-freedom-of-speech-and-hate-crime.pdf, last accessed 27 May 2016.
6. See M.P. Charlesworth, 1943, http://journals.cambridge.org/action/displayAbstract, last accessed June 2015.
7. Socrates, Freedom of Speech and Hate Crime by James Owens, Ph.D. (December 1998), p. 5., available at http://www.solargeneral.org/wp-content/uploads/library/Free-Speech/socrates-freedom-of-speech-and-hate-crime.pdf, last accessed 27 May 2016.
8. See Karen Sanders, 2003, *Ethics and Journalism*. Universidad de Navarra. Sage Publications.
9. Whereas Voltaire insisted on the supremacy of the intellect, Rousseau emphasised the emotions, becoming a contributor to both the Enlightenment and its successor, Romanticism. And whereas Voltaire endlessly repeated the same handful of core Enlightenment notions, Rousseau sparked off original thoughts in all directions: ideas about education, the family, government, the arts, and whatever else attracted his attention. For all their personal differences, the two shared more values than they liked to

acknowledge (http://www.google.com/ The Enlightenment, accessed June 2015).
10. See more: Lonang Institute at (http://www.lonang.com/exlibris/blackstone/), last accessed June 2015.
11. This comment was written by Pekka Korpinen specifically for this book and is published, unedited, with his permission. It has not been previously published.
12. See Anders Chydenius, *Legacy Today 2*. Ed. Juha Mustonen 2006. Electronic book on the homepages of Chydenius-foundation website: http://www.chydenius.net/pdf/worlds_first_foia.pdf, http://www.chydenius.net/julkaisut.htm, accessed June 2015.
13. See Jonathan Israel, 2010, *A Revolution in the Mind*. Princeton University Press, p. 76 and H. Arnold Barton, 1986, *Scandinavia in the Revolutionary Era – 1760–1815*, University of Minnesota Press, pp. 90–91.
14. See more David A. Schultz, 2010, *Encyclopedia of the United States Constitution*, Infobase Publishing.
15. See more from former District Judge Bob Moss at http://www.ruleoflawus.info/freedom_of_speech.htm, last accessed June 2015.
16. See more: http://www.theguardian.com/media/greenslade/2012/jul/04/us-press-publishing-sweden, last accessed June 2015 (Roy Greenslade, 4 July 2012, *The Guardian*).

CHAPTER 5

Freedom of Speech in Books and in Action

DEVELOPMENT OF FREEDOM OF SPEECH IN FINLAND

From the Idea of Free Speech to the Present Law The constitutional 1766 Freedom of the Press Act did not clearly differentiate between the right to print and the availability of documents. At times the prevalent interpretation was that documents were only accessible if they were demanded for the purpose of printing and if printing costs had been deposited. Mathias Calonius, a known Nordic legal scholar of the time, advocated the removal of these obstacles and defended the principle of accessibility.

In the years that followed critique of the government resulted in the curtailment of freedom of the press. In the 1780 Act printers were made liable for offences of press publications. A royal edict of 1804 disallowed objections and dissenting opinions in minutes of proceedings.

After the war with Russia, Finland separated from Sweden and became an autonomous Grand Duchy within the Russian Empire in 1809. At the same time, this event was a step towards the development of an independent Finland. In the old motherland of Sweden, the new form of governance starting in 1809 confirmed not only the freedom of the press but also the principle of availability of information, and thus strongly underlined the existing principles of the Freedom of the Press Act.

Initially in Finland there was no great struggle for freedom of the press or for the availability of documents. In 1829, early on in the period of autonomy, an Act re-established a licence system for printing and advance censorship. However, in 1847 the system was tempered by means of partial availability of documents Acts that related to the protocols emanating from public authorities and governors. Consequently, availability was firmly monitored by officials.

The sort of political press required for the strengthening of public opinion dates to the 1840s in Finland. At this juncture, J.V. Snellman, who later emerged as the national philosopher, came forward to defend freedom of speech. He wrote these famous words in *Saima* (the first newspaper) in 1844: "In our comfortable time, public affairs are decided upon in comfortable chambers, and none of these would become publicly known unless the masters of printing printed them in black on white".[1] Gradually, media became the watchdog over the principle of officialism.

The next milestone, the Press Freedom statute of 1865, also included regulations concerning publication of documents. An official permit was always needed for access to print high-level government documents. A further Act in 1867, during the "regression" of the latter half of the nineteenth century, was based on a system of licensing and censorship. Towards the end of the century controls became ever stricter. Despite some initiatives, the enactment of the Freedom of the Press Act was postponed. Instead, after the general strike of 1906 a constitutional statute on freedom of expression, association and assembly was adopted. At the same time, censorship was abolished. This reform was almost radical at the time and supported society's move towards openness.

After Finland gained independence in 1917 and debate about the form of government was concluded, freedom of the press was deemed a self-evident constituent of the republic's 1919 governmental charter. The principle of accessibility was not included as a regulation. Despite this, the freedom of the press as a vital prerequisite for public intervention in irregularities, as well as for society as a whole, was specifically justified.

It was the first president of the Republic of Finland, K.J. Ståhlberg, who formulated the first proposal on freedom of information. The heavy years of war, 1939 and 1940–45, delayed the enactment of the law, but in 1951 it was finally adopted. The principle of freedom of information now prevailed. The authorities had to justify any demands for secrecy on legal grounds. Ståhlberg himself saw the freedom of information law as an opportunity to "efficiently keep watch on the actions of public authorities".[2]

Present Day In recent times, the meaning of free speech and freedom of information regulations was reconsidered during the 1995 review of fundamental rights under the constitution. The determinants of a democratic society were listed as freedom of opinion, open public discussion, free development and pluralism of mass media, and the ability to publicly criticise the powers that be. Freedom of speech was deemed a political basic right at its core. Its level of protection should be strong and the threshold for curtailment high.

The present 1999 constitutional provisions on freedom of speech secure everybody's right to receive information, opinions and other forms of communication without any hindrance.[3] This expression is in line with international human rights obligations, but it stresses democracy and the opportunity to participate more clearly. Everybody's right of access to information and public documents is also guaranteed. Openness, democracy and legal protection form a chain. The central purpose of the provisions is to guarantee the freedom to form opinions as a prerequisite of a democratic society. Thus, by its very nature freedom of speech is a basic political right.

The 1999 Constitution has a clear provision (Section 12) on freedom of expression and the right of access to information:

> Everyone has the freedom of expression. Freedom of expression entails the right to express, disseminate and receive information, opinions and other communications without prior prevention by anyone. More detailed provisions on the exercise of the freedom of expression are laid down by an Act. Provisions on restrictions relating to pictorial programmes that are necessary for the protection of children may be laid down by an Act.
>
> Documents and recordings in the possession of the authorities are public, unless their publication has for compelling reasons been specifically restricted by an Act. Everyone has the right of access to public documents and recordings" (see The Constitution of Finland 11.6.1999 nr. 731/1999).[4]

Freedom of speech is not tied to any particular form of communication, although traditionally it has been linked with freedom of the press. The provisions have been interpreted taking into account technological developments and have thus been extended to encompass new forms of communication such as television, public and cable broadcasting, although these latter operations can be distinguished from the print media by their technical and economic limitations.

The realm of freedom of speech encompasses all sorts of information, opinions and other communications regardless of their content and without reference to the purpose of their expression or publication. This is comparable to the freedom of speech articles in human rights agreements that strongly safeguard opinions, information and ideas. Consequently, the application of freedom of speech does not differentiate between political, religious, artistic, scientific, commercial, entertainment or other communicative messages. With regard to religious messages it must be pointed out that the constitutional provision (11 §) that guarantees freedom of religion and conscience attests to everybody's right to express their conviction.

In principle, freedom of speech is also connected to commercial forms of communication, although limitations on alcohol and tobacco advertising and other restrictions on advertising laid down by the Consumer Protection Act have been implemented through common legislation without being checked by free speech regulations. Even though advertising and other forms of commercial communication are not deemed to be at the core of free speech, they are protected against unjustified and arbitrary interference like other forms of communication (see Sami Manninen 2011, p. 464). An essential ingredient of free speech is the prohibition of advance censorship. Constitutional provisions prohibit the prior checking of forms of communications and other forms of advance censorship.

As in other countries, freedom of speech is not an absolute fundamental right in Finland, and it can be restricted. However, the constitution stipulates strict preconditions: (1) restrictions must be the subject of laws; (2) restrictions must be specific and (3) acceptable to society; and (4) the core of freedom of speech is out of bounds. Furthermore, (5) proportionality, (6) legal protection and (7) human rights obligations must be adhered to. Since any restrictions must be carefully considered, the system has remained very pro-fundamental rights. The core of freedom of speech above all safeguards political and societal discussion and communication. It is inextricably linked to the construction of the rule of law.

Political rights to freedom, specifically freedom of speech, are connected with the established principle of freedom of information, which has also been secured as a fundamental right. It means that documents in possession of the authorities and other records are public unless there are imperative reasons for restricting their publication. Everybody has the right to receive information about a public document or record. Although publicity of records is the principal rule, it can be departed from for reasons of privacy, commercial confidentiality or national security interests. Publicity is also restricted during the preparatory phases. More specific regulations are to be found in the law governing the publication of official processes.

Finland's reputation as the top-ranking country for press freedom has been compromised by the many rulings and convictions (18 convictions in the 2000s) that Finland had violated free speech. The question is mostly about where to draw the line between free speech and protection of individual privacy. This indicates the need for some repairs in Finnish legal practice as well.

Publicity of Documents The regulations on the availability of official documents as set out in the 1951 law were amended by the 1999 law on the reporting of official processes. The aim was to clarify grounds for secrecy by bringing them all together under one law, enabling the repeal of over 120 secrecy and confidentiality rules across many different laws and statutes. This is a complex area where active safeguarding of sufficient access to information is needed.

From the theoretical point of view there has also been a change: public power has been given a duty, in terms of the principles of fundamental rights reform, to observe transparency and good practice with regard to information administration, as well as to produce and share information. This new strategic objective involves a change from the principle of availability to the principle of information and thus emphasises the public authorities' active duty to promote transparency in governance. The objectives in Finland have been to extend the principle of openness, increase the reporting of preparation processes, promote access to information and clarify the grounds for restricting availability.

FREE SPEECH IN OTHER NORDIC COUNTRIES

Sweden's code of fundamental rights is relatively recent. It was adopted during the constitutional overhaul of the 1970s. A chapter on fundamental freedoms and rights was added to the constitution, including provisions for freedom and equality rights. Chapter 2 (Fundamental Rights and Freedoms) of the *Regeringsformen* protects personal freedom of expression "whether orally, pictorially, in writing, or in any other way".[5] The *Tryckfrihetsförordningen* (Freedom of the Press Act) protects the freedom of the printed press, as well as the principle of free access to public records (Principle of Public Access) and the right to communicate information to the press anonymously. For a newspaper to be covered by this law, it must be registered and have a "legally responsible publisher", a Swedish legal term denoting the person who is ultimately accountable for the printed material.

In terms of the reports by Reporters Without Borders and Freedom House, Sweden has been among the leading countries in freedom of speech rankings from the beginning. Its newspaper market is diverse, with many local and regional outlets. The government offers subsidies to newspapers in order to encourage competition. Media content in immigrant languages is also supported by the state.

The self-regulatory Swedish Press Council has jurisdiction over the print and online sectors. It also operates an ethical code, which is applied to broadcast media by Swedish Radio and Television. Public broadcasting has a strong presence but faces considerable competition from private stations.[6] Private broadcasting ownership is, however, highly concentrated.

As is the case in other top-ranking countries, the line between critical debate necessary for upholding a democratic society and reasonable limitations to free speech that prohibit, for example, incitement to violence towards a minority or a person has recently been the subject of vigorous debate. Mainstream media have been accused of self-censorship in the name of open debate.

A number of court cases concerning racism and populist right-wing movements have established limits to freedom of speech. For example, in 2012 the website editor for the extremist Swedish Resistance Movement was sentenced to a month in jail for intense anti-Jewish criticism posted by a reader (FH). Three journalists were convicted for acquiring an illegal gun during an investigation to shed light on the issue of the thriving underworld arms trade. The journalists took five hours to acquire a gun and turned it over to the police. The court's decision was criticised as a setback to investigative journalism (RSF). The case of Julian Assange has stirred debate as to whether he should be extradited to the USA, where he could face the death penalty for leaking classified government information. After the USA demanded his extradition, he was accused in Sweden of sexual assault and fled the country.

Since Sweden has such a strong historical tradition of free speech and reporting, there is a high threshold for the amendment of laws pertaining to these issues. Thus it has been deemed impossible to make changes to the existing 1991 Fundamental Law on Freedom of Expression that followed the Freedom of Press Act of 1766—although in an attempt to reduce areas of conflict between Swedish and EU law there has been a specific investigation into whether the historical laws have now become outdated by the influx of new media forms such as web portals, blogs and text messages. A task committee decided to essentially stick with present legislation, partly bypassing its instructions from the government.

Recent reforms have improved the situation of the individual in defamation cases. The previous threshold—that particular reasons should exist for defamation claims to be handled in a court of law—has been removed. Further, individuals are no longer responsible for the opposing side's legal costs even if they lose the case. This reform, as well as the concomitant change to the constitution, came into effect at the beginning of 2015. Although the reform strengthens the protection of privacy, it does introduce new kinds of difficulties for media conduct. In practice, reporters often make complaints about harassment and threats, which may indicate a polarising media environment.[7]

Norway's constitution is one of the oldest in the world (1814), which is why its fundamental rights provision is so limited. Constitutional protection is, however, strong with regard to freedom of religion, freedom of the press, the right to vote and personal liberty. Article 100 of the Norwegian Constitution has granted freedom of speech since 1814 and has remained largely unchanged since then. Article 142 of the penal code is a law against blasphemy, but no-one has been charged since 1933—although it was upheld as recently as 2004. Article 135a of the penal code is a law against hate speech, which is debated and not widely used.

Article 100 of the Constitution states:

> No person may be held liable in law for having imparted or received information, ideas or messages unless this can be justified in relation to the grounds for freedom of expression, which are the seeking of truth, the promotion of democracy and the individual's freedom to form opinions. Such legal liability shall be prescribed by law. Everyone shall be free to speak his mind frankly on the administration of the State and on any other subject whatsoever. Clearly defined limitations to this right may only be imposed when particularly weighty considerations so justify in relation to the grounds for freedom of expression.
>
> Everyone has a right of access to documents of the State and municipal administration and a right to follow the proceedings of the courts and democratically elected bodies. Limitations to this right may be prescribed by law to protect the privacy of the individual or for other weighty reasons. It is the responsibility of the authorities of the State to create conditions that facilitate open and enlightened public discourse (The Constitution of Norway 1814, Art. 100).[8]

Denmark's constitution (1953) has been regarded as typical in terms of freedom rights. It protects freedom of association, assembly and speech, as well as the right to vote and freedom of religion. Freedom of speech is granted by Grundloven 77 §: "Any person shall be at liberty to publish his ideas in print, in writing, and in speech, subject to his being held responsible in a court of a law. Censorship and other preventive measures shall never again be introduced" (Constitution Art. 77).[9]

The 1991 Media Liability Act (*Medieansvarloven*) created criminal and civil mandates that mass-media content and conduct must be consistent with the ethics of journalism and the right of reply, and also created the Press Council of Denmark (*Pressenævnet*) which can impose fines and imprisonment for up to four months.

The Danish newspaper *Jyllands-Posten* knew it was testing the limits of free speech and good taste when it published a dozen cartoons of the prophet Muhammad in 2006. But it could never have imagined how much. At least ten people died in protests. Several were killed in Afghanistan as police shot at a crowd besieging a Norwegian peacekeepers' base. Western governments reacted with shock and confusion. In France, home to Europe's biggest Muslim minority—roughly 10 per cent of the population—there was surprise at the relatively conciliatory response of Jack Straw, Britain's Foreign Secretary, who called the publication of the cartoons "insensitive" and "unnecessary".[10] Many in France were baffled at the reluctance of the British and American press to publish the cartoons themselves. At the same time there was little understanding, in many Muslim countries, either of how Western democracies function, or how they have evolved historically towards enshrining maximum personal freedom. Danish protests that there are no laws empowering the government to intervene were met with disbelief.[11]

The above chain of events has sparked numerous comments on media freedom and responsibility. At issue is freedom of expression, even when its use can lead to uncontrollable consequences and examinations of responsibility. These events have been analysed by, for example, British novelist and journalist Philip Hensher, author of *The Mulberry Empire*.[12]

FOUNDATIONS OF FREE SPEECH ELSEWHERE IN EUROPE

Destinations Having dug for the roots of free speech in the Nordic countries, let us now head south to the familiar countries of the old continent. The fundamental rights tradition is also strong in continental Europe.

In so-called "written law" or civil-law countries, constitutions have a high hierarchical position as norms. Hence, fundamental rights are already influential in the preparatory stages of law making and enactment, as well as in the evaluation of lower-level norms. Often the constitutions also stipulate the duties of the public when it comes to economic, social and cultural rights.

Let us start with **the Netherlands**, perhaps the most liberal and multicultural society in Europe. Reporters Without Borders' Press Freedom Index for 2013 has ranked the Netherlands as the second-best nation in the world in regard to freedom of speech and the press. Dutch history has been shaped by very distinct religious views, but as these views begin to dissipate—with about one-third of the inhabitants identifying as Roman Catholics, one-fourth as Protestants, 5 per cent Muslims and the remainder professing no religion at all—the Dutch people are becoming more compromising and tolerant of differences of opinion (*Europa World Yearbook*, 2012). This trend toward acceptance is demonstrated in their constantly changing government policies in relation to free speech and free press. Holland's long history as a colonial power casts a shadow over the country that cannot be dismissed.

Jessica Loechel describes the development of free speech in the Netherlands as follows: "The Netherlands was led early on to an emphasis on international trade. This constant interaction with foreign nations spurred the country's interest in the development of the rule of law in the world. 'The interest of the State demands that there be quiet and peace everywhere and that commerce be conducted in an unrestricted manner', stated Johan de Witt, leading Dutch politician during the mid-17th century. This philosophy has stuck with the Dutch people throughout history and has caused the country to join and support various international organisations, including the European Union of which it is a founding member."[13]

The existing Dutch constitution of 1983 includes a broad and modern set of fundamental rights norms: the first paragraph of Article 7 of the Dutch *Grondwet* grants everybody the right to make ideas and feelings public by printing them without prior censorship, but does not exonerate the author from their liabilities under the law. The second paragraph says that radio and television will be regulated by law, but that there will be no prior censorship of the content of broadcasts. The third paragraph grants a similar freedom of speech to the first for other means of making ideas and feelings public but allows censorship for reasons of decency when the intended audience may be younger than sixteen years of age. The fourth and last paragraph exempts commercial advertising from the freedoms granted in the first three paragraphs.

While the Netherlands' Constitution protects the freedoms of the printing press by granting the right to publish without prior permission, it has a much more restrictive hold over broadcast media. Established in 1928, the Radio Law required that for cultural/religious reasons, programmes that were in bad taste or disturbed the peace were prevented from being broadcast (*Media Policy for the Digital Age*, 30). The broadcasting rules became obsolete during World War II when the Netherlands was occupied by Germany. After the war, in 1947, the pre-war rules were restored with the addition of a licensing fee introduced by the Nazis. This required anyone who owned a radio to pay an annual fee to use their device (*Media Policy for the Digital Age*, 30–31). When television was introduced nine years later, the same rules applied to television broadcasting. In 1967, The Netherlands Broadcasting Law came into effect, ensuring that only public broadcasters were granted legal access to the airwaves.

The Provisional Act on Media Concentrations of 2007 makes it illegal for publishers and media groups to control more than 35 per cent of the newspaper market and no more than 90 per cent of the television, radio, and newspaper programmes combined (*On Media Monitoring*). The Media Authority is a group that serves as the watchdog for all broadcasters in relation to financial and content issues. Under this group there are various other monitoring groups to regulate diversity, fairness and evolution of various mediums (*On Media Monitoring*).[14]

Germany Germany, the current driving force of the EU's development, is the promised land of jurisprudence. The origins of rule-of-law development have initially been dated to the eighteenth century, when the idea of *fiscus*—inherited from Roman law—gained ground. Under this idea public power was perceived as *fiscus*, a legal person, and was thus determined to be subject to the law (Mayers 49, Forsthoff, p. 29 and 112). This, combined with Immanuel Kant's categorical imperative, gradually produced the notion of a liberal rule of law. One of the pioneers to extend conformity to the law and subjective rights to the realm of public governance was Georg Friedrich von Gerber (*Über öffentliche Rechte*, 1852).

Under Bismarck, Germany united to become a federal union, characteristic of which is the concentration of power. The Weimar Republic of 1919–1933 was governed by a constitutional, albeit formal, rule of law.

In the present context, we will leave out the dismal, dictatorial times of the Third Reich (1933–1945). Suffice to say that this period of darkness over human rights led, as if it were a counter-reaction, to the Bonn Constitution (1949) with its emphasis on the rule of law. The aim was to, by all possible means, reject the degradation of the previous era.

Thus German legal thinking has come a long way from the days of Immanuel Kant's categorical imperative to the liberal-democratic *Rechtsstaat* of today. The present political system of Germany has been characterised as a representative democracy. It has been said that the structure of the German federal system laid down in the Bonn Constitution of 1949 reflects a compromise between the supporters of a centralised federal system and those of a decentralised one. It seems that the federal system of united Germany is now caught in the "joint-decision trap", a situation in which beneficiaries of the status quo can block all reforms.

However, it may be that the actual situation is more complex. It has also been argued that at the federal level, strengthening the Council of States—which consists of members of the *Länder* governments—would mean a modification of the principle of the separation of powers.

In Germany freedom of expression is granted by Article 5 of the Basic Law for the Federal Republic of Germany, which also states that there is no censorship and that freedom of expression may only be limited by law. The press is regulated by the law of Germany as well as all sixteen states. The most important and sometimes controversial regulations limiting freedom of speech and the press can be found in the Criminal Code.

As regards to freedom of expression, the situation in Germany is largely positive. Freedom of expression is protected by the German Constitution and basic laws. The biggest limitations on freedom of expression are its strict hate-speech legislation, which criminalises incitement to violence or hatred. Germany has particularly strict laws on the promotion or glorification of Nazism or Holocaust denial, with paragraph 130(3) of the German Criminal Code stipulating that those who publicly or in an assembly approve, deny, or trivialise the Holocaust are liable to up to five years in prison or a fine. Hate speech also extends to insulting segments of the population or a national, racial or religious group, or one characterised by its ethnic customs.

Germany retains penalties for defamation of the President, insulting the Federal Republic, its states, the flag and the national anthem. However, in 2000, the Federal Constitutional Court stated that even harsh political criticism, however unjust, does not constitute insulting the Republic. The Criminal Code, however, remains in place.

While government and political interference in the media sector continues to raise concerns over independence of the media, plurality remains strong among regional newspapers, though due to financial pressure, media plurality declined in 2009 and 2010. Germany has one of the most concentrated TV markets in Europe.[15]

France's fundamental and human rights tradition is strong: we have already traced its roots to the post-revolution Declaration of the Rights of Man and of the Citizen. On this basis freedom of expression is generally protected, although it is limited by strict defamation and privacy laws. Several laws have been passed since 1972 that have further restricted this fundamental right. In addition, France's libel laws make it easy to sue for defamation.

The Declaration of the Rights of Man and of the Citizen—still of constitutional value—states in its Article 11: "The free communication of thoughts and of opinions is one of the most precious rights of man: any citizen thus may speak, write, print freely, save [if it is necessary] to respond to the abuse of this liberty, in the cases determined by the law".[16] In addition, France adheres to the European Convention on Human Rights and accepts the jurisdiction of the European Court of Human Rights.

The Press Law of 1881, as amended, guarantees freedom of the press, subject to several exceptions. The Pleven Act of 1972 (after Justice Minister René Pleven) prohibits incitement to hatred, discrimination, slander and racial insults. The Gayssot Act of 1990 prohibits any racist, anti-Semitic or xenophobic activities, including Holocaust denial. The Law of 30 December 2004 prohibits hatred against people on the basis of their gender, sexual orientation or disability. France does not implement any preliminary government censorship for written publications. Any violation of law must be processed through the courts.

France has some of the toughest hate-speech laws in the EU. The number of legal actions for hate speech multiplied after the 1881 Law on Press Freedom was amended to introduce the offence of inciting racial hatred, discrimination, violence or contesting the existence of crimes against humanity, which has been very broadly interpreted as the right not to be offended or criticised. Some civil society groups have even managed to force the cancellation of public debates in order to prevent potentially libellous or racist remarks.

Since 2004, wearing signs or clothing that overtly manifest a particular religious affiliation has been prohibited in schools. In 2011, France implemented a ban on the *niqab* or face veil in public places. In September 2011, Paris passed a ban on Muslim street prayers, restricting the right of religious expression.

France's privacy law is often described as the toughest in the world. This is because the publication of private details of someone's life without their consent is a punishable offence, with limited ublic-interest defences available. Privacy is safeguarded not only by civil-law provisions but also by the existence of specific criminal offences which indirectly promote the withholding of information and self-censorship and limit the exposure of political corruption.[17]

We can estimate that France's media are generally regarded as free and represent a wide range of political opinion. Still, they face economic, social and political challenges, in particular from the security services and from the country's stringent privacy laws. Since 2009, France's president has appointed the executives in charge of its public broadcasting outlets. This controversial measure was heavily criticised, as it was seen as politicising public broadcasting and brought its executives' independence into question.[18]

Switzerland The Swiss Constitution also guarantees freedom of speech and freedom of information for every citizen (Article 16). Yet the country has made some controversial decisions, which both human rights organisations and other states have criticised. The Swiss animal rights organisation *Verein gegen Tierfabriken Schweiz* took the country to the European Court of Human Rights twice for censoring a TV advert for the organisation, in which the livestock farming of pigs was shown. The organisation won both lawsuits, and the Swiss state was required to pay compensation. Another very controversial law is that persons who refuse to recognise the Armenian Genocide of 1915 are prosecuted. Holocaust denial is also illegal.

Hungary Hungary lies in the heart of Europe. Historically it was founded in the year 1000 with the crowning of King Saint Stephen. In a constitutional sense, and with its present borders, Hungary gained independence after World War I in 1920 following the collapse of the Austro-Hungarian monarchy. On the anniversary of the 1956 popular uprising, Hungary changed its constitution, transforming the country from a People's Republic into the independent and democratic Republic of Hungary on 23rd October 1989.

Modern Hungary is a constitutional and representative republic. In accordance with parliamentary rule, the Hungarian government is accountable to a unicameral parliament that has legislative and budgetary powers and is responsible for political oversight. We have already noted in this book how the political climate has gone through critical change lately—exactly how free speech has been trampled upon in political campaigns will be discussed later in the book. Here we will only examine the legal foundations of freedom of speech in Hungary.

The centre-right Fidesz party, in alliance with the Christian Democratic People's Party (KDNP), has in recent years had a two-thirds majority in the Hungarian parliament. This majority has allowed for changes to be made to the constitution. The Fidesz government has used its majority to make radical changes, including curtailing freedom of speech. At the same time, Hungary's ranking is continuously worsening.[19]

Freedom of speech was already formally protected in Article 61 of the Constitution of 1944:

1. In the Republic of Hungary everyone has the right to freely express his opinion, and furthermore to access and distribute information of public interest.
2. The Republic of Hungary recognizes and respects the freedom of the press.
3. A majority of two-thirds of the votes of the Members of Parliament present is required to pass laws on public access to information of public interest and on the freedom of the press.
4. A majority of two-thirds of the votes of the Members of Parliament present is required to pass laws on the supervision of public radio, television and the public news agency, as well as the appointment of the directors thereof, on the licensing of commercial radio and television, and on the prevention of monopolies in the media sector.[20]

The new Constitution, which entered into force in 2012, enables sweeping restrictions to free speech to be enacted (see also Chap. 7). In order to secure this power Fidesz revised the Hungarian electoral law during 2011–2013, albeit to fierce critique. The law was criticised because, to name but one reason, it clearly favours the biggest party. The Fidesz–KDNP alliance retained its two-thirds majority in the April 2014 parliamentary elections. In February 2015, however, a single by-election broke that majority. Which way will the pendulum swing next?

The European Union has objected to the Hungarian changes as it is feared they will restrict democracy and citizens' rights. Using its dominance of the legislature, the government installed a Fidesz loyalist as president in August of 2010 and increased control over a number of institutions during 2010, including the media (Freedom House 2013). Prime Minister Viktor Orban has accused the EU of interference in the country's internal affairs.

The new constitution significantly delimits the constitutional court's authority as it can no longer act upon amendments to the constitution unless there are technical mistakes in the order of enactment; the court can no longer intervene in the legal content itself. Subsequently, freedom of speech has lost some of its legal protection. To make matters worse, the parliament declared all decisions taken by the constitutional court prior to 2012 null and void.

Party political campaigning in the media is also restricted by the new constitution. Hungarian websites and commercial television stations are prohibited from carrying campaign content during the 50 days before an election (reduced from 60 days), though there are no restrictions on social media sites like Facebook, YouTube and Twitter (Freedom House 2013). The constitution now also requires university students to commit to working in Hungary after graduation in order to receive a government study grant. The atmosphere in society has clearly become more tense as a consequence of these measures.

United Kingdom As there is no written constitution in Great Britain, the evolution of rule-of-law thinking cannot be divided into formal stages. In common-law countries, written law has less significance than tradition. In addition to the Magna Carta, history reminds us of Oliver Cromwell's Ironside troops who advocated the idea of a separation of powers. From these roots, a strong model of a liberal-democratic state of law emerged, which also acts as a safeguard for free speech.

As pointed out earlier, the considerable emphasis on the status of Parliament and civil liberties has been a distinctive feature of British thinking, acting as the background for the traditional liberal-democratic form of governance. One of the milestones of rule-of-law thought was A.V. Dicey's famous work *An Introduction to the Study of the Law of the Constitution* (1885), which emphasised the objectives of halting misuse of power and ensuring the rights of the individual.

UK citizens have a negative right to freedom of expression under the common law. In 1998, the United Kingdom incorporated the European Convention, and the guarantee of freedom of expression contained in Article 10, into its domestic law under the Human Rights Act.

However there is a broad sweep of exceptions including: threatening, abusive or insulting language or behaviour intending or likely to cause harassment, alarm or distress or cause a breach of the peace (which has been used to prohibit racist speech targeted at individuals); sending any article to another person which is indecent or grossly offensive with intent to cause distress or anxiety (which has been used to prohibit speech of a racist or anti-religious nature); incitement to racial hatred; incitement to religious hatred; incitement to terrorism, including encouragement of terrorism and dissemination of terrorist publications; glorifying terrorism; collection or possession of a document or record containing information likely to be of use to a terrorist; treason, including compassing or imagining the death of the monarch or advocating the abolition of the monarchy (which cannot be successfully prosecuted); sedition; obscenity; indecency, including corruption of public morals and outraging public decency; defamation; prior restraint; restrictions on court reporting including names of victims and evidence, and prejudicing or interfering with court proceedings; prohibition of post-trial interviews with jurors; scandalising the court by criticising judges; time, manner and place restrictions; harassment; privileged communications; trade secrets; classified material; copyright and patents; military conduct; and limitations on commercial speech such as advertising. UK laws on defamation are among the strictest in the Western world, imposing a high burden of proof on the defendant.[21]

The well-known British journalist, Peter Preston[22] comments as follows:

> The English polemicist Mick Hume makes the crucial point about press freedom in Britain. It is in the hands of people who say "Of course I believe in a free press BUT". For there is always a "but" or a "however" that lets repression in. And that, in turn, is because we Brits don't have a constitution that secures our rights. On the contrary—and in spite of inflated rhetoric down the ages—we make and muddle things up as we go along. Our freedom is an ability to restrict and penalise when a mood or a crisis takes hold. That's why our reputation abroad drops so dismayingly—for instance, to number 36 last year (2014) on Freedom Houses league table of media liberty, co-equal with Malta and Slovakia. America has its First Amendment and formidable constitution to take away the "but" and the "however". Modern Britain just drifts with the tide.
>
> So when, in 2013, Edward Snowden discloses the secrets of relentless state surveillance to the *Guardian* and the *Washington Post*, what happens next? In the US, there's no thought of shutting down the debate, let alone prosecuting newspapers. On the contrary, and however glumly, administration officials work with journalists to make sure that the essential Snowden leaks can be published. However, in Britain officials from intelligence arrive at the *Guardian*'s offices and watch, in the building's basement, as copies of offending computer discs are destroyed. A courier for Glenn Greenwald,

the main reporter on the case, is arrested in a Heathrow Airport transit lounge and more discs are seized. There is an open threat to revise the long-standing, and long reviled, Official Secrets Act, with sentences that might send editors to prison for ten years. We all believe in press freedom, but …

See, moreover, how one bit of legislation piles on top of another. Here is the Regulation of Investigatory Powers Act which authorises the collection of meta-data—including records of journalist's contacts with their sources. Here is the Bribery Act, which makes it a possible offence to buy one of those sources (in public life) a good lunch. Here is the Data Protection Act, which tends to set privacy and confidentiality above the fact-gathering that every good investigation needs. Of course some good things happen along the way. There is freedom of information and some reform of England's draconian libel laws: but when you throw in the prior restraint of injunctions routinely granted and the chilling operation of contempt of court restrictions, not to mention the growth of secret justice in unreported cases, the balance is still hugely unfavourable. We don't even recite the mantra about believing in freedom very convincingly—even before we get to the "but".

How, though, does a nation that so bears down on the simple trade of journalism come to think of itself as democratic bastion of liberty? Why doesn't this mountain of restrictions affront the ordinary citizen (and newspaper reader)? In part, the problem is cultural, and historic. America, as we've seen over Snowden, doesn't trust the federal government, any more than it trusts big business to behave ethically. Britain, by contrast, is far more trusting. It cherishes a state-run system of health care that America would reject in an instant. It is oddly incurious about the steps authority takes in its name. Its number one fiction hero is a spy, James Bond.

Perhaps, over recent years, some of this complacency has begun to break down. Policing has undergone a long run of scandals. Parliament has been soiled by crookery over expenses. The secret services have put their name to some wretched rubbish (notably over Iraq). The almost saintly image of the BBC has been tarnished by paedophile horrors past and excessive pay-offs to departing executives in the present. But the press hasn't benefited from any of this. The seedy saga of phone-hacking, and of fat payments for information by the tabloid papers, has soured journalism's image too. There are very few heroes left, which means that new laws arrive without adequate scrutiny or defence. Worse, the parallel debate about press regulation—sparked by Lord Justice Leveson's inquiry—has constructed a potential royal charter regulator that the *Guardian*, the exposer of phone hacking, cannot live with because it puts members of Parliament, prone to displays of mass emotion and instant decision-making, in charge of any new Snowden-style crisis.

Naturally the *Guardian*'s views—like my own—tend to reflect what journalists, not lawyers, think. This isn't a clinical or forensic business. You can't take one segment of law in isolation and treat it quite separately from another. Nor can you miss the connections when Westminster attacks the European Convention on Human Rights, the Strasbourg Court, or indeed any international obligation freely entered into long ago. There's something chafing, something profoundly unhappy, about Britain's actual relationship with the rights of freedom. Law after law pulls us one way or another. Terrorist outrages at home or overseas tug us in America's wake, without America's safeguards. Yes, to be sure, we believe in a free press, raucous and unruly as our latest regulator grandly declares. But, but, but. Do we truly believe in the free, unfettered journalism that must exist to give it life?

In the past few years Britain has fallen in freedom of speech rankings, which has given cause for concern. Researchers from watchdog Reporters Without Borders, who compiled the World Press Freedom Index, also highlighted liberal libel laws which allow claimants of any nationality to sue in its courts. Libel "tourism" is seen as a way for the richest to clamp down on freedom of expression.

The UK's slide from 19th to 28th place is partly blamed on the fallout from the phone-hacking scandal at the *News of The World*, which prompted the Leveson Inquiry into press ethics. There were also concerns that the police had attempted to extract information from a number of private companies—including BlackBerry—to identify looters during the London riots.[23]

Ireland Freedom of speech is protected by Article 40.6.1 of the Irish constitution. However, the article qualifies this right, providing that it may not be used to undermine public order or morality or the authority of the state. Furthermore, the constitution explicitly requires that the publication of blasphemous, seditious or indecent matter be a criminal offence, leading the government to pass a new blasphemy law on 8 July 2009.

The scope of the protection afforded by this Article has been interpreted restrictively by the judiciary, largely as a result of the wording of the Article, which qualifies the right before articulating it. Indeed, until an authoritative pronouncement on the issue by the Supreme Court, many believed that the protection was restricted to convictions and opinions and, as a result, a separate right to communicate was, by necessity, implied in Article 40.3.2. This judicial conservatism is at variance with the concept of speech as a democratic imperative.

Italy We have already searched for the roots of the ideals of democracy and republicanism in ancient Athens and the Roman Empire. In this day and age we are faced with a different and altogether more complicated societal reality. Freedom of speech and the press are constitutionally guaranteed and generally respected in practice, despite ongoing concerns regarding the concentration of media ownership.

Where are these ideals found today? Research shows that trust in public authority has plummeted, in particular in Mediterranean countries. According to some sociologists, trust has been at its lowest in Greece at 3 per cent and in Italy at 10 per cent. Willingness to pay taxes is ebbing and corruption levels are high. The purpose of these surveys is not to label these or any other European countries. However, examples show how crucial social trust and social capital are to societal atmosphere and development of the rule of law.

In Italy the Constitution guarantees freedom of speech, as stated in Article 21, Paragraph 1: "Anyone has the right to freely express their thoughts in speech, writing, or any other form of communication". The Article also provides restrictions on acts considered offensive by public morality, as stated in Paragraph 6: "Publications, performances, and other exhibits offensive to public morality shall be prohibited. Measures of preventive and repressive measure against such violations shall be established by law. Such restrictions are enforced through the Italian Penal Code." (see the Italian Constitution of 27 December 1947, Art 21)[24] Even though the Italian Constitution does not specifically refer to broadcasting, it contains a number of provisions that bear upon its regulation.

Giovanna Loccatelli, a freelance Italian journalist based in Cairo, is concerned about the parlous state of journalism in her home country. Italians, whose civilisation once transformed the world, now stare inward.[25]

Media and freedom of speech issues have often recently been personified in media mogul Silvio Berlusconi, who has cut out the middleman between politics and the media by serving as Prime Minister of Italy while holding the majority of shares in Italy's largest free-to-air private TV company, as well as owning the country's largest publisher, largest advertising company and one of its most successful soccer teams, AC Milan. Often accused of using his media powers to deflect criticism, Berlusconi still manages to be mired in controversy and allegations of improper conduct—he has faced numerous accusations of corruption and bribery as well as a series of sex scandals.

The 2004 Gasparri Law on broadcasting has been heavily criticised for provisions that enabled Berlusconi to maintain control of the private media market, largely through ownership of the Mediaset Group, though his resignation from the premiership in November 2011 curtailed his parallel influence over state media. In February 2011 the Constitutional Court struck down a law that effectively guaranteed Berlusconi immunity from prosecution by allowing the prime minister to postpone any trial for up to 18 months. The ruling paved the way for a number of court cases against him to proceed. He finished his community service for tax fraud involving Mediaset in March 2015.

Italy suffers from an unusually high concentration of media ownership for its region. Berlusconi's departure from office late in 2011 helped to reduce this concentration in *de facto* terms in 2012; when in power, he had indirect control over up to 90 per cent of the country's broadcast media through state-owned outlets and his own private media holdings. Berlusconi still controls a significant stake in the private media, as he is the main shareholder of Mediaset, which owns several television channels; the country's largest magazine publisher, Mondadori; and Publitalia, Italy's largest advertising company. Publitalia controls 65 per cent of the television advertising market, giving Berlusconi's channels an advantage in attracting advertising. In addition, one of the country's major nationwide daily newspapers, *Il Giornale*, is owned by Berlusconi's brother. Nevertheless, these outlets suffered considerable losses after Berlusconi left office. Mediaset's profits were down 85 per cent in the first quarter of 2012 compared with the previous year.

Approximately 58 per cent of the population accessed the internet regularly in 2012. Blogs and social media have played a growing role in political debates and news dissemination. In May 2012, prominent blogger and comedian Beppe Grillo's Five Star Movement won the mayoral elections in the town of Parma and a number of other smaller towns, running on an anti-corruption platform that was disseminated largely through social-media tools like Facebook and Twitter.[26]

After a long career in the leadership of Helsinki, Dr. Pekka Korpinen has in recent years spent a lot of time in Rome and has written a book called *Berlusconi's Italy* (2011). Looking at the state of free speech in today's Italy, Dr. Korpinen[27] links, in an interesting way, Italy's media climate with religious traditions and reading culture:

> According to the index of world press freedom 2014 Finland has greatest freedom while Italy is ranked in the 49th place despite slight improvement in

last two years. "The models of respect for media freedom are in the northern Europe. Finland, Norway and the Netherlands have led the index for years. Their success rests on solid constitutional and legal foundations, which in turn are based on a real culture of individual freedoms, a culture that is more integrated than in southern Europe."

One of the problems in Italy is no doubt the still existing feudal features in society. In the media two families are very dominant, Silvio Berlusconi being the head of the other. When he entered politics and became a long time prime minister there were obvious conflicts of interest, which was not properly addressed in Italy. But there are deeper reasons. To understand the limitations of the freedom of expression in Italy the concept freedom has to be divided into two: to negative and positive ones.

In the following I will concentrate in the first hand on the positive freedoms, i.e. on the actual capabilities of the individuals to exercise their formal liberties. In this respect reading and writing skills are essential. These skills are not only learned but also inherited. To learn to live within written information it takes several generations.

It is striking how big differences there are between countries in the history of literacy even though education has been always considered one of the key factors in development and growth. It seems that religions have played a greater role that we think.

In the Jewish communities there is a historic tradition which obliges the fathers to teach their sons to read the Torah. This may be one of the factors behind scholarly success of the Jews. Among other achievements they have won by far most Nobel Prizes per capita in the world. In the Protestant religion it was important that everybody should read the Bible in their own language and have thus a direct dialogue with God.

In Sweden, which included also Finland then, King Charles XI made by church law the literacy a precondition to marriage as early as 1686 with the effect that at the end of 18th century almost all inhabitants were able to read (not necessarily write). Protestantism was closer to the Jewish Religion in many respects than Catholicism. The role of priests and Latin was much more important in the Catholic and Orthodox world. The Bible in local language was considered so dangerous that it was on the Vatican list of prohibited books until the third quarter of the 19th century. Latin was replaced by Italian language only in the 1960's in the church liturgy.

Against this background it is no wonder that two-thirds of the Italians were illiterate in the middle of the 19th century. In the Orthodox east Europe the figure was still lower. The literacy rate increased slowly and the reading and writing culture is still shallow. This has been reflected in among other things in poor Pisa learning skills results for Italy.

It is only natural that printed press never had similar role in society in Italy as in Scandinavia. The main channel to distribute information and influence public opinion is TV in Italy. (I have described this in details in my book Berlusconi's Italy, in Finnish 2011.)

The Berlusconi family has three TV channels with a market share of some 40 per cent of viewing time and 60 per cent of advertising income. If the state owned RAI can be coordinated with private TV channels the political impact is great second only to the concentration of information power in Putin's Russia. One could see for example in 2008 election this kind of coordination taking place.

Italy has a particular history of authoritarian governments and foreign rules. The Popes and the Fascists have left their fingerprints to liberties as well. Before Berlusconi the country was governed some fifty years by "the only alternative" Christian Democrats with close relations to the Holy See. The only serious opposition was initially Moscow controlled Communists with ideas of the dictatorship of the proletariat.

The Italian political system is still very unstable and the election law biased. Both Christian Democrats and the Communists have disappeared. Prolonged economic stagnation has given energy to the populists and extremists such as the Five Star Movement (M5S) that got in its first election appearance in 2013 as much as 25 per cent of the votes. The now ruling Democratic Party got 29.5 per cent of votes but has a simple majority in Parliament (lower house).

The TV dependence is one source of Italian political instability. Internet is, however, about to change the media world. The Five Star Movement is trying to compensate its disadvantageous position in the traditional media by relying heavily on the internet and e-referendums. The problem with the new media and network is the quality of information. And here again we come back to reading culture. With relatively narrow base of critical absorption capacity of the people internet may turn to means to further political unrest and even revolution in some countries.

In **Austria** the old national code of fundamental rights is still valid and is part of the 1867 Constitution, which codifies citizens' rights. Alongside this, the European Convention on Human Rights is keenly observed. Austria has a strong tradition of conformity to law and respect for fundamental rights in accordance with the idea of the hierarchy of norms advocated by the well-known, previously mentioned legal philosopher Hans Kelsen. Austria is high in the present international rankings at 12th place.

Countries that had earlier been liberated from authoritarian rule have also included broad codes of fundamental rights in their constitutions, for example, **Greece** (1977), **Portugal** (1976, 1982) and **Spain** (1978). Article 578 of the Penal Code of Spain prohibits the "glorification or justification, by any means of public expression or dissemination, of the crimes included in Articles 571–577 of this Code or of those who participated in its execution, or performance of acts involving disrepute, contempt or humiliation of the victims of terrorist offences or their families [...]".[28]

Fundamental rights have also played an important role in the constitutional reform of **Eastern Central European** countries that have been liberated from the shackles of socialism. The Constitution of the Republic of **Poland** specifically forbids the existence of "political parties and other organisations whose programmes are based upon totalitarian methods and the modes of activity of Nazism, fascism, and communism, as well as those whose programmes or activities sanction racial or national hatred, the application of violence for the purpose of obtaining power or to influence the State policy, or provide for the secrecy of their own structure or membership".[29] Now, however, the situation seems to be worse in Poland.

Development of the rule of law in Poland, much like Turkey, has since 2015 drifted to the sidelines. A shortcoming in the maintenance of the values of the EU is that it did not used to have a mechanism to monitor the rule-of-law development of the Member States. In Poland, with the Law and Justice Party in power, the broadcasting service and judiciary were both propelled into a more favourable attitude towards the government. This time, having learned from its previous experience with Ukraine, the EU intervened. The EU commission has introduced a mechanism for rule-of-law issues, the Framework for addressing systemic threats to the rule of law. In the worst case the voting rights in the Union decision making of the Member State in question may be suspended. It remains to be seen in the next few years if the Framework will bring results.

Freedom of speech in the **Czech Republic** is guaranteed by the Czech Charter of Fundamental Rights and Basic Freedoms, which has the same legal standing as the Czech Constitution. It is the first freedom of the Charter's second-division political rights.

It is not a long hop from the borders of Europe to the Middle East and **Israel**, where the parliament, the Knesset, passed a law on 11 July 2011 making it a civil offence to publicly call for a boycott against Israel, defined as "deliberately avoiding economic, cultural or academic ties with another person or another factor only because of his ties with the State of Israel, one of its institutions or an area under its control, in such a way that may cause economic, cultural or academic damage".[30] According to the law anyone calling for a boycott can be sued and forced to pay compensation, regardless of actual damages. At the discretion of a government minister, they may also be prevented from bidding for government tenders.

No Free Speech in Russia?

Russia Let us stop on our tour in Russia, a country as large as a continent. It is not possible to grasp Russia's judicial development without at least taking a look at the country's historical stages and familiarising ourselves with its centuries-old traditions and rich culture. Having explored the origins of the Russian state, the era of Kievan Rus', the rise of Moscow, Imperial Russia as a European superpower, the communist era, the time of stagnation and *perestroika*, we can begin to understand modern-day Russia in the third millennium.

Russia's present policy towards Ukraine is at times perplexing. For a better understanding, it is useful to recall events from history: how according to the Rus' *Primary Chronicle* (Nestor's Chronicle) the Russian state was founded in the year 862 in Kiev. Hundreds of years later, when the Ukrainians had been fighting with the help of Russia against the Polish, the Russians and Ukrainians signed a treaty in 1654. The Ukrainians have emphasised that it was a contract between two sovereign countries. The Soviet perception, however, was that it was a unification in which Ukraine joined Russia. In 1954 the Soviet Union celebrated the 300th anniversary of Russia's unification with Ukraine. To commemorate this, the Russian Soviet Federative Socialist Republic (RSFSR) gave Crimea to the Ukrainian Soviet Socialist Republic as a gift. Since 1991 Russia and Ukraine have been in dispute over Crimea, and in 2014 it was annexed by Russia.[31] While these views of history do not legitimise present Russian power politics, they partly explain Russia's information war against the West's perceptions of it. One of the basic questions in communication is how to separate right and true from wrong and manipulated information.

We will leave historical musings and try to offer some examples of the development of freedom of speech and expression in Russia. Russia gained its first printing press in 1553 by order of Ivan IV (1533–1584), commonly known as Ivan the Terrible. The first printers, however, had to flee from Russia to Lithuania due to pressure from the scribes in the book-copying guild (see *Changing Russia?* p. 28).

Even though Orthodox Russia's atmosphere diverged from that of Catholic and Lutheran Europe, the eighteenth-century ideas of Enlightenment did reach the Russian Court. Catherine the Great was in contact with the most famous philosophers of her time, Voltaire and

Diderot amongst them. It has been suggested that Catherine the Great thought that enlightened autocracy would be more effective than messy democratic meetings. This idea later gave the Russian national poet and novelist Alexander Pushkin (1799–1837) reason for his vivid comment: "God save us from seeing a Russian riot, meaningless and merciless!". [See Eloise M. Boyle and Genevra Gerhart (2002), Pushkin's poem 'The Captain's Daughter' (1833–36.)] This line is often quoted and has symbolised—both to his own and later generations—a genius who, regardless of external pressure, managed to maintain his creative freedom. Despite strict censorship, this period is known as the "Golden Age of Russian literature".

In Russia, writers have always been social thinkers and dignitaries. During times of censorship, however, they have had to speak through metaphors. Imperial Russia collapsed in 1917, and from its ruins rose the Soviet Union. To understand long-term development it is useful to pay particular attention to the Soviet era, when legality was formal in nature. Josef Stalin is known to have said that "if we find the guilty one, we will always also find the law according to which he will be punished" (see Kavan 1999, p. 29 ff.).

In a socialist regime, an individual's right to access information or even their position in society were not of paramount importance. Lenin and Stalin understood the dangers posed by writers, and for that reason the deportation and execution of authors was common. There is a popular saying that "in Russia an author is not just an author" (see *Changing Russia?* p. 62).

Later on in the Soviet Union, Khrushchev opened the door to increased cultural freedom. Although censorship remained, authors began to write about "problematic" topics more frequently, and criticism of society was often hidden between the lines. The loosening of ideological shackles was evident as even Aleksandr Solzhenitsyn's depiction of life in one of Stalin's labour camps, *One day in the Life of Ivan Denisovich*, passed censorship and was allowed to be published in 1962.

Mikhail Gorbachev (the General Secretary of the Central Committee 1985–1991) increased the speed of reform. His slogans were "transparency" (*glasnost*), "new thinking" and "democratisation". The Yeltsin era (1991–1999) has been described as democracy under the shadow of misery, when the intelligentsia became impoverished and cultural institutions lost their audience. During this time, Western mass culture invaded Russia in the form of films, TV and literature. Through the internet, Russian youth were also connected to Western influences. According to surveys most Russians were in favour of censorship, but this was never implemented (see *Changing Russia?* p. 163).

The stages of constitutional development can be summarised as follows: according to the 1936 Constitution the Soviet Union was a socialist country. This meant that private ownership and national prejudice had been conquered. Democratic rights could therefore be returned to every person, and persecution of certain classes would end. Although the Constitution also granted freedom of speech and thought, this was an illusion. The reform of the Constitution in 1977 improved the judicial climate and legal protection somewhat, but legal protection was still controlled by procurators and the party organisation. The present constitution, ratified on 12 December 1993, already lists the principles of rule of law and fundamental rights, as well as even freedom of speech and separation of powers in a democratic federal state.

Article 1 defines the rule-of-law principle as "democratic federal law-governed state".[32] Article 2 lays down the rights and liberties of the individual as fundamental values. The constitution also secures the principle of the separation of powers, freedom of speech and other fundamental rights of the citizen, the structure of the federation, the functions of central state organs, and the basic provisions and independence of the court system. To sum up, the constitution follows a structure similar to Western European constitutions (see Hallberg, *Rule of Law*, 2004, p. 117).

Changes in the legal culture and the implementation of objectives would, however, still take a long time—another generation. The previous president of the constitutional court, Marat Baglay, has described[33] the extent of the change required for the consolidation of the rule-of-law principle (*pravovoye gosudarstvo*) to replace the previous socialist system and, on the other hand, how the turbulence in peripheral areas like Chechnya has hampered the quest for harmony in the centrally governed system in pursuance of democracy.

Numerous questions about the relationships between freedom of speech, justice and power relations, as well as irresponsible acts of terror, have arisen in recent years in the aftermath of the murders of known journalists Paul Hlebnikov (2003) and Anna Politkovskaja (2006), the trials of dissidents like Mihail Hodorkovski and, as the latest upset, the cruel killing of Boris Nemtsov, shot in the back on 27 February 2015.

Trust in the realisation of justice in Russia has faltered despite attempts at reforming the system. Implementation problems are aplenty. As Fareed Zakaria shows in *The Future of Freedom* (2003), the biggest shortcoming in democratic development is that pluralism still equates with the struggle between centres of power. A truly democratic, bottom-up counterforce to political rule is lacking, the opposition is silenced and access to information is manipulated. This also has an impact on the achievement of free speech. At the same time, in his book *Putin and the Rise of Russia* (2008, 71), Michael Stuermer, a German columnist, states that the slow formation of civil society is partly the result of the lack of trust towards courts and legal institutions.

Journalist Steven Ellis[34] has analysed the background to freedom of speech and the recent media operating environment in Russia. His cutting criticism broadly corresponds with the views of editors. Ellis comments as follows:

> Media freedom bloomed in Russia following the collapse of the Soviet Union in 1991, but that development was short lived. The ascent of Vladimir Putin to the presidency in 1999 and his return in 2012 following elections decried as fraudulent have left the country with one of the most dire media freedom situations in Europe, characterised chiefly by impunity for attacks on journalists and an increasingly repressive climate.
>
> Russia has been the most dangerous country in Europe for journalists over the past two decades, despite the number killed in Ukraine in 2014, most amid battles between forces loyal to Kiev and pro-Russian separatists. Nearly 65 journalists in Russia have died in connection with their reporting or while on assignment since 1997, when the International Press Institute (IPI) began counting on its Death Watch. However, a lack of full investigations means the true count could be higher. Almost half of those deaths occurred since 2004 and nearly a quarter came amid violence in the North Caucasus region. Most others are attributed to reprisals for covering sensitive issues, particularly allegations of corruption or illegal acts.
>
> When authorities pursue journalists' attackers, justice is often incomplete. In 2014, a court convicted five men in the murder of investigative journalist Anna Politkovskaya, who was gunned down in 2006 in her Moscow apartment building. In proceedings widely criticised by Politkovskaya's family, the court handed the defendants—including three Chechen brothers previously acquitted—lengthy prison terms. A retired police officer was also sent to prison in 2012 for his role in the crime, but no mastermind has been identified, much less punished.
>
> Journalists in Russia regularly complain that authorities misuse criminal provisions to retaliate for critical coverage, accusing journalists of threats, embezzlement or tax crimes. Some authorities have even accused journalists of unlawfully disclosing personal data for having named allegedly corrupt

officials. Journalists covering public demonstrations risk detention and many describe receiving summons from investigators following critical reports, as well as pressure to disclose sources. Journalists are also regularly subject to defamation suits, especially by regional officials seeking excessive payment for alleged damage to reputation.

Recent years, however, have also brought a consolidation of control over the media sector and the online sphere by the state. They have further brought a redefinition of the term "extremism" to apply to almost any criticism of government and broad moves to curb any exercise of the freedoms of expression or assembly that might threaten the existing power structure.

As IPI's 2012–2013 World Press Freedom Review noted: "Authorities met protests against Vladimir Putin's return to the presidency in 2012 with a heavy hand, and the country saw a crackdown on civil society following Putin's inauguration, with parliament passing laws re-criminalising defamation [which was decriminalised in 2011], creating an Internet blacklist, expanding the definition of treason, and requiring organisations that receive foreign funds and that conduct "political activities" to register as "foreign agents", a term synonymous in Russia with "spies".

Lawmakers in 2013 gave authorities sweeping powers to close down websites that advocated "extremist activities" or participation in unsanctioned public demonstrations, and they adopted a provision that prohibits promoting "non-traditional sexual relations" to minors, i.e., any non-negative discussion of homosexuality.

Measures squeezing independent media continued in 2014. In July, Putin signed a law banning commercial advertising on pay cable and satellite television channels, although it was later relaxed for channels that did not broadcast foreign content. Also that month, a new law required bloggers whose sites receive more than 3,000 daily visitors to register with the government. The vaguely worded law also imposes steep fines for posting "unchecked facts", but officials admitted that enforcement would be selective; one told journalists that bloggers who "post kitten pics, speak in a civilized manner and publish no classified information" may be exempt from registration.

Subsequent measures in 2015 subjected certain blogs and online communities to the same regulation faced by mass media outlets, and granted regulators greater power to surveil and censor correspondence on social networks. Other troubling measures followed, including the application of the "foreign agents" registration requirement to NGOs operating media outlets that cover "political activities" and receive more than 25 per cent of their funding from governments or NGOs. Another law limited the amount of foreign ownership in a media outlet to 20 per cent.

In late 2015, authorities targeted media outlets not already covered by those provisions with a new requirement: media outlets must report all foreign funding they receive or forfeit that amount to the government. Authorities also approved a measure to label certain foreign or international organisations "undesirable", thereby preventing them from founding media outlets. That effectively prohibits Russian media from disseminating information those organisations produce and bans local media NGOs from receiving assistance from those organisations.

The impact of these developments can be seen overall in the change in tone of news coverage, which has veered increasingly toward propaganda, particularly with regard to Ukraine. In late 2014, Russia's government effectively weaponised journalism in its geopolitical conflict with the West by creating Sputnik, a vast new state media organisation with hundreds of representatives disseminating news abroad to counter western "propaganda". In recent years, the government created large "troll factories" that flood online platforms with pro-Kremlin commentary.

As Putin continues to bask in public approval following his annexation of Crimea and military intervention in Syria—both welcome distractions from the country's sluggish economy—and as critical voices continue to be silenced, the near future of media freedom in Russia appears bleak.

Various aspects of the contemporary situation in Russia are criticised by multiple international organisations. The Russian constitution provides for freedom of speech and the press; however, government application of law, bureaucratic regulation and politically motivated criminal investigations have forced the press to exercise self-censorship constraints in its coverage of certain controversial issues, resulting in infringements of these rights. According to Human Rights Watch, the Russian government exerts control over civil society through selective implementation of the law, restriction and censure.

The 2002 Federal Law on Counteracting Extremist Activity codifies a definition of "extremism", prohibits advocacy of extreme political positions, imposes liability on organisations that do not disavow the "extremist" statements of their members, and allows government authorities to suspend, without court order, social and religious organisations and political parties.

In 2014, Russia strengthened criminal responsibility for crimes under Article 280 ("public calls for extremist activity"), Article 282 ("inciting hatred or hostility, and humiliation of human dignity"), Article 282 Part 1 ("the organisation of an extremist community") and Article 282 Part 2 ("the organisation of an extremist organisation") of the Criminal Code. Under the strengthened laws, those convicted of "extremist activity" face up to six years in prison.

Recent Activities In the swell of changes the connections between justice and power have not been carefully analysed. As President, Dmitri Medvedev brought up rule-of-law development as a programmatic goal. In pursuit of this, annual St. Petersburg Legal Forum conferences were launched in 2011. These have been big international events. The fifth conference in 2015 discussed, *inter alia*, freedom of speech.

Finn Hanna Smith and many other researchers (2014) at the Aleksanteri Institute in Helsinki have foreseen the increase in internal instability during Vladimir Putin's third term as president. The research concludes that the stability of the system rests rather heavily on the mutual understanding between the citizenry and the power elite, as well as the mutual harmony within the power elite. First Putin and then Medvedev were regarded as having been successful during their earlier terms in creating some sort of stability and hopes of a functioning rule of law.

Many are asking if the situation is now going the other way, considering increased global tension, security measures and the heavy-handed handling of demonstrations. In the background may be the lurking Russian tradition that every leader is free to determine state policy documents. A reflection of the times to come can be found in Putin's policy document from 2013 which stresses Russia's superpower position and its claims to be able to determine the international agenda. The new bill includes interesting elements compared to the 2008 one, which concentrated on the support of modernisation. The heading "modernisation"' was changed to "dynamic economic development" in 2013. In the 2008 document Russia's competitiveness was still associated with democratic development as well as successful development of the rule of law and the implementation of human rights and liberties. These emphases have been replaced by the objective of promoting Russia's viewpoint when it comes to human rights on international fora.

In his memoirs *Najedine s soboi*, Mikhail Gorbachev defends the achievements of *perestroika*. In a January 2015 interview for the German news magazine *Der Spiegel* he argued that *perestroika* and *glasnost* are still strong, although many tend to disagree. Finnish businessman Timo Vihavainen stated, for his part (6 March 2015), that it is possible to speak one's mind in Russia, and that there are websites worth following. In the Soviet era nothing like this could have been imagined.

Dark Clouds, Nevertheless From the point of view of international rule of law development, it is to be hoped that judicial reforms initiated in Russia and sanctioned specifically by the higher courts can continue without setbacks. The old Soviet traditions have been transferred to many Asian countries. Thus, if Russia stays on course with its reforms, not only the country's own development but also other collaborative relations would be supported. However, the recent tenser climate, the disappearances of journalists, centralisation of the flow of communication in the Kremlin and lapses in rule-of-law development all point to the contrary. In their report (3 April 2015), the UN Human Rights Committee called on the Russian government to take action on violations of freedom of speech.

How is Freedom of Speech in North America?

The United States In order to understand the current societal climate and rule-of-law thinking—including the state of free speech—in America, it is necessary to examine the origins of the United States. Until recently, the United States has in many ways been the archetype of a free world, based on a narrative of the new continent in which everything is possible. In his famous book *Democracy in America* (1835–1840), Alexis de Tocqueville idealised the American model of democracy in comparison with the old European aristocratic model which he viewed with contempt.[35]

In his time Alexis de Tocqueville was a modern supporter of democratic revolution, professing liberty and equality and campaigning against despotic governance and centralised power structures. Key roles were given to a free press and freedom of speech as well as an independent judiciary. He advocated decentralised government and warned against "big government". All these features still apply to basic elements of rule-of-law development, but a modern-day traveller to America will miss them.

The origins of the American state are to be found in the phase of independence in 1776. Among others, Joseph Ellis provides a description of this Confederation era in *Founding Brothers* (2000). Conscious efforts were made to avoid the problems of monarchy and aristocracy inherited from Europe by choosing republican democracy and by strengthening the guarantees of individual liberty and freedom of ownership. Freedom of thought and speech were inherent in this environment. Thus, we may find the principles of liberalism and market economy underlying the constitution. The establishment of the Constitution of the United States was tied to the historical events and background of that time.

Making changes to the constitution is to all intents and purposes impossible. Consequently, another route has been invented: that of adding to the constitution by making amendments. The First Amendment was adopted in 1791 to secure free speech. This Amendment has been highlighted, even in the present age of the internet, as the pillar of modern society. It is forgotten that the 1766 Freedom of the Press Act, adopted by the parliament in Stockholm, was the first concerning freedom of speech, and went further than the First Amendment.

Today, the United States is ranked 46th in the Reporters Without Borders Press Freedom Index. The freedom of the "new continent" has suffered setbacks.

Originally, the United States Constitution had no code of fundamental rights. However, it was amended rather soon after (1791) with additional articles commonly known as the Bill of Rights. They protect, *inter alia*, freedom of religion, speech and assembly (First Amendment). Freedom of expression consists of the rights to freedom of speech, press and assembly, the right to petition the government for a redress of grievances, and the implied rights of association and belief. The Supreme Court interprets the extent of the protection afforded by these rights. The First Amendment has been interpreted by the Court as applying to the entire federal government even though it is only expressly applicable to Congress.[36]

There are several common-law exceptions including obscenity, defamation, incitement, incitement to riot or imminent lawless action, fighting words, fraud, speech covered by copyright, and speech integral to criminal conduct; this is not to say that it is illegal, but just that the government may make it illegal.

There also are federal criminal law statutory prohibitions covering all the common-law exceptions other than defamation, for which there is civil-law liability, as well as terrorist threats, making false statements in matters within the jurisdiction of the federal government, spreading false and misleading information (which has been used to punish hoaxes), speech related to information decreed to be related to national security such as military and classified information, false advertising, perjury, privileged communications, trade secrets, copyright and patents.

There are also so-called "gag orders" which prevent recipients of certain court orders (such as those concerning national security letters, stored communications subpoenas, pen registers and trap and trace devices) from revealing them. Most states and localities have many identical restrictions, as well as harassment, and time, place and manner restrictions. In addition, in California it is a crime to post a public official's address or telephone number on the internet.[37]

As the Bill of Rights is still scant and concise in its wording, the status and actions of the Federal Supreme Court have given cause to fineline interpretations. In accordance with the principles of the common-law judicial system, flimsy legislation is to be complemented with judicial interpretation, which then forms a central part of the legal system. The Third Amendment concerning judicial power is the shortest of the additional articles, but it has not prevented the evolution of the courts into the most important users of public power and the prime interpreters of the Constitution. Hence, the famous statement of former President of the Supreme Court Charles Evans Hughes: "We are under a Constitution, but the Constitution is what the judges say it is" (see Linda R. Monk, *The words we live by*, 2003).

Sandra Day O 'Connor,[38] the first woman appointed to the United States Supreme Court, is one of the best-known jurists in the world, and after a remarkable career as a Supreme Court Justice, she is now the chairperson of the board of the National Constitution Center in Philadelphia. She gives a judicial perspective on the meaning of the First Amendment and the recent developments in freedom of speech:

> The First Amendment to the United States Constitution provides that "Congress shall make no law ... abridging the freedom of speech". Despite that seemingly categorical language, protection of speech in the United States is not absolute. The United States Supreme Court has long held that certain categories of speech are not protected by the First Amendment. In Chaplinsky v. New Hampshire, 315 U. S. 568 (1942), the Court surveyed some of the "well-defined and narrowly limited classes of speech" that fall outside the protection of the First Amendment: "the lewd and obscene, the profane, the libellous, and the insulting or 'fighting' words—those which by their very utterance inflict injury or tend to incite an immediate breach of the peace." Id., at 572. Such speech, the Court explained, is "of such slight social value ... that any benefit that may be derived from [it] is clearly outweighed by the social interest in order and mortality." Ibid.

In the age of the Internet courts have continued to wrestle with whether certain speech is protected by the First Amendment. In December 2014, just before this contribution was submitted, the Supreme Court heard argument in Elonis v. United States. Elonis involved a man, Anthony Elonis, who was prosecuted writing a series of violent Facebook posts about his wife. The question was presented whether Elonis's conduct, in and of itself, fell outside the protections of the First Amendment—or whether the First Amendment required the government to prove that Elonis had a subjective intent to threaten his ex-wife.

Cases like these illustrate the difficulty determining the First Amendment's outer bounds.

Although the First Amendment does not protect certain categories of speech, its protections apply to even the most unpopular ideas. The First Amendment, after all, was written in the aftermath of American colonists' rebellion against a detested British King. Shaped by their experience during the American Revolution, the Framers of the Constitution sought to ensure that political dissent could flourish in the United States.

To that end, one of the central tenants of America's First Amendment jurisprudence is that content-based restrictions of free speech pose an inherent danger to democracy. As a general matter, the First Amendment Provides that the Government may not restrict speech because of its subject matter, its content, or its message. Accordingly, content-based restrictions are presumptively invalid. If the Government passes a law which imposes a content-based restriction on speech, it must demonstrate the constitutionality of the law under the exacting "strict scrutiny" test, the Government must demonstrate that a content-based restriction on speech is the least restrictive means of achieving a compelling state interest. See United States v. Playboy Entertainment Group, Inc., 529 U. S. 803, 813 (2000). In practice, it is very difficult for the Government to satisfy that test.

An opinion I wrote shows just how negatively our First Amendment jurisprudence looks at content-based restrictions. In Simon & Schuster, Inc. v. Members of New York State Crime Victims Board, 502 U. S. 105 (1991), the Supreme Court struck down a New York law which required that a criminal's income for works describing his crime be turned over to his victims, or to other creditors. Although the policy behind that law may seem sound, it singled out speech on a particular subject for a financial burden that was not placed on any other speech. Moreover, the speech in Simon & Schuster did not fall within the narrow set of categories the Court had exempted from First Amendment protection—obscenity, fighting words, and the like. The Court thus required the Government to justify the restriction, and held that it failed to do so. Simon & Schuster illustrates that the Government may not suppress or burden speech just because it finds it inconvenient, disagreeable or offensive.

To be sure, the First Amendment's disapproval of content-based speech restrictions sometimes leads the Court to allow patently offensive speech. For example, in 1977, the Court allowed a march by a Nazi organisation to move ahead, despite the fact that the Nazis planned to march in a predominantly Jewish neighbourhood. See National Socialist Party v. Skokie, 432 U.S. 43 (1977). But the First Amendment's tolerance—indeed, its reverence—for political dissent requires courts generally to accept speech that expresses even the most abhorrent ideas.

Although First Amendment admits of very limited exceptions, it has for over two centuries served as a steadfast guardian against Government censorship of unpopular ideas. The First Amendment has thereby allowed a diverse array of voices to flourish in the United States—significantly strengthening American democracy.

The atmosphere in the United States is now permanently tainted by the terror attacks of September 11, which indirectly influenced the development of the political and legal system (see Howard 2001a). After the attacks, the nation was outwardly the most united it had been for a long time, and support for the federal government rose. Security issues naturally came to the fore, and as a result the Anti-Terrorism Act of 2001 was approved. The act contains far-reaching restrictions on fundamental rights and enables the collection of information for official purposes (CIA, INS, military, etc.).

It is not easy for an outsider to fully grasp the complexities of the checks-and-balances system of Capitol Hill. In recent years the war against terrorism has shifted the focus from the ideals of civil liberties to security-focused legal thinking. This development can be viewed as the superpower's "security-oriented" and self-righteous conception of its role in the exercise of power. Now we have seen the long road from the Patriot Act (2001) to the new Freedom Act (2015). The names of these acts are informative: Uniting and Strengthening America by Providing Appropriate Tools Required to Intercept and Obstruct Terrorism, and Uniting and Strengthening America by Fulfilling Rights and Ending Eavesdropping, Dragnet-collection and Online Monitoring.

Later on in the book we will explore the increases in spying, phone tapping and surveillance which have been justified under the rubric of security concerns. Here we will investigate general developments with guidance from journalist Claude E. Erbsen[39]:

The 9/11 attacks on the World Trade Center profoundly reshaped the lives of Americans, and ushered in more than a decade of fear-driven politics, affecting domestic policy as well as foreign policy. Some aspects of the country's traditional press freedom were among the casualties of 9/11, and the Obama administration has been credited with—or rather blamed for—launching more legal actions against journalists and leakers than most of its predecessors combined. It has also seized the telephone records of journalists in AP's Washington bureau in an effort to identify sources of leaked information, and FBI agents impersonated an AP journalist to find a potential school shooter.

Until just before Christmas 2014, a *New York Times* reporter, James Risen, faced the possibility of imprisonment for refusing to testify against—and thus identify—someone who allegedly provided him with information about CIA efforts to sabotage Iran's nuclear program. Another journalist, James Rosen of Fox News, has been named as a possible "co-conspirator" in the investigation of another national security leak.

And this has been happening against the background of a statement by Attorney General Eric Holder that no journalist would end up behind bars on his watch for doing their job, and President Barack Obama's even stronger assertion that no journalist should be "at legal risk" for his or her work. So what's going on?

Constitutionally limited in its ability to prevent publication of what it considers sensitive national security information, the government is going after leakers of such information. And it intimidates other potential leakers by focusing on leak-receiving journalists. The knowledge that the phone records of journalists could be seized, or that a reporter might be forced to identify a source or face jail has an obvious chilling effect on those who might seek to reveal sensitive information. The cloak of anonymity has become very thin and gauzy.

The administration's efforts to shut off leaks, and its perceived lack of transparency have met with strong push back and sharp criticism from within the media world. Jill Abramson, the former executive editor of *The New York Times* has described the Obama administration as "the most secretive White House I have ever been involved in covering".

There is nothing new about a government's desire to keep its secrets secret, and the desire of the press to pry them loose.

What is new in the United States is the way the tragedy of 9/11 has provided the government with a "national security" shield to cover its aggressive pursuit of leakers. And the public, fearful of another 9/11, is not especially upset about it. There has been little public outrage about the government's efforts.

In my personal view this is partly a result of a public perception in which serious journalism—in print, online and on the air—is lumped together with frivolous, gossip-mongering and often completely inaccurate internet rants under an all-purpose "media" umbrella. This reduces their public support.

American journalists are fond of quoting Thomas Jefferson on the importance of a free press:

"were it left to me to decide whether we should have a government without newspapers or newspapers without a government, I should not hesitate a moment to prefer the latter".

That's what he wrote in 1787. But 27 years later, in 1814, he was less positive:

"I deplore... the putrid state into which our newspapers have passed and the malignity, the vulgarity, and mendacious spirit of those who write for them ..."

Replace the word "newspapers" with the broader, all-encompassing "media," and Jefferson's 200-year-old disappointment may resonate somewhat with today's public opinion and help explain why there are no demonstrators in the streets protesting curbs on press freedom.

But let's be fair. Yes, the post 9/11 climate of fear has chilled access, especially on national security issues, and resulted in less openness.

But journalists are not being hauled off to jail by the truckload, or gunned down as they are in some countries. Investigative reporting is still thriving throughout the country with incisive, well researched, and thoroughly documented pieces appearing in national and local media, exposing misbehaviour, malfeasance and incompetence by government officials, corporations and all manner of institutions.

And no one has been prosecuted for publishing what the government would have preferred to have kept secret, including the massive outpourings of WikiLeaks or Edward Snowden.

A significant changing trend in freedom of speech in the United States is the concentration of media house ownership. Of late, big business has gradually amassed TV and radio channels, newspapers and publishing houses. Questions about who owns the media and the potential consequences for freedom of speech and flow of information are more and more current in the United States.

Massive corporations dominate the United States media landscape. Through a history of mergers and acquisitions, these companies have concentrated their control over what we see, hear and read. In many cases, these companies are vertically integrated, controlling everything from initial production to final distribution. This is identifiable elsewhere in the world as well, as we can see in Italy, India, Russia and most Central Asian countries.

This tendency has far-reaching consequences for the preconditions of free speech and the flow of information. Francis Bacon's (1561–1626) famous phrase "knowledge is power"[40] (*scientia potestas est*; see also Chap. 1) explains our concern. Power in turn often means money, which impels us to explore later in the book the interests of moneyed power in manipulating the flow of information. The United States provides illustrative examples.

Who owns the media? That is a relevant question. Broadcasters make billions in profits while using the public airwaves for free. In return, they are supposed to provide programming that fulfils community needs. Instead, lobbyists have successfully fought to make it easier for broadcast companies to gobble up even more free airspace while doing less to serve the public.[41]

Access to high-speed internet service—also known as broadband—has become a basic public necessity, just like water or electricity. Yet despite its importance, broadband access in the United States is far from universal. Millions of Americans still stand on the wrong side of the "digital divide", unable to tap into the political, economic and social resources of the web. Meanwhile, cable and phone companies—which hold virtual monopolies over the infrastructure of the internet—often refuse to roll out high-speed broadband to regions that need it most, and actively seek to block communities from seeking their own broadband solutions.

Consolidation has contributed to tough times for the newspaper industry. When the industry was swimming in profits in the 1990s, big media companies used 14–27 per cent profit margins to buy up other properties rather than invest in the quality of their existing products or innovate for the future. Now they want to make it possible for a given company to own a newspaper and a broadcast station in the same market.

Giant companies like Apple, Facebook and Google are slowly reconstituting the internet's walled gardens of old. As these companies try to steer us to their increasingly closed versions of the internet—and to marketers who benefit from mining our personal information—we must fight for policies that protect our rights as internet users.[42]

General Electric's ownership of NBC is a good example of the way a corporation can influence television content. NBC is a television network which broadcasts to over 200 affiliated stations in the USA, several US television stations and cable stations, and shares in many others as well as media outlets in Europe including Super Channel, Europe's largest general-programming service offering programmes to 70 million homes and 350,000 hotel rooms in 44 countries. It has a Spanish-language news service reaching 21 countries in Latin America and an Asian Service (NBC 1996).

NBC is itself one of the handful of giant global media empires which dominate world media. These media corporations, including Time Warner, Disney, Bertelsmann, Sony and Rupert Murdoch's News Corporation, dominate films, television, cable channels, book and magazine publishing, and music production—that is, most of the means of communication in the modern world (McChesney 1998). Most recently NBC joined with CNET and XOOM.com to form NBC Internet to offer "the seventh-largest Internet site based on user reach" (NBCi 1999).[43]

President Barack Obama often talked about the meaning of freedom, and in *Audacity of Hope*—published before his terms of office—he noted idealistically "that freedom means more than elections, and there are four essential freedoms: freedom of speech, freedom of worship, freedom from want, and freedom from fear" (2006, p. 317). It doesn't seem that these freedoms have been realised in the way that was hoped. On the contrary, tough measures to disperse the recent racial riots and deter reporters' work, for example in Ferguson in the autumn of 2014, indicate that the atmosphere is getting tense (see Freedom House report 2015).

The entanglements of American political culture and the deadlocks created by the burned bridges between the Democrats and the Republicans in Congress—which frequently cripple the President's ability to manoeuvre—are often difficult for an outsider to understand. Obama tried to use his office to hinder media concentration and to increase local TV coverage—objectives that have met resistance from industry groups. The impact of the concentration of media ownership on freedom of speech would require much deeper analysis than the scope of this book allows.[44] The 45th president of the USA, Donald Trump challenged the mainstream media of the country during his 2015 campaign and repelled it. It is, however, too early to analyse as to what kind of permanent standing Trump will take.

Canada is a fascinating country, not only for its vastness but also—to us northern hemisphere inhabitants—for its forest culture. However, from a judicial point of view what is interesting is Canada's historically harmonious co-ordination of two cultures, the English- and the French-speaking. The country has seen occasional disputes, but it can broadly be said to be successfully multicultural. The status of Canada's two official languages dates back to the 1867 Constitution, according to which everyone has the right to use either one of these two languages in the Canadian parliament as well as in the Parliament of Quebec and courts of law. The equal status of English and French as the official languages of the federal state was established in more detail in the Official Language Act of 1969, amended in 1988.

Since 1982 Canada's constitution has contained a bill of fundamental rights. Other laws that protect freedom of speech in Canada, and did so to a limited extent prior to the enactment of the Charter in 1982, include the Implied Bill of Rights and the Canadian Bill of Rights.

In 1982 courts of law were authorised to investigate the constitutionality of laws.

"Section 2(b) of the Charter states that everyone has the following fundamental freedoms: freedom of thought, belief, opinion and expression, including freedom of the press and other media of communication. The section potentially covers a wide range of action, from commercial expression to political expression; from journalistic privilege to hate speech to pornography. The jurisprudence of the Supreme Court has largely been an attempt to carve out, first, the purpose of s. 2(b) (what values it seeks to protect, who should be entitled to its protection?), and second the scope of s. 2(b) (what is "expression"?)."

Section 1 of the Charter, the so-called limitations clause, establishes that the guarantee of freedom of expression and other rights under the Charter are not absolute and can be limited in certain situations. This suggests that the Canadian Charter of Rights and Freedoms guarantees the rights and freedoms set out in it subject only to such reasonable limits prescribed by law as can be demonstrably justified in a free and democratic society. This section is double-edged: it implies that a limitation on freedom of speech prescribed by law can be permitted if it can be justified as a reasonable limit in a free and democratic society; yet conversely it implies that a restriction can be invalidated if it cannot be shown to be reasonable.

Is Free Speech a Utopian Idea in Latin America?

Introduction During the last few decades democracy and human rights have progressed in small steps in Latin America. Military dictatorships have been overthrown and most countries are on the road to democracy. The journey, however, remains a long one. Since problems are endemic, there is good reason to ask whether the state of freedom of speech is much better compared to former despotic times. There have also been backward steps; of those we will provide a short overview.

This introductory description has been compiled by the late Ilkka Heiskanen,[45] Finland's former ambassador to Chile. He writes that only a few countries in Latin America get a clean bill of health from the organisations that monitor the realisation of freedom of speech. Freedom House, for example, regards only Costa Rica, Suriname and Uruguay as free; Cuba is amongst the ten least free countries and the scores of Ecuador, Honduras, Mexico and Venezuela are bad. Freedom of expression is quite good in the English-speaking Caribbean.

> The limitations to free speech emanate from four sources: traditional censorship by public authorities, other governmental or judicial actions, distortions created by relations of media ownership and self-censorship due to organised crime.
> Actual censorship legislation exists only in Cuba, where the media is controlled by government, citizens' access to information is curbed and journalists have been detained. But even in Cuba the attitude towards social media has improved in recent years.
> Although most Latin American countries don't have censorship legislation, the public authorities use other means to prevent critical publicity. A popular method is suing for libel. In Ecuador journalists have been sentenced to jail and made to pay huge sums of compensation for insulting the president. To boot, some newspapers have been brought to trial for omitting to report on events and meetings that the government deems important. Ecuador's new communication law sets strict limits to the flow of information.
> In addition to political and legal pressure, some governments resort to economic means. One method is to intensify government—and the businesses' under its control—advertising in compliant media. In Argentina the government has even prohibited enterprises to advertise in opposition-friendly media.
> An efficient method of curbing free speech is the government purchase and control of critical media, either directly or through intermediaries. Venezuelan government, for example, has purchased the GloboVision TV channel.
> The purchase of newsprint and printing ink has often been made more difficult through import and currency regulations. In Venezuela this is commonplace, and in Argentina a long political and legal battle has been waged over the ownership of the biggest manufacturer of newsprint.

Violence directed at media representatives is a growing problem in Latin America. Despite the legislative and practical reforms to protect journalists carried out by many states, specifically violence by drug dealers continues. According to the Organisation of American States (OAS) Special Rapporteur on freedom of expression, some 100 media workers have been murdered on the continent during the last five years. Especially dangerous countries are Mexico and Honduras.

In Mexico murders and disappearances of journalists, violence against them and the impunity of perpetrators is common. This leads to self-censorship: the media owners and editors do not want to place their workers in danger, and journalists are afraid to report e.g. on drug-related crime.

Central America, in particular Honduras and Guatemala, is also dangerous to journalists. Media avoids the topics of corruption and the connections of authorities to drug lords. Violence and threats are happening also in Venezuela, Colombia and Brazil.

The free flow of information is curtailed by centralised media ownership and governance in most Latin American countries. Chile has no censorship legislation nor are the lives of journalists threatened, but the concentration of printed media ownership into the hands of two groupings limits the dissemination of different opinions. After the change in ownership many provincial newspapers are viewed as local copies of the main newspapers. Criticism has been levelled against the concentration of TV station ownership in Mexico.

Attempts at curbing the internet are also prevalent. In Argentina and Brazil service providers (search engine or website) may be held criminally liable for their users' content.

The OAS affiliated Inter-American Commission on Human Rights, Special Rapporteur on freedom of expression and Inter-American Court of Human Rights monitor the state of freedom of expression on the continent, but some countries have made it known that they will no longer adhere to the recommendations and court decisions of this system of human rights.

Argentina has been in turmoil in recent years. Ingmar Ström,[46] who has kept an eye on the country's politics ever since he was stationed at the Finnish Embassy in Buenos Aires, evaluates media developments in the country.

> Argentina is an example of a country where a powerful government, for all practical purposes, was able to divide the political sector, people and media, in two. During the terms of presidents Néstor and Cristina Kirchner (May 2003 – December 2015) the motto of power politics became "we want all" (*vamos por todo*). The attitude was highlighted in February 2015 when president Cristina Fernández de Kirchner in her all-network radio and TV speech used the expression "'we and the others'".

In this kind of a presidential system "'the others" are all those who do not support the official ideology. Due to the prolonged polarisation during the Kirchner rule, the independent media, notably the main dailies in Buenos Aires *Clarín* and *La Nación*, adopted an increasingly critical stance while the governmental views were distributed by *Página/12* newspaper and several radio and TV channels. Public TV channels run current affairs programmes whose main purpose seemed to be slandering the opposition.

The express targets of the leadership's contempt were "the big corporations which also are in the business of shaping opinions". The government got a far-reaching influence on the media sector. For example, one of the objectives of the 2009 Media Law was to prevent the concentration of TV and cable licenses in big corporations. Specifically, the law aimed to break up the Clarín media conglomerate.

In its report on 2014 the Argentine Freedom of Speech + Democracy Foundation (LED) listed 451 cases where the authorities had infringed on freedom of speech, an increase of 81% over the previous year. Over 2.3 billion pesos (some 230 million euros at the time) were spent on public sector advertising on TV, radio and in printed media, totaling an increase of 3,800% during the Kirchners. Public advertising was almost exclusively channeled to media supporting government policies. Hence, about 80% of the radio stations were estimated to be in the hands of owners in tune with the government.

In December 2015 centre-right coalition Let's Change candidate Mauricio Macri put an end to the Kirchnerist period. Having won the presidential elections with a 3 point margin, Macri immediately set out to fulfil his campaign promises by trying to bridge the gap between people thinking differently and completely reversing the media policies.

Argentina has attracted international attention in other ways as well. Assistant Professor Rogelio Alaniz has written on the "silent protest march" attended by some 400 000 people which was held in Buenos Aires the day before, in commemoration of federal prosecutor Alberto Nisman. Nisman was found dead in his bathroom on 18 January 2015. Many believed that he had come too close to the truth about a terror attack in 1994 that killed 85 people. The people not only protested against the present state of affairs but also gave a message to the future politicians who will run the country in a few months' time (see Rogelio Alaniz in *La Nación* on 19 February 2015).

Brazil Let us stop in South America's most populous country. Brazil is the only Portuguese-speaking country in South America, with its roots dating back to its colonisation by Portugal in 1549. Historically, the first step to freedom of speech was taken when the 1824 Constitution was enacted, though it was later banned by the Vargas dictatorship and severely restricted under the military dictatorship of 1964–85. Here is a brief look at the development of freedom of speech. Nowadays freedom of expression is a constitutional right, but in the past censorship has occurred since the state's first use of the press. In 1808, Portugal brought the first press to Brazil after fleeing Napoleon's forces, and with it the first set of press restrictions. Statements contradictory to good morals were prohibited, as well as expressions of dissatisfaction with the government. The monarchy censored the colonists in order to protect people they felt were ignorant, a sentiment that was echoed centuries later.[47]

In 1888, Brazil was the last country in the world to abolish slavery, just a year before the Portuguese monarchy was overthrown. The first federal republic established after the monarchy was replaced by a dictatorship in 1930, known as the Estado Novo or Vargas Era after Getulio Vargas who led the government until his suicide in 1954. During both the Vargas Era and the military regime which came to power in 1964, Brazilians were subject to torture, censorship and suppression of free thought. This proved particularly problematic for Brazilian citizens, whose freedom of speech was explicitly protected in the constitution of 1946, as stated in Article 141:

> The manifestation of thought is free and shall not be dependent upon censorship, except as regards public spectacles and amusements, and each of these shall be responsible in the cases and in the form which the law may establish, for any abuses they may commit. Anonymity is not permitted. The right of reply is assured. The publication of books and periodicals shall not be dependent upon licence from the public power. However, propaganda for war, or violent processes to overthrow the political and social order or prejudices of race or of class shall not be tolerated.[48]

Historically, free speech in Brazil has never been more restricted than it was during the military regime, which lasted from 1964 to 1985. Apart from adding Article 151 to the constitution, various laws were passed limiting the liberties of citizens, the most restrictive being the National Security Law of 1953[6] and the Institutional Acts of 1964.

The National Security Law redefined crimes against the state, and banned any political organisations that conflicted with the values of the military regime. Citizens could be indicted for being a "threat" to national security; citizens who witnessed "threatening" acts without denouncing them could also be punished under the new law. Under the Institutional

Acts, a person could be tried without knowing their action was illegal. The Institutional Acts were enforced by the military in an effort to lead the country towards a better democracy, while methodically violating the constitutional rights of its citizens.

This restricted right to free speech was further restricted in 1967, when Article 151 was added to the Constitution, making "undermining the democratic order" an offence punishable by "the suspension of [free speech] rights ... for a period of two to ten years".[49] It was during this period that several laws were passed that systematically and unconstitutionally restricted the rights of citizens; they remained until Brazil became a democracy in 1985.

Brazil's current stance on free speech has been in place since 1988, when the country's seventh constitution redefined the freedom of expression for the third and final time as follows (Constitutional text enacted on October 5, 1988, with the alterations established by Revision Constitutional Amendments Nos. 1, 1994 to 6, 1994, by Constitutional Amendments Nos. 1, 1992 to 90, 2015, and by Legislative Decree No. 186, 2008):

IV—The expression of thought is free, anonymity being forbidden.
V—The right of reply is assured, in proportion to the offence, as well as compensation for property or moral damages or for damages to the image.
IX—The expression of intellectual, artistic, scientific, and communications activities is free, independently of censorship or license.
X—The privacy, private life, honour and image of persons are inviolable, and the right to compensation for property or moral damages resulting from their violation is assured.[50]

Brazil has experienced the establishment of a 'post-redemocratisation' constitutional framework that undoubtedly grants freedom of speech and of the press. The country has prepared the ground for the establishment of a social communication system that is in line with the most advanced international regimes in the field.

Brazil's Federal Constitution guarantees broad access to information from different and multiple sources within a democratic environment where freedom of speech and the press is assured. However, the country still faces some gaps in its media regulatory framework.

The 1988 Constitution relies on a piece of infra-constitutional legislation dating from 1962. Therefore it does not respond to the new Brazilian social and political challenges or to the technological revolution that the communications and information sector of today has undergone. The country still needs to go further in diversifying its information sources, expanding them to government and community communication channels.

Article IV of the Constitution of Brazil establishes that the "expression of thought is free, anonymity being forbidden". Furthermore, the "expression of intellectual, artistic, scientific, and communications activities is free, independently of censorship or license" (see endnote 50). However, there are legal provisions criminalising the desecration of religious artefacts at the time of worship, hate speech, racism, defamation, calumny and libel. Brazilian law also forbids "unjust and grave threats".[51]

Despite these principles, reality showed a different face when the slums of Rio de Janeiro had to give way to the football World Cup of 2014 and arrangements for the Olympics in 2016. The evictions of inhabitants and the clearances of the slums were widely known, but the Brazilian media still chose their words very carefully when reporting on the progress of the arrangements for the Games.[52]

In fact, the biggest reason freedom of the press is not heavily debated in Brazil is the lack of precedent. The state has always been involved with the press, and the relationship is a delicate one: the press cannot survive without the government. This is due to a combination of factors, including the low readership of Brazilian newspapers and a dependency on advertising and government financing. Despite Brazil's economic boom, both now and when it became a Federal Republic, Brazil has been known for having one of the lowest levels of newspaper readership, not only compared to developed nations, but to other Latin American nations as well.

Brazil fell nine places to 108th on the 2013 World Press Freedom Index, after falling 41 places in 2011, which Reporters Without Borders attributes to the country's "badly distorted media landscape"[53] and violence against journalists. Reporters Without Borders also listed Brazil as South America's deadliest country for media personnel in 2013, due to the unsolved murders of five journalists. By March of 2014, four more journalists in Brazil had been murdered, indicating an increase in violence against journalists in the country, a trend that is not surprising in view of the country's violent history.

There is some cause for concern about the development of Brazil, although it remains a democratic country. Dilma Rousseff, the country's first female president, was elected in 2011 and again in 2014. Her popularity has now significantly declined: the Senate voted her out of office in September 2016 and she faces charges for breaking financial laws.

Searching for Freedom of Speech on the African Continent

A Different Type of Environment Africa is a heterogeneous stage of diverse peoples and crises. Poverty and the instability of political conditions in the continent determine the advancement of its judicial systems. Another factor is colonisation, which is why there are lingering traditions of different European judicial systems. The importance of rule-of-law principles in crisis management and reconstruction efforts is also a significant issue.

From a legal perspective, it is interesting to note that the colonial powers aimed to plant their own systems within colonies as soon as possible. All the major European countries, including France, Great Britain, Belgium, Germany, Portugal and Italy had their own colonies. Britain pursued its common-law system, whereas countries with more statute-based systems applied their own principles of civil law (Joireman 2001, 581ff.).

Each colony adopted unequivocally the judicial system of its mother country. There were two main reasons: first, the aboriginal population was forced to submit to the system of the mother country; and second, the local governing elite often allied with colonial authorities in order to maintain its position.

So in order to understand the differences, it is important to examine the development of the rule of law in a cultural and social context. A number of studies of African countries with both statutory and common-law traditions have concluded that in the battle against corruption and maladministration, education and access to information have more impact than the basic differences between legal systems.

Colonial rulers had differing attitudes towards the education and adaptation of the aboriginal population to new government systems. Today, the importance of legal training and rule-of-law principles is widely understood, and there are related development programmes. The most important issues are education and the functioning of institutions. Here too, access to information, an integral aspect of the concept of freedom of speech, has a key role to play.

The majority of African constitutions provide legal protection for freedom of speech; however, in practice these rights are exercised inconsistently. The replacement of authoritarian regimes in **Kenya** and **Ghana** has substantially improved the situation in those countries. On the other hand, **Eritrea** allows no independent media and uses draft evasion as a pretext to crack down on any dissent, spoken or otherwise. One of the poorest and smallest nations in Africa, Eritrea is now the largest prison for journalists; since 2001, fourteen journalists have been imprisoned in unknown places without trial.

Sudan, Libya and **Equatorial Guinea** also have repressive laws and practices. In addition, many state radio stations (which are the primary source of news for illiterate people) are under tight control, and programmes—especially talk shows providing a forum to complain about the government—are often censored. **Somalia** provides legal protection for freedom of speech but it does not apply in practice.

Despite the **Tunisia**n revolution that led the Arab Spring, freedom of speech is still a controversial issue and a subject of uncertainty in that country. Artists, journalists and citizens still face many kinds of harassment when they try to express their ideas freely. To make things more complicated, there is a lack of experience and tradition on the part of African judges and the legal system in the field of free speech.

The events of the Arab Spring are an example of how social media, enabled by new technology, mobilised crowds in all North African countries. The counter-reactions of the ruling governments were next in the chain of events; the resolve of the protesting citizens, however, paved the way forward. In **Yemen** the President stepped down as a result of the protests. In **Egypt** one uprising led to another, and eventually to a military government. **Syria** has drifted into a full-blown, long-term civil war, as resolve has held on both sides. The effects of social media and new forms of communication on the Arab Spring and especially Egypt—the most influential country in the region—will be analysed in Chap. 8 (The Arab Spring—Disruption or Development in Egypt).

The political history of many of the countries in the Middle East and North African (MENA) region has been one of strong presidents and weak legislatures. We believe that the democratic movements of the Arab Spring created the opportunity to reconstitute the political system in a way that marks a fundamental break from the presidential systems of the past [see *Semi-Presidentialism as Power Sharing, Constitutional reform after the Arab Spring* (2014), published by the International Institute for Democracy and Electoral Assistance (International IDEA)].

The failure of the constitutional systems in place before the Arab Spring can be attributed to a combination of three factors. First, presidential power was largely unlimited. Second, the system of government did not allow the legislature to act as an effective check on presidential power. Third, many pre-Arab Spring countries were single-party states, in which much of the bureaucracy and many state institutions were dominated by the president's political allies and supporters (see IDEA p. 9).

The systematic monitoring of the African media environment has in the last few years begun with publications by the African Media Barometer (AMB), one of the most recent being a 2013 piece on South Africa. The following abstract characterises the method of the AMB.

The African Media Barometer (AMB) is an in-depth and comprehensive description and measurement system for national media environments on the African continent. Unlike other press surveys or media indices the AMB is a self-assessment exercise based on home-grown criteria derived from African Protocols and Declarations like the Declaration of Principles on Freedom of Expression in Africa (2002) by the African Commission for Human and Peoples' Rights. The instrument was jointly developed by fesmedia Africa, the Media Project of the Friedrich-Ebert-Stiftung (FES) in Africa, and the Media Institute of Southern Africa (MISA) in 2004 (AMB 2013).

AMB is an analytical exercise to measure the media situation in a given country which at the same time serves as a practical lobbying tool for media reform. Its results are presented to the public of the country concerned to press for an improvement of the media situation using the decisions and declarations of the Assembly of the African Union, and other African standards as benchmarks. The recommendations of the AMB reports are then integrated into the work of the 19 country offices of the Friedrich-Ebert-Stiftung (FES) in Sub-Saharan Africa and into the advocacy efforts of other local media organisations like the Media Institute of Southern Africa.

South Africa South Africa is probably the most liberal of the African countries as regards freedom of speech; however in light of South Africa's racial and discriminatory history, particularly the era, the Constitution of the Republic of South Africa of 1996 precludes expression that is tantamount to the advocacy of hatred on certain listed grounds.

The current president of South Africa, Jacob Zuma, is an old-school freedom fighter of the ruling ANC party, whose words and massive presence reflect the country's eventful history of conflict. The late Nelson Mandela, the previous president, was a different type of benevolent character who earned worldwide respect. It was a moving experience to visit Mandela's cell on Robben Island, where he spent eighteen of his twenty-seven years in prison. Fellow prisoner Ahmed Kathrada described the conditions in the prison in his memoirs (*Memoirs, The story of prisoner no. 468/64,* 2004). The cell was only 2.4 metres long. One lamp was lit in the middle of the ceiling, day and night. Only thoughts and memories were there to keep you company. During the first years there was no connection to the outside world, never mind freedom of expression. Still these people carried on without breaking, and through all those years Mandela never lost his vision of reconciliation.

Nowadays freedom of speech and expression are both protected and limited by a section in the South African Bill of Rights, Chapter 2 of the Constitution. Section 16 of the Constitution makes the following provisions: (1) Everyone has the right to freedom of expression, which includes (a) freedom of the press and other media; (b) freedom to receive or impart information or ideas; (c) freedom of artistic creativity; and (d) academic freedom and freedom of scientific research. The right in subsection (1) does not extend to: (a) propaganda for war; (b) incitement of imminent violence; or (c) advocacy of hatred that is based on race, ethnicity, gender or religion, and that constitutes incitement to cause harm.[54]

Section 32 of the Constitution specifically protects the right to access information that is held by the state or held by another person and required for the exercise or protection of any rights. The Promotion of Access to Information Act 9 was to give effect to this right—good on paper, but not necessarily in practice.

However, these freedoms, including those relating to the media, are not enforced. Thus, there is no obligation by the state to actively promote and enforce these rights. In addition, the limitations to freedom of expression are not clearly defined. It is on these two points that the environment for freedom of expression is vulnerable.

Compared with other countries in the region, South Africa is in a better position in terms of not having excessive laws that restrict journalistic practice. There are no legal requirements to becoming a journalist. There is no criminal defamation act in South Africa, nor are there insult laws to the same degree as in other countries; defamation is instead a civil matter (see AMB 2013). Section 205 of the Criminal Procedure Act can, in theory, compel journalists to reveal their sources of confidential information, but this is seldom used in practice and the judicial system tends to side with journalists in such instances.

South Africa does have the Promotion of Access to Information Act (PAIA), which legally guarantees all citizens the right of access to information, although this is in practice not enforced. Of concern currently is the controversial Protection of State Information Bill, which, if passed, may undermine people's access to certain kinds of information in the name of national security. PAIA does make it a right that public information be made available unless it is to be used for litigation purposes, which does somewhat limit people's access to information. The Act also covers private information.

According to a new report South African access to information has fallen further from its already worryingly low levels of compliance. The 2013 "shadow report" was issued by the PAIA CSN, the civil society network that monitors the Promotion of Access to Information Act. Only 16 per cent of information requested was released in full text. The South African National Assembly adopted a revised Protection of State Information Bill on 12 November 2013.

The state does not seek to filter or block internet content, although courts have been known to take action after the fact if such content amounts to hate speech, defamation, and so on. Broadcasting in South Africa is governed by the Electronic Communications Act of 2006 and the Broadcasting Act of 1999. At face value, this legislation is world class in terms of international best practice, setting out three tiers of broadcasting—public, commercial and community—and emphasising the importance of content and ownership diversity. However, it is not well implemented, especially as regards commercial broadcasters, as there is little diversity in this sector. Alongside the three public/state television stations provided by the SABC, e.tv remains the only commercial free-to-air television station. The satellite subscription service provided by DStv monopolised this sector until 2010, when TopTV entered the market with cheaper prices (see AMB 2013).

It seems, as a historical paradox, that right now South Africa is falling into another era of darkness. The following account of developments in the media environment in the last couple of decades is given by South African journalist Raymond Louw.[55]

> Evolution of African Media over the Past 20 Years—South Africa.
>
> Twenty years ago, in 1994, when the liberation movement, the African National Congress (ANC), triumphed over the white nationalists in the general election that finally swept away apartheid and brought freedom to the masses of Africans and other races in South Africa, most of the 100 laws censoring the media that had come with apartheid were also removed and press freedom restored.

Journalists revelled in the liberated environment but there was little partying because they had actually enjoyed an incremental freedom process over the previous four years after the lifting of the bans outlawing the liberation movements and the release of Nelson Mandela from a life sentence in February 1990.

The removal of the banning orders meant that the media could report on the statements and activities of ANC members and those of other parties which had been strictly prohibited during most of the 42 years apartheid was in force. The police and other authorities had backed off from applying the restrictive laws still on the statute books.

The English-language newspapers, which had battled against apartheid-era censorship, constantly consulting lawyers and devising tactics to avoid breaking the laws, found themselves in a new environment where their previous outright opposition to a vicious apartheid government had to be abruptly returned into one where the new rulers were encouraged to introduce the freedoms they had promised.

More importantly, the change meant an end to the harassment, beatings, torture and jailing of journalists who stood up to apartheid and who tried to tell the public what was really going on.

The change in the Afrikaans-language press was overwhelming and extremely dramatic. Through all the years of Nationalist Party domination, their newspapers had supported the government's apartheid policies and its attacks on press freedom and the English-language press. Though the restrictions applied to them equally, they had supported them as "patriotic South Africans" and cheered on the government's accusations that their English counterparts were guilty of conduct verging on treason.

Overnight they became avid supporters of press freedom. They feared they would be subjected to harsh treatment similar to blacks by the National Party Government but that this could be prevented by Afrikaners having the freedom to publicise any inroads on them as well as their culture and language and so embarrass the government. In the event, their fears were groundless. The ANC needed them as much as they needed the ANC. Also, President Mandela had instituted a policy of reconciliation, insisting on the rejection of any retribution or revenge.

Freedom House, the New York-based informational monitor of freedom, welcomed the new freedoms instituted in South Africa and elevated the freedom rating of the country to "free", so much more wholesome than the "partly free" classification it was given during apartheid.

The switch to a democracy in 1994 changed the attitudes of government officials to the press and information was more readily supplied. In this climate, the media flourished, using their freedoms with telling effect to expose bad governance, abuse of power, corruption and other evils which had begun to surface.

Among voters, anger was growing and a new phenomenon arose, "service delivery" protests. People in the impoverished townships—low-cost housing developments built as apartheid appendages to 'white' cities and villages—and in the shanty-towns that had grown alongside them, embarked on angry demonstrations, blocking roads with burning tyres and rocks as they protested nepotism, corruption, lack of services and failure to fulfil promises, especially in local government. With the police being called in to restore order and doing so fiercely, the news pictures that were published and the videos that were broadcast took on the aspects of former apartheid repression.

A major corruption scandal currently involves President Jacob Zuma whose luxury country estate at Nkandla in KwaZulu-Natal received "security upgrades" from government departments costing about R246-m (approximately $24-m). Newspapers were especially contemptuous of the security tag being applied to a swimming pool, a cattle enclosure (*kraal*) and a chicken coop as well as other structures. So was the Public Protector, Thuli Mandonsela, who a few days short of a month ago published a damning 400-page report on what had been done by the government at Nkandla. Apart from the improper behaviour of officials, the maladministration, the excessive expenditure and other official failings she found that Zuma had improperly benefited and should repay some of the money spent. An aspect of her report that was especially appealing to journalists was her lavish praise of the *Mail and Guardian* for uncovering the scandal and other papers for continuing to publicise it.

Meanwhile, opposition politicians were, at the time of writing, trying to establish the legality of the National Prosecuting Authority's withdrawal of more than 700 charges of fraud and corruption against Zuma before he became President in 2009.

With corruption and other failings of government regularly publicised in the press, embarrassing the politicians involved as well as the government in general, hostility towards the press began to grow among officials, cabinet ministers and others in the ruling ANC. The press was increasingly accused of being in political opposition and unpatriotic. The ANC proposed that Parliament set up a state-appointed Media Appeals Tribunal to deal with complaints against the media, an idea promptly denounced by journalists who saw it as an instrument of control. The ANC back-tracked on this proposal after the Press Council revised its self-regulatory procedures to provide for more public participation in the process now called co-regulation. But it failed to withdraw it, leaving it on the table as an ominous reminder of what could happen.

Since 1994 the ANC government has passed several laws that impinge on press freedom and which have raised the ire of the media. It has also provided for the broadening of the application of official secrecy classification, again raising strong opposition from media ranks. The strongest opposition has been directed against the Prohibition of State Information Bill, which has given birth to a powerful freedom of expression NGO, the Right to Know (R2K) campaign.

In addition, the SA National Editors' Forum is still trying to persuade the government to review and repeal or amend about 12 apartheid-era restrictive laws which are still on statute books and which are viewed as unconstitutional. Journalists are awaiting an opportunity to test the validity of these laws before the Constitutional Court, the guardian of South Africa's Constitution, which is regarded as one of the best of its kind in the world. It has made a number of important rulings against the government on constitutional grounds in the past.

As government attitudes to the press continued to harden, and media focussed on the increase in restrictive laws, Freedom House exclaimed over the more intense hostility of government politicians towards the press, and withdrew the country's "free" press status, downgrading it once again to "partly free" in 2010.

The South African press is undergoing financial strains similar to those of newspapers in other parts of the world as a result of the growing attraction of social media. Circulation figures have been badly hit and the scope of news coverage has contracted.

But while the financial future of the press raises concern, there is also growing alarm over attempts to exert political influence over news media. The Gupta family, close friends of President Jacob Zuma who were given special permission to fly in from India a large wedding party to a top security Air Force Base, causing further criticism, has started a daily paper, *The New Age*, and a 24-hour TV news service, ANN7, both of which are suspected of eventually seeking to promote the ANC government.

At the state broadcaster, the SA Broadcasting Corporation, where allegations have also been made of improper state political influence, the staff has recently been instructed to structure news coverage on a basis of 70% "positive" and 30% "negative" material. Though not specifically directed towards news coverage of the government, it would inevitably relate to this coverage. The directive drew accusations that the broadcaster was influenced by government complaints that the media's emphasis on "negative" news is "unpatriotic".

There is also disquiet in media circles over the conduct of Dr. Igbal Survé, chairman of Sekunjalo Holdings, a black peoples' consortium which recently bought the Independent media group which owns the largest number of important titles in the country. Survé summarily dismissed editor Alide Dasnois of the daily *Cape Times* for publishing as a lead story criticism by the Public Protector of one of Sekunjalo's companies and using a four-page "wrap-around" to tell the story of Nelson Mandela's death on the same day. Survé apparently ignored the fact that the wrap-around was regarded as publishing master-stroke especially when *Time* magazine singled it out as one of the 14 top Mandela front pages in the world that day. Survé denied the dismissal, saying he had offered Dasnois other options, but his action was widely condemned as unacceptable managerial interference in the paper's editorial independence, and that this boded ill for editorial independence in all the company's papers. Since then the two more senior journalists have been dismissed while others including editors have left the company finding it an unattractive environment.

Similar fears have arisen at the Times Media Group, recently taken over by an investment company run by Andrew Bonamour who describes himself as a "long term investor". Journalists are alarmed over his criticism of the company's newspapers being too focussed on politics which he claimed had alienated readers. He elaborated: "You don't always want to read about politics, there is other stuff that is news and relevant".

Despite what is seen as attempts to temper newspaper criticism of government, journalists in papers like the *Mail and Guardian* and some of the other titles have continued to uncover corruption, maladministration and abuse of power—all showing worrying growth in South Africa—and given it wide publicity. Their courage is to be applauded.

But as the 20 year review period comes to an end with this recent chronicle of alarming managerial approaches to press coverage, the optimism generated by the arrival of democracy in 1994 has become clouded if not tinged with pessimism for the future of press freedom in South Africa.

Freedom of Speech Under Pressure by the Asian Great Powers

Background The most populated of the continents, Asia offers an explorer indescribable scenery, layers of history and grandeur as well as poverty, rapid economic growth as well as various types of societal problems—which are not easy to research as accurate information is scarce. The Finnish books by well-known linguist and diplomat G.J. Ramstedt, based on his journeys to China, Japan, Mongolia and the Central Asian countries (1898–1912), were an inspirational depiction of the Asian region for Finnish people.

The Asia of today is a very different world of old traditions and new technology; a world of contrasts. Several Asian countries provide formal legal guarantees of freedom of speech to their citizens. These are not, however, implemented in practice in some countries. There is no clear correlation between legal and constitutional guarantees of freedom of speech, and actual practice among Asian nations. These developments will be analysed more closely in the following section.

India The Indian Constitution guarantees freedom of speech to every citizen, and there have been landmark cases in the Indian Supreme Court that have affirmed the nation's policy of allowing free press and freedom of expression to every citizen. In India, citizens are free to criticise politics, politicians, bureaucracy and policies. Although the formal aspects of these freedoms are comparable to those in the United States and Western European democracies, India ranks quite low in the freedom of speech indices. (Press Freedom Index 2013, Reporters Without Borders ranking: 140/179; difference compared to the previous year: −9.)

Article 19 of the Indian Constitution states that: "All citizens shall have the right to freedom of speech and expression; to assemble peaceably and without arms; to form associations or unions; to move freely throughout the territory of India; to reside and settle in any part of the territory of India; and to practise any profession, or to carry on any occupation, trade or business."

These rights are limited so as not to affect: the integrity of India, the security of the state, friendly relations with foreign States, public order, decency or morality, contempt of court and defamation or incitement to an offence.[56] Article 19 of the constitution guarantees freedom of expression as long as it is not used to oppose India's "sovereignty and integrity"(see endnote 56). On the whole, journalists are free and know how to defend their rights on the streets and in the courts. (The Constitution of India was adopted by the Constituent Assembly on 26 November 1949, and came into effect on 26 January 1950.)

Freedom of speech is restricted today by the National Security Act of 1980 and in the past by the Prevention of Terrorism Ordinance (POTO) of 2001, the Terrorist and Disruptive Activities (Prevention) Act (TADA) from 1985 to 1995, and similar measures. Freedom of speech is also restricted by Section 124A of the Indian Penal Code 1860, which deals with sedition and makes any speech or expression of contempt towards government punishable by upwards of three years in prison.[57]

Nonetheless, the gulf between different parts of India is growing. In New Delhi journalists enjoy freedom and safety, but for example in the central state of Chhattisgarh, where the rule of law has broken down, they are increasingly exposed to obstacles and dangers including police abuses and powerful local officials. In the frequent armed clashes between Naxalite (Maoist) guerrillas and security forces, journalists in Chhattisgarh are often branded as "traitors" by the guerrillas and as Maoist supporters by the police.

Internet use is expanding rapidly, with the number of users increasing to around 300 million by 2014. Wireless internet, especially mobile-phone internet, is also developing quickly as the price of smartphones falls. But since the 2008 bombings in Mumbai, the Indian authorities have been tightening internet surveillance and legislation, including the 2000 Information Technology Act. Online free expression is threatened by new "IT Rules" issued in April 2011 by the Ministry of Information Technology and Communications. Internet service providers are required to withdraw offensive content—including content that is obscene, harassing, libellous, hateful, harms minors or infringes copyright within 36 hours of being notified by the authorities or risk prosecution. Social networks and internet service providers must state that such content is banned in their terms of service. This has the effect of turning technical intermediaries such as telecom companies, service providers, social networks and search engines into police auxiliaries and web censors. The definition of illegal content is very vague.

The interior ministry, which is responsible for national security, is trying to get real-time access to all BlackBerry communications, including its corporate email service, called BlackBerry Enterprise Server (BES). RIM insists that it does not have access to the encryption keys used by BES clients.

The government is reportedly also planning to ask Google and Skype to provide it with a way to monitor their internet telephony (VoIP) services. Last September, the interior minister warned that it might force RIM, Google and Skype to set up servers in India in order to facilitate surveillance by the security agencies.

The Business Standard 2012 review demonstrates that more than a third of news channels in India are owned by politicians or political affiliates, who use their channels as "political vehicles" to influence the course of local elections. Nearly 60 per cent of the cable distribution systems in India are owned by local politicians. "Owning a news entity has become a practical necessity for political parties in India."[58]

The two laws covering interception are the Indian Telegraph Act of 1885 and the Information Technology Act of 2000, as amended in 2008. The Telegraph Act mandates that interception of communications can only be done on grounds of a public emergency or for public safety. If either of these two preconditions is satisfied then the government may cite any of the following five reasons to justify their intervention: "the sovereignty and integrity of India, the security of the state, friendly relations with foreign states, or public order, or for preventing incitement to the commission of an offense" (The Indian Telegraph Act (Amendment) *ACT, 2003*. NO. 8 OF 2004. 9 January 2004).

In 2008, the Information Technology Act copied many of the interception provisions of the Telegraph Act, but removed the preconditions of public emergency or public safety, and expanded the powers of the government to order interception for the investigation of any offence. The IT Act thus very substantially lowers the bar for wiretapping.

In a landmark 1996 judgement, the Indian Supreme Court held that telephone tapping is a serious invasion of an individual's privacy, and that the citizen's right to privacy has to be protected from abuse by the authorities. Given this, governments must have explicit permission from their legislatures to engage in any kind of broadening of electronic surveillance powers. Yet, without introducing any new laws, the government has surreptitiously granted itself powers—powers that Parliament has not authorised it to exercise—by sneaking such powers into contract provisions and subordinate legislation.

We can conclude by quoting Suketu Mehta, Associate Professor of Journalism at New York University and the author of *Maximum City: Bombay Lost and Found* (2013): "India is in the throes of what Salman Rushdie rightly calls a 'cultural emergency'. Writers and artists of all kinds are being harassed, sued and arrested for what they say or write or create. The government either stands by or does nothing to protect freedom of speech, or it actively abets its suppression. In recent years, the government has cast a watchful eye on the Internet, demanding that companies like Google and Facebook prescreen content and remove items that might be deemed 'disparaging' or 'inflammatory,' according to technology industry executives there".[59]

In India's neighbouring countries, like **Iran,** there is a tendency to restrict freedom of speech on religious grounds. Blasphemy against Islam is illegal in Iran. According to the Press Freedom Index for 2007, Iran ranked 166th out of 179 nations. Only three other countries—Eritrea,

North Korea and Turkmenistan—had more restrictions on news media freedom than Iran. The government of Ali Khamenei and the Supreme National Security Council imprisoned 50 journalists in 2007 and all but eliminated press freedom. Reporters Without Borders (RSF) have dubbed Iran the Middle East's biggest prison for journalists.

Pakistan has had similar developments. However, Article 19 of the Constitution of Pakistan guarantees freedom of speech and expression, and freedom of the press with certain restrictions. Blasphemy against Islam is illegal in Pakistan.

China—A Country Like a Continent In Western countries people frequently ask if there are laws at all in China. However, their system of legislation is one of the oldest traditions in the world. All dynasties of times gone by had their own legal and penal codes.

Historical Background to the Judicial Tradition History books reveal that before the Common Era, during the Qin dynasty, a "legal school" or legalism (*fajia*), already existed. Alongside Taoism and Confucianism, particularly, this so-called legalism was one of the most important domestic doctrines. The government built a strong state through law.[60]

The Confucianism of law mostly took place during the period of the Han dynasty. Social values were combined with the code of conduct. Also the connection between humans and nature was noted (an influence from Taoism). It is therefore said that the context of contemporary Chinese legal thinking cannot be understood without knowing even a little about Confucius' (circa 500 BCE) ethics and the five Chinese constant virtues: Rén 仁 (benevolence), Yì 義 (righteousness or justice), Lǐ 禮 (propriety), Zhì 智 (wisdom) and Xìn 信 (fidelity). Confucianism has emphasised hierarchical traditions and has portrayed the hardworking citizen as an ideal, which partly explains China's orderly culture and economic productivity (see Jyrki Kallio 2014).

Tradition has had a great influence on China's judicial development. Hierarchism, collectivism and a family-oriented outlook are still present in society. The centre of power is to this day viewed as one body. The law mostly takes the form of criminal law, and the penalties have been severe, as in eighteenth-century Europe. In recent history there was the Manchu law period of 1740–1905, the Kuomingtan law until 1949, followed by the revolutionary period during which there was a Soviet-style legal system.

When examining the recent history of legal development in China, we must first consider the era of the People's Republic before the Cultural Revolution. At that time, the role of the judicial system was understood as a means to facilitate the transfer to a communist system. During the Cultural Revolution (1966–1976), the principle of legality was given up and some state organs were abolished. As a result, and crucially, the judicial system became less predictable. Freedom of expression had no place in this system. Since 1978, the era of reform and the opening up of the economy has prevailed.

Constitution One of the most important policies from the time of opening up was the implementation of the 1982 Constitution (*xianfa*). Researchers do not usually consider it binding in the sense that we are accustomed to in Western countries.[61] The relevance and meaning of the constitution may be debated, but it can certainly be demonstrated that the amendments gradually paved the way towards a rule of law.

It is worth noting the consistency with which, through partial reforms since the 1982 constitutional acts, the country moved towards a socialist market economy in 1993, and set the rule of law as an objective in 1999. A constitutional amendment that would give equal status to private and state property was adopted in 2005.

These amendments are essential to the integration of more of a spirit of the modern rule of law within the constitution. This means implementing the principles of a market economy in a socialist system. Professor Luo Haocai, one of China's best-known judges and justice theorists, describes the development as follows (2009 p. 24): "Although the so-called 'Legalist' philosophy came into being in China as early as two thousand years ago, it is only in the last thirty years that the 'rule of law' has been freed from ideological 'forbidden zones'. From then on, the academic community not only differentiated between the 'legal system' and 'the rule of law', but also carried out thorough discussions concerning the content of the rule of law".

Freedom of speech has been regulated by law in China as well, but is still far from reality. Article 35 of the Constitution of the People's Republic of China reads: "Citizens of the People's Republic of China enjoy freedom of speech, of the press, of assembly, of association, of procession and of demonstration".[29] There is heavy government involvement in the media, with many of the largest media organisations being run by the Communist

Party-led government. References to democracy, the free Tibet movement, Taiwan as an independent country, the Tiananmen Square massacre, the Arab Spring, certain religious organisations and anything questioning the legitimacy of the Communist Party of China are banned from use in public and blocked on the internet. Web portals including Microsoft's MSN have come in for criticism for aiding these practices, including banning the word "democracy" from its chat-rooms in China.

Due to their close geographical proximity to Hong Kong, parts of southern China are able to receive broadcast signals from television channels in Hong Kong, where China's censorship does not apply. However, comments that the Communist Party feels uncomfortable with are cut out and replaced with TV commercials before they can reach consumers' TVs in mainland China. According to the *Beijing News* there are 2 million internet policemen, also known as "analysts of public opinion". The most recent case to test the credibility of these regulations is the September 2014 demonstrations in Hong Kong.

What is the Trend in China? The next stage of reform is about to begin, as on 12 November 2013 the third plenary session of the Communist Party of China's 18th Central Committee ratified a reform programme with more than ten sections. Its objective is to bring the public and private sectors closer to one another and improve communication between them. The programme has been in the National People's Congress for ratification since the spring of 2014, when almost 300 different actions for reform were listed. It is still difficult to evaluate the programme's significance for the tight restrictions on freedom of speech.[62]

The change from databases and fax machines to mobile devices and cloud computing have dramatically influenced the ways in which governments, businesses and citizens interact. Incorporating ICT into government helps strengthen the efficiency, accessibility and integrity of public services, and may bring about ground-breaking changes in public administration. The central government of the People's Republic of China has recognised the importance of utilising ICT to achieve better governance. When it comes to **promoting freedom of speech**, close attention should be paid to ICT projects in the provinces that are strictly supervised by central government, such as the Hangzhou Information and Communication Technology Programme of 2013.

The reverse side of a centralised government system is, however, a tendency to limit and control communication, social media and the internet. There is little reason for any unrealistic optimism when it comes to the development of free speech in China, as it is still difficult to assess the significance of the new reforms. Let us conclude this overview on a Chinese note with a verse by one of China's best-known poets, Qu Yuan: "Long, long had been my road and far, far was the journey. I would go up and down to seek my heart's desire".[63]

Mongolia is a fascinating destination between the two great powers of China and Russia. Genghis Khan (born Temujin, died 1227), founder of the Mongolian state, conquered most of Eurasia, including China. In the West, his conquests reached parts of Russia, South India, Iran and the Caucasus. The Mongol Empire continued to grow under the rule of his descendants, eventually becoming the largest empire in the history of the world (see *Changing Russia?* p. 14–6). History has taught us that nothing lasts forever, not even the millennial Roman Empire.

The interesting thing about Mongolian history is the fact that Genghis Khan was thought to have respect for law (*yasa*) even eight hundred years ago, and he worked for the consensus of his sub-commanders (*kuriltai*). From that period the codification of this customary law of the nomads was inherited and preserved during the Manchu period that followed. After the revolution of 1921 justice took a socialist form with characteristics of Asian as well as European cultures.

Disengagement from the shadow of communism started in 1989 as crowds gathered for a demonstration at Sukhbaatar Square in Urga—known today as Ulaan Baatar—leading to the resignation of the government. The constitution was changed in 1990 and the first multi-party election was held for the State Great Assembly (*Hural*). The Assembly first declared the protection of property, ratified a number of laws and started a process of constitutional reform that led to ratification of a new constitution in 1992. Freedom of speech also gained a constitutional footing.

Today's Mongolia is an independent republic based on a multi-party system. The unicameral parliament has 76 members. According to the principle of separation of powers, the government is responsible for governing and courts are independent. The head of state is the president, who symbolises the unity of the nation. In 2012 the Democratic Party (DP) formed a government together with two smaller groups. The re-elected President Tsakhiagiin Elbegdorj, who is a member of the DP as well as a member of the Great Hural, is still in office. The chairman of the Great Hural is Zandaakhuu Enkhbold.

Mongolia has been particularly interested in the Nordic welfare state and its democracy, equality and low levels of corruption. Reforming the government and increasing transparency are its primary goals, and it is for this reason that we included Mongolia as a destination on this world tour. In this land of two cultures, in the midst of traditions, nomadism and the rising mining industry, there are still many twists and turns along the road to free speech and functional justice.

Along the Silk Road in Central Asia

Common Heritage, Different Cultures All five Central Asian countries, **Kazakhstan, Kyrgyzstan, Tajikistan, Turkmenistan** and **Uzbekistan,** have their own historical and cultural backgrounds. However, because these countries differ in their level of economic development, as well as in terms of natural resources and overall circumstances, their development prospects cannot be analysed from the same perspective.[64]

Even though the Central Asian states share some common characteristics, they also host a number of cultural and societal differences which we have to take into consideration when analysing rule-of-law development in these countries. Of their shared historical experience, it has been said that "although the basic circumstances of these five countries are incomparable, they all have one thing in common: a Soviet heritage which is still visible today throughout their legal system and procedure laws" (see Schuhmann, *Law in Transition* 2011, 74). National characteristics have also been visibly incorporated into the countries´ respective constitutions.

The transitional period, and the associated national strategies, legislative programmes, new constitutions and amendments, and the tendency towards strong national governments are something that the five states have in common. Moreover, the situation is still in flux: power structures are being shaped within rapidly changing circumstances, and the countries are still getting used to solving national problems. Because of this, international assessments and indicators measuring rule-of-law development cannot sufficiently demonstrate the relevance of different development projects. We have witnessed significant progress in all five countries, including a new constitution in Kyrgyzstan.

Kazakhstan In the leading country of the region, Kazakhstan, we can clearly observe the following characteristics which deviate from the norm: government powers are limited; freedom of assembly and the freedom of opinion and expression are too circumscribed; there is a lack of due process in administrative proceedings; and civil justice is not free of corruption.

Kazakhstan proclaims itself a democratic, secular, legal and social state where the individual, their life, rights and freedoms are most important. The preamble to the Constitution emphasises the importance of "freedom, equality and concord" and Kazakhstan's role in the international community.

In a press conference held on 12 July 2012 the UN High Commissioner for Human Rights, Ms Navi Pillay, criticised the excessive use of force and the related abuse of power that occurred during the tragic events that took place in Zhanaozen in December 2011. Fifteen people died and over 100 were injured during the Zhanaozen and Shetpen riots. She also stated that a comprehensive, national human rights action plan involving key ministries, state institutions and civil society organisations, addressing all the recommendations emanating from the international human rights system—especially those relating to weaknesses in rule-of-law institutions—would be the best way to begin the process of carefully planned and coordinated reform.

The status of private individuals and citizens is, in principle, well secured in Section II of the Constitution (Art. 10–39). The fundamental human rights provision can be found in Art. 12: "Human rights and freedoms shall be recognized and guaranteed in accordance with Constitution. Human rights and freedoms shall belong to everyone by virtue of birth, be absolute and inalienable, and define the contents and implementation of laws and other regulatory legal acts".[65] The Constitution makes separate reference to foreigners and stateless persons (Art. 12). Other civil rights and freedoms and the right of everyone to be treated equally before the law are also guaranteed in the Constitution. Rights of participation are restricted to the country's citizens (Art. 33). Electoral legislation has undergone several changes since the 2007 parliamentary elections.

The constitutional guarantee of freedom of speech and the prohibition of censorship are limited by criminal responsibility for defamation and by the special protection afforded to the President and public officials (Art. 10–1 and 317–1 of the Criminal Code). This legal situation has raised concerns among national and international media experts.[66]

Kyrgyzstan The Kyrgyz legal system has undergone considerable changes over the past few years. In 2007 a new constitution, which increased presidential powers and strengthened the status of the parliament, was accepted by referendum. This, however, led to a deterioration in the human rights situation and, with the situation escalating into crisis and widespread demonstrations, President Kurmanbek Bakiyev was eventually forced to resign on 15 April 2010. A new constitution, which reinforced the principles of parliamentarism, was approved by referendum on 27 June 2010.

The ethnic violence experienced in Southern Kyrgyzstan in the summer of 2010 resulted in hundreds of people losing their lives and the mass displacement of civilians. An independent inquiry into the events was carried out in 2010–2011. The WJP Rule of Law Index from 2011 illustrates, for instance, the following concerns: (1) corruption especially has caused problems in relation to accountable government; (2) in the section covering fundamental rights, arbitrary interference needs to be addressed, and equal treatment and absence of discrimination are factors clearly in need of reform; and (3) when it comes to the development of open government and regulatory enforcement, there have been significant problems in relation to the stability of legislation and access to information.

Tajikistan The World Bank Indicators assessment of rule-of-law development in Tajikistan during the years 1996–2011 does not give a positive picture. At first, Tajikistan experienced a clear upturn in its rule-of-law development, but the situation then declined, showing signs of recovery only in 2009. Every now and then there has been unfortunate news of the torture of witnesses.

The Constitutional Court was established in 1994 to protect the Constitution and individual rights and freedoms, and to enforce the rule of law. In 1995 the Court began hearing cases, and in March 2008 its jurisdiction and standing were significantly expanded as a result of the amendments made to the Law on the Constitutional Court. Part II of the Constitution provides in detail for individual rights and freedoms, as well as for individual economic, educational and social rights.
In **Turkmenistan** the World Bank's Worldwide Governance Indicators from the years 1996–2011 illustrate the following general development trajectories through six governance dimensions: (1) Voice and Accountability—scores have been fairly consistent, but remain at very low

levels when compared internationally; (2) Political Stability and Absence of Violence—scores have been at a relatively higher level during the intermediate years. According to these indicators, compiled on the basis of multiple international sources, Turkmenistan's values on the other dimensions—(3) Government Effectiveness, (4) Regulatory Quality and (5) Control of Corruption—have not risen from their internationally compared low levels.

In Turkmenistan the state owns all domestic media, and President Niyazov's administration controls them by appointing editors and censoring content. Niyazov personally approves the front-page content of the major dailies, which always include a prominent picture of him.

Uzbekistan The World Bank's Rule of Law Indicator from the years 1996–2011 shows a more positive outlook for Uzbekistan than its neighbours. However, during the past few years no progress has been achieved. The constitution entails very detailed provisions for securing fundamental and human rights, for ensuring equality before the law and for prohibiting discrimination. The constitution also regulates specifically for nationality and ensuring legal protection for foreign citizens and stateless persons during their stay in Uzbekistan, as well as for personal rights and freedoms, political rights, economic and social rights, and guarantees of human rights and freedoms and the duties of citizens.

The Institute for Monitoring of Current Legislation under the President of the Republic of Uzbekistan, founded in 2005, plays a significant role in terms of preparing legal acts and researching legislation. The main tasks of the Institute consist of conducting a comprehensive legal review of draft laws, analysing the improvement of the legal basis for reforming and modernising the country, and monitoring the realisation of norms and principles of the constitution in law. The law in action may be different. President Karimov's regime uses an informal system of state censorship to prevent the domestic media from reporting on the widespread use of torture by the police, poverty and the Islamic opposition movement. No improvement in the state of freedom of speech in the country has been observed following the death of President Karimov in autumn 2016.

Conclusion What stands out to an external observer when assessing the Central Asian constitutions is the detailed way that citizens' status and fundamental rights are described. Development in terms of realising fundamental and human rights has often been measured by how freedom rights such as freedom of opinion and freedom of assembly have been secured, and on the other hand to what extent economic, social and cultural (ESC) rights have been realised. There is of course need for development in all these areas.

Despite detailed provisions, criticism has been voiced concerning the realisation of basic protection of the law, with the latest concern being about Kazakhstan where freedom of assembly is far too restricted (see the statement made by UN High Commissioner for Human Rights, Navi Pillay, 12 July 2012 in Astana).

The declaration "Placing Human Rights at the Heart of EU Action" (19 June 2012) by 50 NGOs, including NGOs from each of the five Central Asian states, describes well the gap between regulated rights and their practical implementation. The NGOs argue for a better dialogue between society and public authorities when the rule-of-law state is being built.

Light and Shadows in the Southeast Asian Countries

Many Different Lands and Cultures Let us now pass through some other Asian countries, although this overview will only begin to scratch the surface. Barriers to freedom of speech are common, and vary drastically between countries. They include the use of brutal force in cracking down on bloggers in Myanmar (Burma), Vietnam and Cambodia; *lèse-majesté* in Thailand; the use of libel and internal security laws in Singapore and Malaysia; and the killing of journalists in the Philippines. Freedom of expression is significantly limited in North and South Korea. Freedom of speech has improved in Myanmar in recent years, but significant challenges remain. The Constitution of Brunei Darussalam does not contain any section or provision for a Bill of Rights for citizens. Freedom of expression and the press is mainly governed by the Sedition Act.

South Korea The South Korean constitution guarantees freedom of speech, press, petition and assembly for its nationals. However, behaviours or speeches in favour of the North Korean regime, communism or Japan can be punished by the National Security Law—though in recent years prosecutions under this law have been rare.

A strict election law takes effect a few months before elections prohibiting most speech that either supports or criticises a particular candidate or party. People can be prosecuted for political parodies and even for wearing a particular colour (usually the colour of a party).

Japan Freedom of speech is guaranteed by Article 21 of the Japanese Constitution. There are few exemptions and a very broad spectrum of opinion is tolerated by the media and authorities. In 2013 Japan passed an Act on the Protection of Specially Designated Secrets and is now developing the implementing regulations. The law was recently critiqued by the United National Human Rights Committee (see Freedom info.org report.) Does Japan really have an information security problem?

In **Cambodia** "Khmer citizens shall have the freedom to express their personal opinions, the freedom of press, of publication and of assembly. No one can abusively take advantage of these rights to impinge on the dignity of others, to affect the good mores and customs of society, public order or national security. The regime of the media shall be regulated by law" (Chapter III, Art. 41; http://www.wipo.int/edocs/lexdocs/laws/en/kh/kh009en.pdf). Freedom of expression and press is limited by the second sentence of the article. The country has ratified and incorporated international human rights laws into its domestic law. However, the government exercises tight control over print and broadcast news outlets by using legal provisions against criminal defamation and incitement, so as to discourage media organisations seeking free expression, and encourages self-censorship.

In **Indonesia** the freedom to associate and to assemble, to express written and oral opinions, and so on, is regulated by law. The Indonesian Constitution does not detail the right to freedom of expression, which is just a general umbrella provision, and the details of implementation or procedures are regulated through government or ministry acts, including the Press Law.

In **Laos**, Laotian citizens have the right to freedom of speech, press and assembly, and have the right to set up associations and to stage demonstrations which are not contrary to the law.

Article 44 of the constitution guarantees the freedom of press and expression; however defamation and misinformation are criminal offences, and individuals who break the law can be sentenced to lengthy terms of imprisonment or even face possible execution.

In **Malaysia** free expression is guaranteed by Article 10 (1.a) of the constitution: every citizen has the right to freedom of speech and expression. However in the same article, clause 2 (a) states that the "restrictions are necessary in the interest of the security of the Federation or any part thereof, friendly relations with other countries, public order or morality and restrictions designed to protect the privileges of Parliament or of any Legislative Assembly or to provide against contempt of court, defamation or incitement to any offence" (http://www.rsog.com.my/media/558.pdf). Therefore, there are restrictions on these rights. The Sedition Act and harsh criminal defamation laws are regularly used to impose restrictions on the press and other critics of the government. Violations of these laws are punishable by several years in prison.

Myanmar's constitution was suspended during military rule in 1974. The new Constitution of 2008 stipulates that a two-chamber parliament (Assembly of the Union) elect the President and two Vice-Presidents. Nevertheless, the Constitution emphasises the predominant role of the armed forces in decision making and one-quarter of the seats in each chamber is reserved for representatives of the armed forces. Similarly, ministerial posts had earlier been reserved for serving generals. The first general elections—which were boycotted by the main opposition group National League for Democracy (NLD)—were organised in 2010. Civilians have gained some ground since then and the general elections of November 2015 were hailed as a further step towards democracy.

The human rights situation of minorities in Myanmar remains poor. There have been clashes between groups, with an element of ethnic cleansing present. The dominance of the Burmese population over Karen, Shan, Raksine, Mon, Rohingya, Chin, Kachin and other minorities has frequently led to protests and uprisings. However, ceasefire agreements in 2011 and 2012 with rebels of Karen and Shan groups, and in 2013 with Kachin rebels, indicate a new determination to end the conflicts.

The current Constitution (Chapter VIII, Section 354) guarantees the freedom of speech as follows: "Every citizen shall be at liberty in the exercise of the following rights, if not contrary to the laws, enacted for Union security, prevalence of law and order, community peace and tranquillity or public order and morality: to express and publish freely their convictions and opinions". Clause (a) of section 354 upholds freedom of expression, but it is restricted by vague conditions relating to "Union security, prevalence of law and order, community peace and tranquillity" (see Constitution of the Republic of the Union of Myanmar (2008), Burma, Printing & Pub. Enterprise, Ministry of Information 2008).

The reforms in Myanmar since 2011 have relaxed many of the restrictions on the press. However, legal restrictions still exist, including in the criminal code, the Official Secrets Act and other laws that can punish journalists. In 2012 Aung San Suu Kyi made constitutional reform one of her party's priorities, although even then it was not entirely clear what changes she wanted to make.[67] Lasting peace with the many ethnic insurgencies remains elusive.[68]

The **Philippines**' constitution supports freedom of expression and press, (Art. III Bill of Rights, Section 4): "No law shall be passed abridging the freedom of speech, of expression, or of the press, or the right of the people peaceably to assemble and petition the government for redress of grievances". However, libel is a criminal offence under the penal code, which can punish journalists with prison terms and large fines.

In **Singapore** every citizen has the right to freedom of speech and expression.

This article—Article 14 of the Singapore constitution—is identical to Article 10 of the Malaysian constitution, as Singapore was previously part of Malaysia.

Thailand It is necessary to stay longer in Thailand, where large demonstrations and debate on freedom of speech have recently taken place. The constitution includes a special and more detailed norm on "Liberties in Expression of Persons and Mass Media", Section 45: "A person shall enjoy the liberty to express his or her opinion, make speeches, write, print, publicize, and make expression by other means. The restriction on the liberty under paragraph one shall not be imposed except by virtue of the provisions of the law specifically enacted for the purpose of maintaining the security of the State, safeguarding the rights, liberties, dignity, reputation, family or privacy rights of other persons, maintaining public order or good morals or preventing the deterioration of the mind or health of the public".

While the Thai constitution provides for freedom of expression, by law the government may impose restrictions to preserve national security, maintain public order, preserve the rights of others, protect public morals and prevent insults to Buddhism. Defamation is a criminal offence, and parties that criticise the government or related businesses may be sued, setting the stage for self-censorship. Recently, in 2015, actors were sentenced to long terms of imprisonment because of the play *Wolf Bride*'s associations with the royal house.

Censorship has expanded considerably, starting in 2003 during the Thaksin Shinawatra administration, and after the 2006 military coup. Under an Emergency Decree in the three southernmost provinces, the government may restrict print and broadcast media, online news and social media networks: "The closure of a newspaper or other mass-media business in deprivation of the liberty under this section shall not be made. The prohibition of a newspaper or other mass-media business from presenting information or expressing opinions in whole or in part or imposition of interference by any means in deprivation of the liberty under this section shall not be made except by virtue of the law enacted under paragraph two.

The censorship by a competent official of news or articles before their publication in a newspaper or other mass media shall not be made except during the time when the country is in a state of war; provided that it must be made by virtue of the law enacted under paragraph two. The owner of a newspaper or other mass-media business shall be a Thai national. No grant of money or other properties shall be made by the State as subsidies to private newspapers or other mass media".[69]

So we can consider that the Thai Constitution does guarantee freedom of expression; however the repeated use of the phrase "except by virtue of provisions of the law"—in, for example, article 112 of the criminal code, or the *lèse-majesté* law—is a popular issue in terms of restricting freedom of expression. It violates section 45 of the constitution. According to that law anyone who defames the royal family can be sentenced to up to fifteen years' imprisonment. Defamation is also a criminal offence and can be punished with fines and prison terms of up to two years.

In **Timor Leste** every person has the right to freedom of speech and the right to inform and be informed impartially. The exercise of freedom of speech and information is not to be limited by any sort of censorship. Freedom of expression and the press are protected under both sections 40 and 41 of the constitution. However, a penal code known as "defamatory false information" is a threat to journalists.

Vietnam guarantees freedom of expression and the press in Article 69 of its constitution. However, when we look at the Article 33, under chapter III of Culture, Education, Science and Technology, it states: "Work in the field of information, press, radio, television, cinema, publishing, libraries and other means of mass communication is to be developed by the State-Cultural of information; activities detrimental to the national interests and which undermine the fine personality, morality and way of life of the Vietnamese people are prohibited". This makes freedom of expression and the press seem vague. Articles of the criminal code which restrict the dissemination of anti-government propaganda, the use of pseudonyms and anonymous sources also represent a threat to journalists.[70]

AUSTRALIA, THE FINAL DESTINATION OF OUR WORLD TOUR

Australia does not have explicit freedom of speech protection in any constitutional or statutory declaration of rights, with the exception of political speech, which is protected from criminal prosecution under common law per *Australian Capital Television Pty Ltd v Commonwealth*.[71] An implied freedom of speech was also recognised in *Lange v Australian Broadcasting Corporation*.

In 1992 the High Court of Australia judged in the case of *Australian Capital Television Pty Ltd v Commonwealth* that the Australian Constitution, by providing for a system of representative and responsible government, implied the protection of political communication as an essential element of that system. This freedom of political communication is not as broad a freedom of speech as in other countries, but rather a freedom whose purpose is only to protect political free speech. This freedom of political free speech is a shield against government prosecution, not against private prosecution under the civil law. However, not all political speech appears to be protected in Australia.[72]

In 2014 the Australian parliament debated changes to national security laws intended to keep Australians safe. Many journalists had hoped that Parliament would not rush to adopt laws that infringed fundamental rights and risked criminalising the legitimate activities of whistle-blowers, journalists and human rights activists.[73] Under the proposed amendments, anyone who discloses information related to a special intelligence operation could face up to five years in prison. The penalty increases to ten years if the information endangers lives. The legislation, which passed the lower house with support from the main opposition Labour Party, is vague as to what exactly could be considered a "special intelligence operation"; but in a post-Snowden and WikiLeaks world, we know that simply describing something as "special" or "classified" does not mean it should automatically be free from scrutiny. Conservative Prime Minister Tony Abbott warned that the balance between freedom and security may have to shift (see endnote 73). The proposed legislation also outlaws copying, transcribing, retaining or recording intelligence materials, which critics say is a direct response to former damaging leaks by National Security Agency contractor Edward Snowden, and vastly expands the government's power to monitor computers.

This legislation is the first of a series of laws aimed at "beefing up" the government's security powers, including a controversial proposal to make it a crime for an Australian citizen to travel to any area overseas once the government has declared it off-limits (see Matt Siegel, Sydney Wed Oct 1, 2014).

Some journalists have also written columns criticising this new legislation: punishing those who leak security information or publish it can be problematic as it suppresses information that may be vital for the exercise and protection of human rights, accountability and democratic governance. "It's very dangerous to democratic values to introduce such sweeping laws to gag publication of sensitive materials. The United Nations Human Rights Committee has noted that governments must take 'extreme care' to ensure that laws relating to national security are not invoked 'to suppress or withhold from the public information of legitimate public interest that does not harm national security' or to prosecute journalists, researchers, activists, or others who disseminate such information".[74]

THEORY AND REALITY

There are many sayings in the world about travelling to broaden your perspective, such as "The more you hike the more hills you see"; according to a Finnish proverb "you do not get fat out there in the world, but you do get wiser". Have we gained any wisdom after taking note of how free speech is defended with eloquent presentations while the everyday reality is quite different? The first note along our journey was about how theory and reality sit side by side in Northern Europe and how the reality is tougher the further we travel.

Social conditions and traditions that are reflected in the judicial culture and the way power is exercised explain differences in the development of free speech. It is relevant to note the connection between freedom of speech and judicial development: where, as we noted in the beginning, "speech is free and also justice is respected". Therefore, freedom of speech cannot be analysed—still less promoted—without tackling general questions on the exercise of power and justice first.

This context brings to mind another saying, apparently the motto of Frederick the Great: "*Esse, non videri*"—it is better to be something rather than to just appear so. This leads one to wonder whether, if fundamental rights to free speech are trampled on, and human rights obligations are not fulfilled, it would be better to lower the bar closer to reality—representing surrender—or to continue to strive to change reality?

The answer is of course obvious: we must not give up universal objectives and free speech as a fundamental right that belongs to everyone. The apex of reform is abiding by our principles and better implementing laws. For each individual, the point is having the strength to withstand ideological influence and even subtle persuasion. Without slipping towards idealism, the question is about acting on the interests that lie behind restrictions, shaping centralised types of governance to a more democratic form and increasing the transparency of the decision-making process. The next chapter examines the meaning of human rights and international cooperation. The power of change is at grassroots level, where the people are, but we may still entertain hopes.

Notes

1. See Eero Vartiainen, Publishing *Saima*: J.V. Snellman and His Influence on Finnish Nationalism Between the Years 1844–1846. Providence College, 2007.
2. For the background to the freedom of information legislation and the role of K.J. Ståhlberg, see Ståhlberg, Suomen hallinto-oikeus, Sisäasiain hallinto 1931, p. 180.
3. See Constitution of Finland at http://www.finlex.fi/fi/laki/kaannokset/1999/en19990731.pdf, accessed 5 September 2016.
4. Available at http://www.finlex.fi/fi/laki/kaannokset/1999/en19990731.pdf, accessed 30 August 2016.
5. See Regeringsformen 1974 and most recent reforms RP 2009/10:80.
6. See more at Accountable Journalism initiative homepage: http://www.rjionline.org/MAS-Press-Councils-Sweden#sthash.m0ghqZF1.dpuf, last accessed 27 May 2016.
7. See more at the homepage of the Swedish Parliament at http://www.riksdagen.se/sv/Dokument-Lagar/Utskottens-dokument/Betankanden/Arenden/201314/KU17/, last accessed 27 May 2016 (Riksdagen, 10 April 2014).
8. Available at https://www.stortinget.no/en/In-English/About-the-Storting/The-Constitution/, accessed 30 August 2016.
9. Available at http://www.servat.unibe.ch/icl/da00000_.html, last accessed 20 August 2016.

10. *The Guardian* 3 February 2006, available at https://www.theguardian.com/media/2006/feb/03/pressandpublishing.religion5, last accessed 30 August 2016.
11. In both Yemen and Jordan, editors who republished the cartoons (which have now appeared in 22 different countries) were promptly arrested and their newspapers were shut down. http://www.economist.com/node/5494646, last accessed June 2015 (Feb 9th 2006, *The Economist*).
12. See more at http://www.theguardian.com/media/2006/feb/04/mainsection.garyyounge;, last accessed June 2015, Philip Hensher and Gary Younge, 4 February 2006, *The Guardian*.
13. See Jessica Loechel, last updated April 30 2013, Free Speech and Free Press Around the World, available at https://freespeechfreepress.wordpress.com/the-netherlands/, last accessed 30 August 2016.
14. See more at Free Speech and Free Press Around the World Project homepage at http://freespeechfreepress.wordpress.com/the-netherlands/, last accessed June 2015.
15. A summary of the present state of freedom of speech in Germany is available at https://www.indexoncensorship.org/2013/08/germany-a-positive-environment-for-free-expression-clouded-by-surveillance/), accessed June 2015.
16. The Declaration of the Rights of Man and of the Citizen (*Déclaration des droits de l'homme et du citoyen*), passed by France's National Constituent Assembly in August 1789, is a fundamental document of the French Revolution and in the history of human and civil rights.
17. See more at the Index on Censorship homepage at https://www.indexoncensorship.org/2013/08/france-faces-restrictions-on-free-expression/, accessed June 2015.
18. A summary on media Freedom in France is available at https://www.indexoncensorship.org/2013/08/france-faces-restrictions-on-free-expression/, last accessed June 2015.
19. Press Freedom Index, Reporters Without Borders 2014: 64/179; 2013: 56; 2012: 40.
20. Available at http://legislationline.org/documents/action/popup/id/5350, accessed 5 September 2016.
21. Find more sources at Wikipedia at http://en.wikipedia.org/wiki/Censorship_in_the_United_Kingdom, accessed June 2015.
22. This comment was written by Peter Preston specifically for this book and is published, unedited, with his permission. It has not been previously published.
23. Read more at the *Daily Mail*: http://www.dailymail.co.uk/news/article-2092173/World-Press-Freedom-Index-2011-U-S-U-K-drop.html#ixzz3C9Trotvu http://www.dailymail.co.uk/news/article-2092173/

24. World-Press-Freedom-Index-2011-U-S-U-K-drop.html (26 January 2012, *Daily Mail*), last accessed June 2015.
24. Available at https://www.senato.it/documenti/repository/istituzione/costituzione_inglese.pdf, accessed 5 September 2016.
25. See http://www.theguardian.com/media/greenslade/2014/feb/18/italy-newspapers (Roy Greenslade, 18 February 2014, *The Guardian*, accessed June 2015.
26. See Freedom of the Press 2013 http://www.freedomhouse.org/report/freedom-press/2013/italy#.Uu-Pwvl_vHU, last accessed June 2015.
27. This comment was written by Pekka Korpinen specifically for this book and is published, unedited, with his permission. It has not been previously published.
28. Available at http://en.wiki2audio.com/wiki/Freedom_of_speech_by_country+Spain, accessed 5 September 2016.
29. Constitution of China Art. 35: http://www.hkhrm.org.hk/english/law/const03.html.
30. Law for the Prevention of Damage to the State of Israel through Boycott – 2011 available at https://www.adalah.org/uploads/oldfiles/upfiles/2011/boycott_law.pdf, accessed 5 September 2016.
31. Kari Ketola, an expert in Russian business relations, and Timo Vihavainen, a professor of Russian Studies, give us many interesting views in their new book '*Changing Russia?*' (2015).
32. Constitution of Russian Federation available at http://www.venice.coe.int/webforms/documents/default.aspx?pdffile=CDL(2003)018-e, accessed 5 September 2016.
33. In an interview for Hallberg's book *Rule of Law*, 2004 p. 118.
34. This comment was written by Steven Ellis specifically for this book and is published, unedited, with his permission. It has not been previously published.
35. Find more references for Tocqueville at Wikipedia at http://lt.wikipedia.org/wiki/Alexis_de_Tocqueville, last accessed June 2015.
36. See Cornell University Law School homepage at https://www.law.cornell.edu/constitution/billofrights, accessed 27 May 2016.
37. See the UNOFC homepage at https://unofc.wordpress.com/2012/10/04/by-country-freedom-of-speech-censorship-defamation-laws/, accessed 27 May 2016.
38. This comment was written by Sandra Day O'Connor specifically for this book and is published, unedited, with her permission. It has not been previously published.
39. This comment was written by Claude E. Erbsen specifically for this book and is published, unedited, with his permission. It has not been previously published.

40. Available at http://www.iep.utm.edu/bacon/, accessed 5 September 2016.
41. See Human and Environmental Institute homepage for more information and references at: http://www.herinst.org/envcrisis/media/ownership/nbc.html, last accessed 27 May 2016.
42. See Free Press homepage at http://www.freepress.net/ownership/chart.
43. See case study: General Electric http://www.herinst.org/envcrisis/media/ownership/nbc.html.
44. See Bloomberg at http://www.bloomberg.com/apps/news?pid=21070001&sid=a1PvN0L9y37M, last accessed June 2015.
45. This comment was written by the lateIlkka Heiskanen specifically for this book and is published, unedited, with his permission. It has not been previously published.
46. This comment was written by Ingmar Ström specifically for this book and is published, unedited, with his permission. It has not been previously published.
47. See Free Speech Press at http://freespeechfreepress.wordpress.com/south-america/brazil/, 21 April 2014, accessed 27 May 2016.
48. The Constitution of Brazil of 1946 available at https://archive.org/stream/ConstitutionOfTheUnitedStatesOfBrazilTogetherWithTheAccompanying/Brazil2_djvu.txt, accessed 5 September 2016.
49. Available at https://freespeechfreepress.wordpress.com/south-america/brazil/, accessed 5 September 2016.
50. Available at https://freespeechfreepress.wordpress.com/south-america/brazil/, accessed 5 September 2016.
51. Available at http://www.worldlibrary.org/article/WHEBN0018933534/Freedom%20of%20speech%20by%20country, accessed 5 September 2016.
52. http://www.hrw.org/news/2014/06/25/brazil-investigate-police-response-world-cup-protests, last accessed June 2015, Human Rights Watch: Brazil: Investigate Police Response to World Cup Protests, Demonstrators, Journalists Injured in Confrontations with Police, 26 June 2014.
53. Available at https://freespeechfreepress.wordpress.com/south-america/brazil/, accessed 5 September 2016.
54. See Emperor Thembu and Votani Majola, *Press Freedom in Post-Apartheid South Africa*, Anchor Academic Publishing, 2015. During the era of apartheid in South Africa, the press was severely curtailed and subject to repressive laws. The dawn of democracy liberated the press in more ways than one. The study examines the extent to which, in practice, a free press in South Africa is able to report freely without hindrances.

55. This comment was written by Raymond Louw specifically for this book and is published, unedited, with his permission. It has not been previously published.
56. The Constitution of India available at http://lawmin.nic.in/olwing/coi/coi-english/coi-4March2016.pdf, accessed 5 September 2016.
57. Find more references at Wikipedia at http://en.wikipedia.org/wiki/Freedom_of_speech_by_country, last accessed June 2015.
58. Read more on comments made by Parthasarathy Shome, who was appointed an adviser to the Finance Ministerwith the rank of Minister of State, has authored several books on tax policies and was a professor with the Indian Council for Research on International Economic Relations. See www.parthoshome.com/index.html.
59. See more at http://www.nytimes.com/2013/02/06/opinion/indias-limited-freedom-of-speech.html?_r=0, accessed 5 September 2016.
60. Tauno-Olavi Huotari and Pertti Seppälä (1993) have elaborated on this cultural development in their book.
61. See Donald C. Clarke, *Puzzling Observations in Chinese Law: When is Riddle Just a Mistake?*, *Understanding China's Legal System*, New York and London 2003.
62. See *Global Times*. 2014a. "China must chart own course to rule of law". *Global Times*. 21 October, 2014. http://www.globaltimes.cn/content/887350.shtml, accessed 21 October, 2014.
    Global Times. 2014b. "'Rule of man' tradition changed by new law blueprint". *Global Times*. 30 October, 2014. http://www.globaltimes.cn/content/889069.shtml, last accessed 19 November, 2014.
    Husa, Jaakko. 2015. *A New Introduction to Comparative Law*. Portland: Hart Publishing.
    Ruskola, Teemu. 2012. Legal Orientalism, *Michigan Law Review*, Vol. 101, No. 1 (Oct., 2012), 179–234.
63. Qu Yuan Chinese: 屈原; 343–278 BC was a Chinese poet and Minister who lived during the Warring States period of ancient China. He is known for his contributions to classical poetry and verses, especially through the poems of the *Chu Ci* anthology (also known as *The Songs of the South* or *Songs of Chu*). http://www.goodreads.com/book/show/714142.Li_Sao
64. See Hallberg, *Rule of Law, Prospects in Central Asia* 2013.
65. See http://www.parlam.kz/en/constitution.
66. See Advocacy letter, Kazakhstan: Broadcasting draft law threatens free expression, Article 19, 30 November 2011. www.article19.org/resources.php/resource/2906/en/Kazakhstan:-broadcasting-draft-law-threatens-free-expression.

67. See *Foreign Policy* at: http://www.foreignpolicy.com/articles/2014/03/38/why_burma_is_heading_downhill_fl, last accessed June 2015.
68. See *The Economist* at http://www.economist.com/node/21600119/print, last accessed 27 May 2016.
69. The decree was issued under Section 218 of the Thai Constitution, which concerns public safety, national economic security, or averting public calamity (*Bangkok Post* 13 Aug 2003).
70. Source: Freedom House, available at https://freedomhouse.org/report/freedom-press/2013/Vietnam, last accessed June 2015.
71. See however http://www.comlaw.gov.au/Series/C2004A02562 (Freedom of Information Act 1982), last accessed June 2015.
72. See RSF homepage at http://en.rsf.org/australia-wikileaks-reveals-sweeping-30-07-2014,46727.html (RSF 30 July 2014; Australian court imposes generalized news blackout on bribery case), last accessed June 2015.
73. See Reuters at http://www.reuters.com/article/2014/10/01/us-australia-security-idUSKCN0HQ2WX20141001, Australia passes security law, raising fears for press freedom, by Matt Siegel, 1 October 2014, last accessed June 2015.
74. See a comment made by Elaine Pearson, theguardian.com. Monday 22 September 2014 available at https://www.theguardian.com/commentisfree/2014/sep/22/australias-counter-terror-laws-will-restrict-our-free-speech-and-free-press, accessed 5 September 2016.

CHAPTER 6

Human Rights Obligations: From Ideas to Reality?

THE EUROPEAN CONVENTION ON HUMAN RIGHTS (ECHR)

Historical Background After the Second World War the Council of Europe was established to strengthen Western European co-operation. Respect for human rights and fundamental freedoms were included in the Statute of the Council of Europe (1949) as a condition for membership. In 1950 member states signed the Convention for the Protection of Human Rights and Fundamental Freedoms, also known as the European Convention on Human Rights (ECHR), which is largely based on the earlier United Nations Universal Declaration of Human Rights (1948) and the early draft of the International Covenant on Civil and Political Rights.

Today, practically all Eastern and Central European states are full members, while the remaining countries (e.g. members of the Commonwealth of Independent States) have observer status, still benefiting from various co-operation programmes. Indeed, the transition to democracy in Eastern and Central Europe after the fall of the Berlin Wall has brought tremendous challenges to the Council of Europe: from the sixteen original member states, its constituency has grown to 47 (the situation since 2005). Most of the new members are transitional—and hence fragile—democracies. In 1997, the Council of Europe established new monitoring and verification

© The Author(s) 2017
P. Hallberg, J. Virkkunen, *Freedom of Speech and Information in Global Perspective*, DOI 10.1057/978-1-349-94990-8_6

mechanisms for the assessment of its member states' compliance with their membership commitments and obligations.

The ECHR entered into force in 1953 after it had been ratified by a sufficient number of states. At the beginning of 2010 10 new states ratified the Convention, including Russia, so Europe is not the only area of application (see background: Tuomas Ojanen and Martin Scheinin, *Perusoikeudet,* 2011s. 875 ss.).

The Convention established the European Court of Human Rights (ECtHR). Any person who feels their rights have been violated under the Convention by a state party can take a case to the Court. Judgements finding violations are binding on the states concerned, and they are obliged to execute them. The Committee of Ministers of the Council of Europe monitors the execution of judgements, particularly to ensure payment of damages awarded by the Court to applicants.

Content of the ECHR Signed on 4 November 1950, the Convention guarantees a broad range of human rights to inhabitants of member countries of the Council of Europe, which includes almost all European nations. These rights include Article 10, which entitles all citizens to free expression. This right includes the freedom to hold opinions, and to receive and impart information and ideas.

Here we once again arrive at the question of how to search for the balance between freedom and responsibility on an international level. The starting point is the ideology of free speech and its restrictions must always be based on careful consideration, the principles of rule of law and a democratic society. This is why this book emphasises the significance of also monitoring rule-of-law development when evaluating the fulfilment of international human rights principles. The Convention guarantees the right to freedom of expression, subject to certain restrictions that are "in accordance with law" and "necessary in a democratic society".

ECHR Article 10 Freedom of expression reads:

1. Everyone has the right to freedom of expression. This right shall include freedom to hold opinions and to receive and impart information and ideas without interference by public authority and regardless of frontiers. This article shall not prevent States from requiring the licensing of broadcasting, television or cinema enterprises.

2. The exercise of these freedoms, since it carries with it duties and responsibilities, may be subject to such formalities, conditions, restrictions or penalties as are prescribed by law and are necessary in a democratic society, in the interests of national security, territorial integrity or public safety, for the prevention of disorder or crime, for the protection of health or morals, for the protection of the reputation or rights of others, for preventing the disclosure of information received in confidence, or for maintaining the authority and impartiality of the judiciary.

The restrictions on the exercise of freedom of expression and information that are admissible according to Article 10, para. 2, fall into three categories:

- those designed to protect the public interest (national security, territorial integrity, public safety, prevention of disorder or crime, protection of health or morals);
- those designed to protect other individual rights (protection of the reputation or rights of others, prevention of the disclosure of information received in confidence);
- those that are necessary for maintaining the authority and impartiality of the judiciary.

This list may appear to be an extensive one, but it should be noted that, in order to be admissible, any restriction must be prescribed by law and be necessary "in a democratic society". The Court has repeatedly stressed the importance of testing whether interference is necessary in the context of European supervision.

For example, the Council of Europe's *Explanatory Report* of the Additional Protocol to the Convention on Cybercrime states that the "European Court of Human Rights has made it clear in the *Lehideux and Isorni v France* judgement of 1998 that the denial or revision of 'clearly established historical facts—such as the Holocaust—[...] would be removed from the protection of Article 10 by Article 17' of the ECHR".

Each party to the Convention must alter its laws and policies to conform to the Convention. Some, such as Ireland or the United Kingdom, have expressly incorporated the Convention into their domestic laws. The guardian of the Convention is the ECtHR. This court has heard many cases relating to freedom of speech, including cases that have tested the professional obligations of confidentiality owed by journalists and lawyers, and the application of defamation law, a recent example being the so-called "McLibel case".

Monitoring System The ECHR is generally regarded as the most efficient international human rights monitoring system, as it allows for individual applications, contracting states' complaints against each other, and the ECtHR's advisory opinions on judicial questions. In practice, private appeals are the most important monitoring mechanism.

The monitoring system was renewed in 1998 and 2004. First, the then existing part-time European Commission of Human Rights and the Court were united by Protocol 11 into a full-time institution responsible for deciding cases as well as possible compensations for damage. In 2004 a threshold, among other things, was introduced in order to make the Court's operation more efficient, by ruling that an individual application would not be tried unless the appellant had suffered significant disadvantage; what significant disadvantage means is open to interpretation. When it comes to cases, however, some degree of screening has proved necessary; annually, tens of thousands of appeals are sent to the ECtHR, the vast majority of which are dropped early on in the process.

In the following piece, Jean-Paul Costa,[1] President of the International Institute of Human Rights (Strasbourg) and former President of the European Court of Human Rights (30 July 2014), reflects on the general significance of the ECHR and the working culture of ECtHR.

> As it is well-known, freedom of expression (or freedom of speech) is mentioned in all the international instruments concerning Rights and freedoms, and firstly in the Universal Declaration of 1948 (art. 19). Under the European Convention on Human Rights, 1950, ("the Convention"), it is guaranteed by Art. 10.
> As it is common for the political rights of the Convention, Art. 10 includes two paragraphs:
> § 1 is devoted to asserting the principle, in very strong, general terms; § 2 contains some exceptions which permit the interference to be compatible with the Convention, but subject to the triple (and cumulative) condition that the interference be (i) prescribed by law, (ii) pursuing a legitimate aim, those legitimate aims being made explicit in the paragraph 2 itself, and (iii) necessary, according to the standards of a democratic society, in order to comply with the interests, public or private, constituting a legitimate aim.

The keys of interpretation of Art. 10 by the Court (which states *in concreto* by adjudicating individual applications against defending States), since the nineteen-seventies on, have been the following:

a. A wide meaning given to the very principle, and a narrower interpretation of § 2 exceptions, in order to make people take more advantage of the freedom guaranteed;
b. A strict judicial review of notions such as law (prescribed by law), which must be clear, accessible, foreseeable, necessary (necessity implying a proportionality test—sometimes the Court's judgments use the terms of "a pressing social need" justifying the necessity), the legitimate aims (their list under § 2 has been considered as limitative, rather than indicative, which would have opened too wide the field of exceptions).
c. A little space usually granted to the so-called national margin of appreciation: in assessing the quality of the law, the legitimate character of the aims, or the necessity of the interference, domestic authorities, especially national courts, have to abide by the Court's case-law, which is harmonizing the various possible national approaches under the common flag of an extensive value and scope of freedom of speech.

Moreover, two more aspects have recently developed in the Court's case-law:

d. The privileged room given to the press and the media (either the newspapers or broadcasting or TV, more recently internet and the social networks). The press is currently qualified as "the watchdog of democracy" (*Barthold v Germany,* 1985), given the important public interest of a free information of the population;
e. The importance granted to the protection of journalistic sources, without which the information would be limited or would be affected by a "chilling effect" (see *Goodwin v UK*, 1996, *Fressoz and Roire v France*, 1999, or *Sanoma v the Netherlands*, 2010, and many other authorities).

Nevertheless, freedom of speech is not without limits.

First of all, the Court is obliged due to the very wording of both paragraphs of Art.10, to practice more often than not a balancing exercise, sometimes delicate and dividing the sitting judges between them. Admittedly, if the law does not exist, or has an insufficient quality, the judgment will simply conclude that the interference was incompatible with the Convention. Similarly, whenever the "aim" is not belonging to the categories listed in §2, there has been a manifest violation of Art. 10. On the contrary, if the conditions "prescribed by law" and "pursuing a legitimate aim" are fulfilled, the proportionality test becomes decisive, and is not always easy.

Among the "legitimate aims", some of them are more frequently overcoming the alleged necessity of the interference, in a democratic society, under the meaning of the Convention. While protection of "morals" (see

Handyside v UK, 1976), for example, has now become less weighty, "the protection of the reputation and rights or others" is still a strong possible obstacle to the exercise of freedom of expression, notably because such aim does reflect another right guaranteed by the Convention, the right to respect for private and family life under Art. 8 (see the various *Von Hanover v Germany* cases, 2004 and 2012, where the conflict was between the right to respect for one's own image and the interest of public information). It is more difficult to arbitrate when two liberties, of an equal value, are in conflict, that when a liberty is conflicting with public order.

Sometimes the balance is difficult to strike, for instance when it matters of defamation. Usually, political persons are less protected than ordinary citizens (see *Lingens v. Austria*, 1988, where the political person was Kanzler Kreisky, compared with *Lindon and others v France*, 2007, where the political man "defamed" was Mr Le Pen).

Finally, from my personal experience of the jurisprudence of the Strasbourg Court in this field, and more generally from the activities of the Council of Europe, I have drawn or strengthened some conclusions and feelings:

  a. Legally and politically, freedom of speech is crucial, in particular since it enables to discover, and fight against, violation of other basic rights. The words "in a democratic society" are very significant in that respect, in as much as such a freedom is in danger when a State becomes authoritarian or when specific circumstances incite a regime to derogate, *de jure* (under Art. 15 of the Convention), or *de facto*, to its obligations under Art. 10.
  b. Usually, Judges of the ECHR are "judges for freedom" : they tend to rule more in favour of liberty than in favour of the exceptions to it. Nevertheless, the just equilibrium is depending on subjective factors, which explains that in some important cases the deciding panel is divided, even very much so (see for instance the Grand Chamber case of *Pedersen and Badsgaard v. Denmark*, 2004: no-violation of Art. 10 by just 9 votes to 8).
  c. Some important matters such as protection of the child against pedophilia, or the fight against the dangers of hate speech, must strongly prevail over freedom of expression.
  d. Certainly, the influence of the Court's jurisprudence has strongly contributed to modify, and still does it, the practice and sometimes legislation of the member States.

If compared with the situation thirty or twenty years ago, freedom of speech is currently better protected at domestic level, not only but widely, thanks to the Court's case-law. It is a remarkable achievement.

I allow myself to quote the title of my book (in French) "*La Cour européenne des droits de l'homme Des juges pour la liberté*", Paris, Dalloz, 2013.

From this account we can see how the protection of and restrictions on freedom of speech should be carefully considered on a case-by-case basis, and the interests that would be protected by the restriction against the importance of free speech should be weighed. This composition may vary depending on what kind of communication is the target of the restriction. The weight of free speech is smaller when the targets are, for example, advertising, licensed radio service or—to mention another extreme—pornographic expression (Manninen, *Perusoikeudet* p. 480).

The ECtHR has granted state parties a relatively wide margin of appreciation where free speech restrictions target, for example, advertising or other communication concerned with industrial and commercial activity (see, for example, EIT *Casado Coca* 1994 § 50, EIT *Hertel* 1998 § 47 and EIT *Verein gegen Tierfabriken* (Vgt) 2001 § 69). This wider margin of appreciation (cf. Manninen p. 480) has also allowed for protection of morals (see EIT *Wingrove* 1996 § 58 and EIT *V.D. and C.G.* 2006) and respect for religious convictions (for example EIT *Tatlav* 2006 § 23).

In the following account, a member of the Supreme Administrative Court of Finland, and former judge of the ECtHR, Dr Matti Pellonpää,[2] reflects on the dialogue between national courts and the ECtHR and the preconditions for cohesive judicial customs.

> Freedom of speech is recognized as a fundamental human right in international human rights conventions and other documents. Freedom of speech, however, is not only important as an individual right but at the same time also as an "institutional guarantee" of democracy. The European Court of Human Rights (the "Court" or the "ECHR") has repeatedly recalled
> "... that the freedom of expression, enshrined in paragraph 1 of Article 10, constitutes one of the essential foundations of a democratic society and one of the basic conditions for its progress. Subject to paragraph 2 of Article 10, it is applicable not only to 'information' or 'ideas' that are favourably received or regarded as inoffensive or as a matter of indifference, but also to those that offend, shock or disturb. Such are the demands of that pluralism, tolerance and broadmindedness without which there is no 'democratic society' ..." (e.g. *Castells v Spain*, judgment of 23 April. 1992, § 42).
>
> The role of freedom of speech as an internationally recognized and protected human right on the one hand, and as a more general guarantee of democracy on the other, is connected with inherent tension. As democracy in today's world still principally operates at the level of sovereign nation states, the question arises how external supervision, inherent in international control, can be combined with this reality. How can international bodies such as the ECHR effectively protect freedom of speech as an individual right in a manner which is conducive to democracy, at the same time respecting the plurality of sovereign states. Hereinbelow I put forward some

thoughts in this respect in light of the practice of the European Court of Human Rights, but I believe similar considerations apply more generally to the relationship between international and national level in the context of freedom of speech. As to the freedom of speech case-law of the ECHR more generally, I refer to the Contribution of the Court's former President Jean-Paul Costa in this volume.

A key notion in the definition of the relationship between the ECHR and the national level is the principle of subsidiarity. To quote another former President of the Court, Sir Nicolas Bratza, subsidiarity "requires a shared responsibility which involves establishing a mutually respectful relationship between Strasbourg and national courts and paying due deference to democratic processes" (speech at the Brighton Conference in April 2012). Thus there is a division of labour, meaning that both levels have their respective roles. From the point of view of the ECHR these roles are determined by what is called the "margin of appreciation". According to Sir Nicolas, margin of appreciation is a "a valuable tool devised by the Court itself to assist it in defining the scope of its review" (idem.). In short, margin of appreciation means that the strictness of the control exercised by the ECHR varies depending on whether the margin is "broad", "narrow" or something between, the extent of the freedom of the states and national courts being the other side of the coin. In the definition of the width of the margin of appreciation the Court has the last word, but it must use this power in a manner which is conducive to the mutual respect between the two levels.

As to the criteria in the application of the margin of appreciation, one should take as the starting point the basic philosophy, or the value system, of the Convention. As stated by Paul Mahoney, now judge of the Court, a number of years ago:

The Convention is grounded on a certain political philosophy, namely that political democracy is the best system of government for ensuring respect of fundamental freedoms and human rights (Paul Mahoney, "Marvellous Richness of Diversity or Invidious Cultural Relativism", HRLJ 1988, 1 at 3).

Thus, when the ECHR refers to freedom of speech as one of the essential foundations of democracy it can be assumed to have in mind political democracy as the system best compatible with the values behind the Convention. This necessarily influences the width of the margin of appreciation. Whenever political speech in a strict sense is supressed or threatened, the Court should be vigilant and leave the member states only a narrow margin of appreciation, since political democracy cannot allow too many national variations in this respect. Political persons when entering politics must accept more and sharper criticisms than ordinary citizens when it comes to what they have said as politicians, for example, in connection with an election campaign (e.g. *Lingens v Austria*, judgment of 8 July

1986). However, when one removes further from the core area of political discussion, which is the case when some aspects of the private life of a politician rather than the political standpoints he or she has taken, is criticised, the national courts and other authorities legitimately should have more leeway, as the essential foundations of democracy are not likely to be at issue, the Convention's value system correspondingly tolerating more diversity between member states. As in this kind of situation, moreover, the freedom of speech of one person may run into collision with the right to private life of another person, i.e. a right also protected by the Convention, the national level may be better placed to make the balancing between the conflicting interests in light of the local circumstances,

This would suggest that in situations necessitating balancing the freedom of speech against another protected Convention right, typically right to private life, the role of the ECHR should be that of defining the relevant criteria to applied in the balancing exercise, leaving the concrete application of those criiteria to the national courts and authorities.

This is actually what the ECHR has done. In two important Grand Chamber judgments rendered on 7 February 2012, *von Hannover (No. 2)* and *Axel Springer AG v Germany*, in both of which at issue was freedom of press (Article 10) and its balancing against private life of individuals (Article 8), the Court stressed that both rights deserve "equal respect" and that national courts and other authorities should carry out a balancing exercise in light of criteria developed in the Court's case-law. These criteria include, among others, "the contribution made by the photos or articles in the press to a debate of general interest", and the special role of the press as a "watchdog" especially in relation to politicians. When the balancing exercise has been undertaken in conformity which such criteria the ECHR, according to the Grand Chamber precedents, "would require strong reasons to substitute its view for that of the domestic courts" (von Hannover, § 107).

Noteworthy is not only the outcome of the cases but also the way in which these important precedents came about. They did not result from a unilateral dictate by the ECHR but from a "dialogue" between national courts and the ECHR. In particular the consecutive *von Hannover* judgments involving the saga around Princess Caroline of Monaco constituted a series of judgments by the ECHR and German courts, especially the Constitutional Court, whereby both were influenced by each other, so much so that President Spielman was inspired to make a comparison to a violin concerto. In his speech at the opening of the judicial year of the Strasbourg Court in January 2014, President Spielman, addressing himself in particular to the guest speaker of the day, President Vosskuhle of the German *Bundesverfassungsgericht*, stated, inter alia as follows:

If you would allow me to draw a comparison, I sometimes see our courts as the soloists in the Concerto for Two Violins in D minor of Johann

Sebastian Bach. In that Concerto the two soloists are intertwined, sometimes alternating the melodic line, carrying different tunes and rhythms, yet ultimately—and this is the important point—joining together and combining to produce a particularly harmonious piece. What a splendid example of musical dialogue.

Although dialogue between the ECHR and national courts has not always been as harmonious as in this eloquent description, a mutually respectful interaction between Strasbourg and the national level is important in the further development of the European human rights system. As to freedom of speech, the Court has already made a significant contribution. Its case-law and its interpretations of freedom of political discussions has strengthened the foundations of rule of law in new democracies. Also in countries such as Finland, which usually figures very high in international rankings of freedom of speech/press, the impact of the Court's case-law is clearly discernible while in the 90s it still would have been a rare occasion to see references to the Court's case-law in freedom of speech related cases, the situation is very different now. This has improved the reasoning of decisions and thereby their acceptability by the parties, but, I believe, it has also improved the conditions for our courts to participate in the European dialogue and broader discussion between courts.

Of course, the world is not ready, and also the case-law and relations between national level and European and other international supervision in the field of freedom of speech is susceptible of new developments in light of technological and other developments in the society. As an example a reference can be made to the case of *Delfi As v Estonia* (Chamber judgment of 10 October 2013) which, after having gone through the national courts system and a chamber of the ECHR, is at the time of the writing pending before the Court's Grand Chamber. It concerns the liability of a news portal for anonymous comments allowed to be made on its webpage. The forthcoming judgment is likely to be the next important Grand Chamber precedent in the field of freedom of speech, but it certainly will not remain the last.[3, 4]

There is no further need to discuss the topic of the Court's working culture. In general, we may merely note that it has been emphasised in the precedent of the Court and in the work of the judges that freedom of speech bears important significance in a democratic society.

The Court has ascertained that freedom of political debate is at the very core of the concept of a democratic society, and considered it important that everyone has the right to participate in the exchange of thoughts and opinions which is characteristic of a democratic society, making it possible to freely criticise the exercise of power in the press and other public statements. Sami Manninen, who refers to precedents, comments on the background of praxis (EIT *Handyside* 1976 § 49, EIT *Oberschlick* 1991 § 57, EIT *Castells* 1992 § 43 and EIT *Lyashko* 2006 § 41, cf. *Perusoikeudet* 2011, p. 461).

The Margin of Appreciation Concerning Media The most difficult cases have concerned restrictions on the freedom of the press, in which the Court has held that "the national margin of appreciation is circumscribed by the interest of democratic society in ensuring and maintaining a free press" (see Council of Europe 2001). However, on that note, the Court has also specifically stressed that "this margin goes hand in hand with European supervision, whose extent will vary according to the case. Where there has been an interference with the exercise of the rights and freedoms guaranteed in paragraph 1 of Article 10, the supervision must be strict, because of the importance of the rights in question". The demarcation of boundaries may best be illustrated with some practical examples. Let us start with a couple of cases that demonstrate the limits of a reporter's use of language.

The first case in which the Court had to take a decision on the merits in respect of freedom of expression and information in the press was in the *Sunday Times* (No. 1) case against the United Kingdom. In this case, the Court held, in April 1979, that there had been a violation of Article 10 by reason of an injunction restraining the publication in the *Sunday Times* of an article concerning a drug and the litigation linked to its use. The injunction, based on the English law on contempt of court, was not found to be "necessary in a democratic society".

In the previously mentioned *Oberschlick* (No. 2) case 1997, the Court was to confirm this finding. Here, a journalist had been convicted of insult. In an article commenting on a speech delivered by a politician, he had called the man an "idiot". For the Court, the politician concerned had "clearly intended to be provocative and consequently to arouse strong reactions". Consequently, while "the applicant's words [¡] may certainly be considered polemical, they did not on that account constitute a gratuitous personal attack as the author provided an objectively understandable explanation for them derived from the politician's speech [¡]". The Court held that the word "idiot" (*Trottel*) "does not seem disproportionate to the indignation knowingly aroused"[5] by the politician in his speech. The conviction of the journalist was therefore in breach of Article 10 (see *Oberschlik*-case No. 2/1997).

As regards broadcasting, lines have been demarcated with more flexibility as licensing systems are an option in the field; the ECHR has specifically established that (Article 10, para.1) "this Article shall not prevent States from requiring the licensing of broadcasting, television or cinema enterprises". In a judgement in 1993, the Court for the first time examined a public monopoly on broadcasting in the case of *Informationsverein Lentia and others v Austria*. It found a violation of Article 10. The Court accepted that the Austrian monopoly system was capable of contributing to the quality and balance of programmes through the supervisory powers over the media conferred by the national regulatory authorities.

The Radio ABC case, heard in 1997, led the Court once again to consider the broadcasting monopoly in Austria, as it had in the *Informationsverein Lentia* case. The Court concluded by noting "with satisfaction that Austria has introduced legislation to ensure the fulfilment of its international obligations",[6] namely a law on regional broadcasting enacted in 1997, bringing the monopoly situation in Austria to an end.

In a case declared inadmissible in 1994, the Commission accepted that a prohibition on broadcasting live interviews or spoken statements by persons representing or expressing support for organisations linked with Sinn Fein affected the way in which the applicant, a local councillor, was able to impart information. The prohibition therefore constituted an interference with his Article 10 rights.

Access to Information An important aspect of freedom of speech is everyone's right to have access to information, which in many countries has also been secured with legislation concerning openness of officials. When, as for example in Finland and Sweden, access to public records is the main rule, exceptions from this principle must be interpreted tightly. Some grounds, like national security and commercial confidentiality, have been found acceptable.

For example, in the *Leander* case, the applicant complained that the Swedish authorities kept secret information on him, which was not disclosed on grounds of national security. In its judgment in 1987, the Court concluded that there had been no violation of Article 10.

In 1997, the Commission declared inadmissible an application concerning refusal to allow a company free access to court archives for the purpose of obtaining information about potential borrowers to sell to financial institutions. For the Commission, Article 10 of the Convention does not give any person or firm the absolute right to access archives containing information on the financial situation of a third party, or require the authorities to communicate such information to anyone who so requests.

On the Criteria for Limitations Protection of general interest has already been mentioned. As a flexible concept, it of course allows for some margin of appreciation—often tested in the ECtHR. In 1995, the Court found that Article 10 had been violated in the *Piermont* case, which concerned an expulsion measure from French Polynesia together with a prohibition on re-entry and a measure prohibiting entry into New Caledonia taken against a German member of the European Parliament. In this case, the Court ruled that "a fair balance was accordingly not struck between, on the one hand, the public interest requiring the prevention of disorder and the upholding of territorial integrity and, on the other, [the applicant's] freedom of expression (see *Piermont* case 1995).[7]

In 1991, the Commission considered an application concerning the applicants' conviction for renting or selling obscene video films. The Commission held that the interference was justified for the protection of morals and necessary in a democratic society. In 1992, the Commission declared there had been no violation of Article 10 regarding limitations imposed on a doctor for advertising his private medical practice in the press, and that they were not disproportionate to the legitimate aim of protecting patients' health, as well as the rights of others—namely other doctors.

Conclusion We may note that for obvious reasons political expression is given particular precedence and protection. The demarcations may seem overly exact from a global perspective. Artistic expression—vital for fostering individual fulfilment and the development of ideas—is also robustly protected. To ensure that free expression and debate is possible, there must be protection for elements of a free press, including protection of journalistic sources. The right to free expression would be meaningless if it only protected certain types of expression, so—subject to certain limitations—the right will protect both popular and unpopular expression, including speech that might shock others.

How Does the European Union (EU) Protect Freedom of Speech?

Some History of the European Union When examining the normative background of the EU, we can distinguish the following main elements. The first fundamental objective has been peace. This was evident already in Robert Schuman's declaration of 1950 and the treaty establishing the European Coal and Steel Community of 1951. The second leading idea is liberty, which is also set out in the Treaty of Rome [Art. 6 of the TEU (1991)]. The other fundamental principles are democracy, the rule of law and respect for human rights and fundamental freedoms, which are also expressly written into the preamble of the TEU. In addition to these main elements, there are other fundamental values.

When assessing the application of membership criteria, it should be noted that the EU has not presented any clear definition of democracy. However, many documents refer to the Final Act of the Commission on Security and Cooperation in Europe (CSCE) summit held in Helsinki in 1975—even if this Act rather consisted only of a set of principles—and especially to the Charter of Paris of 1990, which comprised more detailed definitions of democracy criteria.

Expansion of the EU In connection with the latest enlargement process of the EU, it was interesting to see how the original, very general political criteria (democracy and rule of law, human rights, respect for minorities, transparency)—part of the so-called Copenhagen criteria 1993 (see *Rule of Law* 2004 p. 149)—were given more concrete shape as negotiations progressed. In the end, the issues discussed included themes such as deficiencies in legislation, functioning of the administration, structure of the judiciary, length of proceedings, corruption, freedom of speech, and so on.

In the summer of 1997, the European Commission presented a statement in the Agenda 2000 document on the ten countries—excluding Cyprus, Malta and the still-pending Turkey—that were applying for membership of the EU at the time. The statement was concerned with meeting the Copenhagen criteria. In terms of freedom of speech—considered a political right—the following shortcomings were noted among the applicants:

legislation concerning defamation and libel that may limit freedom of the press (Poland, Romania, Czech Republic); government interference with administration of public TV channels limits freedom of speech (Romania); imbalance in the broadcast time allocated to the government and the opposition (Slovakia, Bulgaria, Hungary); and attention paid to lack of private TV channels (Hungary).[8]

The rule of law is possibly now addressed in more practical terms even in Europe, the birthplace of the rule-of-law principle. However, some scholars have raised the question of possible double standards in Europe: new Member States are subject to strict scrutiny, whereas there are even greater deficiencies in, for example, the treatment of minorities in some of the old Member States. Thus, it would be appropriate to consider the entire liberal European establishment.

We might consider that the EU itself should start investigating prospects for creating rule-of-law monitoring and evaluation systems. There are many reasons for this. First, the EU has demonstrated inconsistency during the enlargement process as the candidate countries have been carefully evaluated on the basis of the functionality of their legal systems, while the old Member States have not been subject to such evaluations. Second, one must bear in mind that rule-of-law principles and especially the roots of freedom of speech were both developed first and foremost on the European continent and are indeed a part of the EU "brand". Europe might want to uphold its leading role as a promoter of free speech and democracy.

Freedom of Speech in European Law Article 11 on freedom of speech and communication of the Charter of Fundamental Rights of the EU is also concerned with the very core of European free speech. According to the article, everyone has the right to free speech. This right includes the right to freedom of opinion and the right to receive and distribute information and thoughts without interference from officials, irrespective of regional borders. Freedom and diversity of the media is respected.

The status of fundamental and human rights, and therefore also the right to free speech, was non-existent in the early days of the EU justice system, but has strengthened. This evolution has been slow because the EU's first purpose was to function as an economic community. According to the Treaty of Rome, the European Economic Community (EEC) was first and foremost to serve the economic interests of its member states.

As a matter of fact, popular representation is only referred to as a common value for the first time in the 1990s. Expansion of this line of activities and the strengthening of common values that would affect citizens' rights were only introduced later. The power potential of the EU has indeed often been observed as a normative-power type of system based on strong institutions and innovation.

Only in the later expansion stage did the assessment of Central and Eastern European countries' eligibility for membership based on the 1993 Copenhagen Criteria —specifically the securing of the right to free speech—begin to arise from political criteria.

Ever since then, the status of international human rights treaties has strengthened—albeit slowly—in EU justice culture. Although the EU has not yet been a party to any human rights treaty, the ECHR has been regarded as a minimum standard for any comparable fundamental rights in European law. The ECtHR has also established that the system of fundamental rights of the EU has evolved to meet the European human rights treaty system (EIT decision 2005, the case of *Bosphorus*).

The treaty system that makes up the basis of the EU has been reformed in recent years with, among others, the Lisbon Treaty that entered into force in the beginning of 2009. It affirmed the fundamental and human rights dimensions of the Union and gave full legal effect to the Charter of Fundamental Rights of the EU, proclaimed in 2000 (Allan Rosas, *Perusoikeudet* 2011 p. 197 ff.).

Dr. Niilo Jääskinen,[9] Former Advocate General of the Court of Justice of the European Union, Member of the Supreme Administrative Court of Finland, discusses the developments of recent years in the following account. He is currently back in office as judge at the Supreme Administrative Court of Finland. He gives us a:

> Vision of the realities of European freedom of speech Freedom of communication in EU law:
>
> European Union law (EU law) offers double protection for the freedom of communication. First, as a general principle, derived in essence from Article 10 of the European Convention of Human Rights (ECHR), and second, as a fundamental right in accordance with Article 11, entitled "Freedom of expression and information", of the Charter of Fundamental Rights of the European Union (Charter), which became legally binding when the Lisbon Treaty entered in force in December 2009.
>
> What I mean here by "freedom of communication in EU law" are the rights protected by Article 11 of the Charter. This article consists of two paragraphs. The first paragraph reads as follows: "Everyone has the right

to freedom of expression. This right shall include freedom to hold opinions and to receive and information and ideas without interference by public authority and regardless of frontiers." It corresponds in substance with Article 10 (1) ECHR and must be interpreted in accordance with it. The second paragraph states that "freedom of and pluralism of media shall be respected". This provision lacks a counterpart in Article 10 ECHR.

Apart from Article 11, there are also other Articles in the Charter that are relevant for the freedom of communication. These include the provisions on freedom of thought, conscience and religion (Article 10), on freedom of assembly and association (Article 12), on freedom of arts and sciences (Article 13), on the freedom to found educational establishments (Article 14(3)), on cultural, religious and linguistic diversity (Article 22) and on the right of access to documents (Article 42). All of these give supplementary protection to the freedom of communication.

No limits, restrictions or exceptions to the various rights protected by Article 11 of the Charter are spelled out in that provision itself, contrary to its counterpart in the ECHR. Therefore, in the framework of the Charter, they must be based either on its Article 51(1) concerning limitation on the exercise of the rights and freedoms recognised by the Charter, or on its Article 54 prohibiting abuse of rights. Moreover, in practice freedom of communication must be balanced with other fundamental rights recognised by the Charter such as respect for privacy (Article 7), right to data protection (Article 8), freedom to conduct a business (Article 16), right to property, including intellectual property (Article 17), and the fundamental right to non-discrimination (Article 21).

EU law also includes legislative acts which pertain to the freedom of communication such as directive concerning the provision of audiovisual media services (2010/13), directive on electronic commerce (2000/31), directive on the harmonisation of certain aspects of copyright and related rights in the information society (2001/29), framework decision on combating certain forms and expressions of racism and xenophobia by means of criminal law (2008/913/JHA), and directive on combating the sexual abuse and sexual exploitation of children and child pornography (2011/93).

Freedom of communication in accordance with Article 10 ECHR was recognized as a general principle of EU law in the ERT judgment (C 260/89). Thereafter that principle in its all various dimensions has been applied in different field of EU law by the Court of Justice of the European Communities, since 2009 that of the European Union.

Firstly, the freedom of communication has played a twofold role in the law relating to the four freedoms, in particular with regard to free provision of television services and free movement of press products such as newspapers. On the one hand, the Court has accepted national rules restricting advertising and marketing if that is necessary to promote diversity of media, in other words limiting rights now protected in the first paragraph of Article 11 of the Charter in order to foster the values protected in its second paragraph. More generally it can be observed that commercial communications, though protected by Article 11 rights, are afforded lesser protection than for example political speech.

However, on the other hand, restrictions on internal market freedoms can also be a means to limit freedom of communication (Familiapress, C 368/95). Moreover, in *Sky Österreich* (C 283/11) the Court considered that the public's right to receive information of events of particular interest overrode the relevant economic operator's right based on an exclusive licence to broadcast the event and in UPC *Telekabel Wien* (C 314/12) that the public's right to receive information was weightier that a copyright holder's right to prevent any illicit dissemination of the protected content. However, as a rule, freedom of communication cannot be invoked against the copyright holder's exclusive right to decide over dissemination of the protected content (Laserdisken, C 479/04).

Secondly, the Court established in *Connolly v Commission* (C-273/99P and C-274/99 P) that also EU officials enjoy freedom of expression. However, the provisions in the EU staff regulations can validly foresee a requirement of prior authorisation for EU official publishing books or articles having a link to their office, but such authorisation may be denied only in exceptional situations and on serious and objective grounds. It can be observed that EU law tolerates here deeper restrictions of freedom of expression than for example the Finnish constitution which prohibits all forms of prior censorship. Yet political speech is afforded particular protection in EU law when the freedom of expression of MEPs is concerned (Patriciello, C 163/10).

Freedom of communication as a fundamental right has led to some issues of balancing in relation to fundamental rights to privacy and data protection. In *Satakunnan Markkinapörssi and Satamedia* (C 73/07) the Court adopted a rather wide definition of journalism that the Member States may exclude from full application of EU data protection law principles. Despite of this, data protection rules restrict also dissemination of information that has already entered public domain. The Court ruled in *Google Spain and Google* (C 131/12) that in general a data subject's right to privacy prevails over an internet user's freedom to seek information unless the data subject plays a particular role in public life.

The importance of the right to receive information has been emphasised in the context of internet service providers. The Court held in *Scarlet Extended* (C 70/10) and *SABAM* (C 360/10) that operators providing access to internet or providing data-hosting services cannot be made subject of generalized surveillance obligation regarding the traffic or hosted data as it would infringe, inter alia, the internet users' right to receive information. Nevertheless, it was found in UPC *Telekabel Wien* (C 314/12) that internet access providers can be ordered to block access to certain sources wherefrom illicit copies of films were distributed if this can be made in a way not preventing Internet users' access to legal information.

EU law does not protect abusive exercise of freedom of communication rights. The Court ruled in *Deckmyn and Vrijheidsfonds* (C 201/13) that in the striking of a fair balance between the copyright holder's rights and a person's freedom of expression to use the protected work in order to create a parody of it attention must also be paid to the fact that a parody may associate the original work with racist or xenophobic content in conflict with the legitimate interests of the right holder.

The Charter of Fundamental Rights The legal basis for freedom of speech is, as presented above, the obligations of the ECHR and articles of the new Charter. Currently, all members of the EU are signatories to the European Convention on Human Rights in addition to having various constitutional and legal protections for freedom of expression at the national level. The Charter has been legally binding since 1 December 2009, when the Treaty of Lisbon became fully ratified and effective. Citizens of the European Union enjoy freedom of speech, of the press, of assembly, of association, of procession and of demonstration. Article 11 of the Charter, in part mirroring the language of the Universal Declaration of Human Rights and the European Convention on Human Rights, provides that:

1. Everyone has the right to freedom of expression. This right shall include freedom to hold opinions and to receive and impart information and ideas without interference by public authority and regardless of frontiers.
2. The freedom and pluralism of the media shall be respected.

The European Court of Justice takes into account both the Charter and the Convention when making decisions. According to the Treaty of Lisbon, the European Union should accede to the European Convention as an entity in its own right, making the Convention binding not only on the governments of the Member States but also on the supranational institutions of the EU.

In addition to Article 11 of the Charter, we should also mention Article 52 on the scope and interpretation of these rights and principles. According to the Article, any limitations must be provided by law, while respecting the essence of those rights and freedoms. According to the principle of proportionality, limitations may be provided for only if they are absolutely necessary and in line with the general public interest recognised by the Union or to protect the rights and freedoms of other people.

In principle, *de jure* development appears to be evolving in the right direction, but what is the situation in practice, *de facto*? As we consider the numerous violations of the right to free speech within the foundational source of this ideology, Europe, we are looking for answers. The Council of Europe, as well as the institutions of the EU, are slow and even powerless in practice to tackle the problems of signatory states in the very core of the European continent like, for example, Hungary.

Freedom of Speech in the United Nations (UN) Treaties

Roots of the Global Protection of Human Rights International action for the protection of human rights began in the nineteenth century. The first human rights obligations were concerned with the abolition of the slave trade. The Charter of the League of Nations adopted after World War I did not formally recognise human rights, but already at this point attention was paid to arrangements concerning the protection of minorities. The crimes against humanity committed during World War II led to remarkable progress in the development of human rights as the International Military Tribunal of Nuremberg was established.

International work for the protection of human rights began properly with the founding of the UN and the adoption of the Universal Declaration of Human Rights in 1948. The two most important human rights treaties based on the Declaration were adopted in 1966: the International Covenant on Civil and Political Rights (CP Covenant) and the International Covenant on Economic, Social and Cultural Rights (ESC Covenant). In addition, there are other treaties of more limited application such as conventions against discrimination, for example the International Convention on the Elimination of All Forms of Racial Discrimination (1965), the Convention against Torture and Other Cruel, Inhuman or

Degrading Treatment or Punishment (1984) and the Convention on the Prevention and Punishment of the Crime of Genocide (1948).

Most agreements are of limited application as regards either subject matter or persons covered, e.g., the Convention on the Elimination of All Forms of Discrimination against Women (1979) and the Convention relating to the Status of Refugees and its Protocol (1951 and 1967).Many specialised agencies of the UN also link directly to the implementation of human rights (e.g., UNESCO, ILO, FAO, UNICEF, WHO). To mention some examples, the Convention against Discrimination in Education of UNESCO was adopted in 1960 and the UNESCO Recommendation concerning Education for International Understanding, Co-operation and Peace and Education relating to Human Rights and Fundamental Freedoms in 1974.

The most important ILO conventions on fundamental rights in working life include those on the prohibition of forced labour and slavery (Nos. 29 and 105), the conventions relating to freedom of association and collective bargaining (Nos. 87 and 98), the conventions on discrimination in working life (Nos. 100 and 111) and the convention restricting the use of child labour (No. 138). The convention that prohibits the worst forms of child labour was approved at the International Labour Conference in 1999. A separate declaration on fundamental principles and rights at work was adopted at the 1998 Conference.

The International Covenant on Civil and Political Rights (ICCPR) is a multilateral treaty adopted by the United Nations General Assembly. It commits its parties to respect the civil and political rights of individuals, including the right to life, freedom of religion, freedom of speech, freedom of assembly, electoral rights and rights of due process and a fair trial.

The United Nations General Assembly adopted the ICCPR and opened it for signature, ratification and accession on 16 December 1966. The Covenant, which entered into force on 23 March 1976, acknowledges that the recognition of the inherent dignity and inalienable rights of all members of the human family is the foundation of freedom, justice and peace in the world.

Currently, 167 states are party to the ICCPR, while 24 UN member states have not yet ratified or acceded to the ICCPR: Antigua and Barbuda, Bhutan, Brunei, Burma, China, Comoros, Cuba, the Federated States of Micronesia, Fiji, Kiribati, Malaysia, Marshall Islands, Nauru, Oman, Palau, Qatar, Saint Kitts and Nevis, Saint Lucia, São Tomé and Principe, Saudi Arabia, Singapore, Solomon Islands, Tonga and the United Arab

Emirates. In total, these 24 states are home to over 20 per cent of the world's population.

The number of signatories and ratifying states raises the question of violations of free speech piling up in those countries that have opted out of the Covenant.

Seventeen of these states have not even signed the ICCPR—a particularly concerning revelation in the case of Burma, Malaysia and Saudi Arabia, which are home to over 110 million people. Signature indicates the willingness of a state to continue in the treaty-making process, qualifying it to proceed to ratification, acceptance or approval. Most importantly, signature obliges the state to refrain, in good faith, from acts that would defeat the object and purpose of the treaty. The seven states that have signed but not ratified or acceded to the ICCPR are China, Comoros, Cuba, Nauru, Palau, Saint Lucia, and São Tomé and Principe. Despite becoming a signatory in October 1998, almost twelve years ago, China still has not ratified or acceded to the Covenant. States that ratify or accede to the ICCPR are granted a time-frame within which to seek domestic approval for the treaty and to enact the necessary legislation to give effect to it.

All ratifying states have a duty to implement the rights contained in the Covenant into domestic law, providing a means by which citizens can seek redress for violations of those rights.[10]

The ICCPR has its roots in the same process that led to the Universal Declaration of Human Rights. A "Declaration on the Essential Rights of Man" had been proposed at the 1945 San Francisco Conference—which led to the founding of the United Nations—and the Economic and Social Council was given the task of drafting it. Early on in the process, the document was split into a declaration setting out general principles of human rights, and a Convention or covenant containing binding commitments. The former evolved into the UDHR and was adopted on 10 December 1948.

> "The States Parties to the present Covenant, including those having responsibility for the administration of Non-Self-Governing and Trust Territories, shall promote the realisation of the right of self-determination, and shall respect that right in conformity with the provisions of the Charter of the United Nations."

Drafting continued on the Convention, but there remained significant differences between UN members on the relative importance of negative civil and political versus positive economic, social and cultural rights.

These eventually caused the Convention to be split into two separate covenants, one to contain civil and political rights and the other to contain economic, social and cultural rights. The two covenants were to contain as many similar provisions as possible, and be opened for signature simultaneously. Each would also contain an article on the right of all peoples to self-determination.

Article 19 of the ICCPR, concerned with securing free speech, reads:

1. Everyone shall have the right to hold opinions without interference.
2. Everyone shall have the right to freedom of expression; this right shall include freedom to seek, receive and impart information and ideas of all kinds, regardless of frontiers, either orally, in writing or in print, in the form of art, or through any other media of his choice.
3. The exercise of the rights provided for in paragraph 2 of this article carries with it special duties and responsibilities. It may therefore be subject to certain restrictions, but these shall only be such as are provided by law and are necessary:
    a. For respect of the rights or reputations of others;
    b. For the protection of national security or of public order (order public), or of public health or morals.

In fact, Article 19 does include certain restrictions that it may be subject to, such as respect for the rights and reputation of others, protection of national security or of public order, health or morals.

The possible criteria of limitations to free speech are subject to fierce debate. They include child pornography, hate speech, defamation, direct and public incitement to commit genocide, advocacy of national, racial and religious hatred, and incitement of discrimination, hostility and violence.

Even though these internationally binding criteria are clear underlying structures for restrictions on freedom of speech, they may be interpreted differently in different cultures and exceptional societal circumstances. Therefore the monitoring of the fulfilment of international obligations and their violations should be strengthened. Freedom of speech should gain a more significant place on the international agenda.

The world remembers how in 2011 the Egyptian government ordered service providers to shut down all international connections to the internet. The Arab Spring revolutions in Egypt and Tunisia, and the fall of

Muammar Gaddafi in Tripoli and Libya, have triggered changes in social consciousness and worldwide movements—from Occupy Wall Street to countries all around the world—leading governments to feel threatened about the potential impact of such movements on nations and regions. We are now seeing the result in the emergence of strict laws all over the world clamping down on online democracy.

The Monitoring Systems of the UN Human Rights Treaties For most treaties, periodic reports are presented to committees that monitor their implementation; complaint systems for individuals also exist for many treaties. Usually, the periodic reports presented every four years are a good indicator of progress in signatory states. Although they have been prepared by the governments of the member states, human rights committees have made their activities more open to the influence of non-governmental organisations (NGOs). Through this type of activity, many problems become transparent.

The individual complaint system for the ICCPR is based on an optional protocol. The optional nature of the protocol means that the complaint system is not an obligatory part of the Covenant.

Of the 167 signatory states of the ICCPR, 113 are parties to the Optional Protocol (2010). The Human Rights Committee, an independent expert body with eighteen members established by Article 28 of the Protocol, processes the complaints. The Committee convenes annually for nine weeks and also reviews the periodical reports of the signatory states, in addition to individual applications.

The nature of the Committee's decisions differs from the legally binding decisions of the ECtHR. The Optional Protocol of the ICCPR does not include a notion that the decisions of the Committee are binding. In practice, this has meant that the Committee usually debates, in a free format, different ways of compensating for violations (see Tuomas Ojanen and Martin Scheinin, *Perusoikeudet* 2011 p. 898). These decisions, however, do have a general influence as statements of an expert body on how the Protocol should be interpreted.

How Interpretations Evolve and Strengthen the Right to Free Speech In 2011, after two years of consultation and debate, the UN Human Rights Committee determined how to interpret the "freedoms of opinion and expression" guaranteed by Article 19 of the ICCPR.

Their General Comment (Report of UN Human Rights Committee Comment No. 34) elaborates four important components of the right of access to information: (1) states must make every effort to ensure prompt, easy, effective and practical access to state-controlled information in the public domain; (2) they should proactively put in the public domain information about government functions as well as other information of public interest; (3) they must provide for appeals against failures to respond to requests as well as against explicit refusals; and (4) the right applies to information held by all public bodies—including the legislative and judicial branches—and may extend to private entities that carry out public functions.

The Comment, incorporating a recommendation from the Justice Initiative, also makes clear that states may not, consistent with the Covenant, suppress or withhold from the public information of legitimate public interest that does not harm national security. In other words, states should not classify such information, but instead should release it upon request and should publish it proactively. This marks significant progress. Moreover, states may not prosecute journalists, researchers, environmental activists, human rights defenders, or others, for having disseminated such information. It is implicit that this duty extends even to information that has been formally classified.

As a sign of the intensity of debate around Article 19, it is notable that this document runs to fifteen pages and 54 paragraphs—compare this to the three paragraphs that constituted the last General Comment on freedom of expression, issued in 1983. Michael O'Flaherty, the HRC member responsible for shepherding the drafting of the Comment, said that after two years of work the Committee had achieved "as strong a statement as was possible".[11] The value of the comments cannot be denied, but they are still only recommendations of a general nature. Leaving the option of individual application to be decided at state level weakens the meaning of this Covenant. It will be years before the world abides by these Comments.

The commentary on freedom of expression benefited from written and oral contributions from more than 70 NGOs—including the Open Society Justice Initiative—as well as governments, national human rights institutions and academics. The Comment addresses several key aspects of Article 19, including:

- The significance of freedom of expression and information as a "meta-right" upon which other rights rely.
- Government obligations to protect freedom of expression and to make information available.
- The right of journalists and others to disseminate information, as well as the rights of individuals to receive information.
- Recognition of the changing nature of modern media and developing technologies.
- The importance of media independence.
- The General Comment affirms that media freedom is entitled to high standards of protection, and that the protections afforded to traditional media extend in full to new media. It calls on states to "take all necessary steps to foster the independence of these new media and to ensure access of individuals" to it.

One of the most dramatic advances is the Comment's assertion that "prohibitions of displays of lack of respect for a religion or other belief system, including blasphemy laws, are incompatible with the covenant"[12] although restrictions on such speech may be justified in the specific circumstances envisaged in Article 20(2) of the Covenant, which prohibits "incitement to discrimination, hostility or violence". While "hostility" is a vague term, the Committee could not disregard this explicit treaty language.

This statement is particularly significant in light of the fact that four of the eighteen experts on the Committee are from North African countries (Algeria, Egypt, Morocco and Tunisia) that are members of the Organization of Islamic Conference (OIC). The OIC has, for the past several years, been rigorously lobbying the UN Human Rights Council to adopt resolutions calling on states to criminalise defamation of religion.

FREEDOM OF SPEECH AND OTHER ORGANISATIONS FOR INTERNATIONAL CO-OPERATION

International Interests Along with globalisation and freedom of movement, many issues that were earlier of a purely national nature have now become international. Globalisation tends to increase social inequality if states, businesses and organisations do not take the welfare and security of people into account in their actions. From the citizens' perspective, attention has to be paid to, for example, international crime, immigration, economic life and administration, as well as the functioning of the judiciary. States are increasingly dependent on one another.

To develop criteria for good governance there have been two different, although complementary, traditions. The first concentrates on good governance as a procedure which promotes democracy, respect for human rights and equality. This has been the approach particularly in the Nordic countries, but also in international organisations such as the OECD/DAC working group on participation, democracy and good governance. The second tradition has emphasised efficiency, where good governance has been defined as principles concerning the reliability and efficiency of administration. This tradition is manifested clearly in the policy which determines the country shares of the World Bank's IDA-13 credit.

Both traditions deal with the functioning of the rule of law, although there are differences in their emphases. In practice, support for the legal sector has accounted for the greatest share of the finances allocated by the World Bank for reforms of public administration in Africa. The preconditions for the development of good governance and the possibility of finding applicable indicators to measure its success are a big challenge. For example, preconditions derived from the principles of the UN with respect to human rights, working conditions and the environment have been set for companies who wish to join the Global Compact programme.

Continental Co-operation The Charter of the Organization of American States (OAS) was adopted in 1948. Human rights have been concretised by the American Declaration of the Rights and Duties of Man (1948), which has been used to interpret the Charter. The European Human Rights Convention served as a model in the preparation of the American Convention on Human Rights (1969).

As a pan-American security organisation, the OAS has adopted a proactive stance in support of democracy. It recognises that the solidarity of American states requires that each member be a "representative democracy", proactive in its efforts to preserve democracy among its members. The fact that all OAS members in Latin America have become progressively more democratic in recent years has been a fundamental factor in its development over the last decade.

According to the Charter of the Organization of African Unity (OAU), a pan-African security organisation, the promotion of human rights is one of its foremost missions. The African Charter on Human and Peoples' Rights was adopted within the framework of the Organization in 1981. The OAU has made progress towards enhanced African capacities for conflict prevention and peace-keeping. Nowadays there is a new organisation for co-operation between African countries, the African Union (AU).

The Arab Charter of Human Rights (1994) was formulated by the League of Arab States, but it has not entered into force. The Southern African Development Community (SADC) has endorsed democratic principles and committed its members to democracy, respect for human rights and the supremacy of the rule of law.

The *Commonwealth of Nations* is a 54-member community of countries, most of which were once part of the British Empire. The Commonwealth provides its members with a useful platform for dialogue and collective action. It works to advance democracy within its member states through democracy assistance programmes, and it can resort to the suspension of membership for flagrant violations of democratic principles. In the past the Commonwealth has adopted a proactive anti-apartheid stance, and forced South Africa to withdraw from its membership in 1961. It also imposed sanctions on Rhodesia in 1965.

The Organisation for Security and Co-operation in Europe (OSCE), a trans-Atlantic security organisation, has strengthened its confidence-building, conflict-prevention and fact-finding mechanisms for investigating threats to stability in Europe. While it has neither the structures nor the military capability for peace enforcement and peace-keeping, it is rather a forum for pan-European discussion and co-operation, especially concerning human and minority rights issues.

Economic Integration We have examined the ways the EU protects freedom of speech. These days there are many systems in the world that only promote economic integration, not really taking into account freedom of expression in their activities—but not overlooking it completely either.

The removal of trade barriers, connected to the present phase of globalisation, began after World War II. The rebuilding of the world economy began at the Bretton Woods conference in 1944, when the first international institutions to promote international trade and settlements and steady economic growth were founded. The International Monetary Fund

(IMF) and the International Bank for Reconstruction and Development (IBRD)—or World Bank—were created in 1946. The General Agreement on Tariffs and Trade (GATT) was signed in the following year. In the course of several rounds of negotiation, the Agreement developed into the complex GATT system which became the World Trade Organization (WTO) at the beginning of 1995. Now it is the most important trade-related intergovernmental organisation.

The *Economic Commission of West African States* (ECOWAS) is a regional economic organisation established in 1975. ECOWAS broadened its mandate in 1993 to include responsibility for the prevention of regional conflicts such as those in Liberia and Sierra Leone. Since 1990, it has taken an increasingly assertive role in conflict prevention and resolution: in 1997, for instance, it was designated to bring about the restoration of the constitutional government in Sierra Leone. ECOWAS subsequently authorised the intervention of a West African peacekeeping force, ECOMOG, to restore the democratically elected government to power in 1998.

The *Asia-Pacific Economic Co-operation* (APEC) forum, a regional economic organisation established in 1989, and the South Asian Association for Regional Co-operation, founded in 1985, provide regular fora for the broadening of dialogue beyond economic matters, but have not so far specifically addressed the issue of democracy.

The *Association of Southeast Asian Nations* (ASEAN)—the most established organisation in the region—was originally created to promote economic co-operation, and has shied away from more explicit involvement in the promotion of democracy. However, the ongoing democratisation of the Philippines and Thailand, and the 1998 transition in Indonesia—ASEAN's largest and most powerful member—may signal the beginning of a more assertive role.

MERCOSUR is an interesting phenomenon among regional trading blocs in the tendency towards democracy, and its decisive influence in the 1996 crisis in Paraguay deserves a mention. Founded in 1991 by Argentina, Brazil, Paraguay and Uruguay to foster regional integration and trade, the political influence of MERCOSUR also makes it influential in non-economic matters. Higgins (2003, p. 14) writes that the Protocol of Ouro Preto, which established a revised institutional structure for MERCOSUR, is very much the national legal one for domestic implementation. These rules cannot be denominated community laws as they lack hierarchical superiority.

Conclusions A realistic comment is required at this point. So far, the rule of law has not been prevalent as a global concept or strategy. When the Universal Declaration of Human Rights was adopted at the United Nations there were only about 50 member states, while today there are some 200 member states applying human rights obligations. In a large number of these states the concepts of the rule of law and freedom of speech are relatively poorly known, and the concept of sovereignty, closely linked to state formation and independence, receives the most attention.

This observation does not detract from the need to consider legal development at the international level too, but it should be noted that the significance of these legal values has been greater in regional than in global arrangements. It is thus difficult to summarise the influence of human rights instruments in brief statements. There are, however, general observations on the nature of human rights obligations, especially freedom of speech, which have affected the research process for this book.

Human rights obligations have been characterised as being universal, indivisible, interdependent and inter-related, in accordance with the principles of the Vienna Human Rights World Conference of 1993. One of the major achievements of the Vienna Declaration was that it managed to move the international debate forward and shift the focus again onto the implementation of the principles of the Universal Declaration.

At the same time, it must be borne in mind that the two core human rights instruments of the UN, the CP and ESC Covenants, were adopted as separate documents in 1966. Maybe it was also assumed that the implementation of economic, social and cultural rights would result in greater financial costs than that of civil and political rights. Many of the factors that led to the creation of two separate instruments are now vanishing.

Nowadays the economic, social and cultural rights, too, are applied in the courts, even though their implementation mechanism is considered more incomplete. The ratification of the CP and ESC Covenants has recently been proceeding at the same pace. Finally, subsequent human rights conventions, as well as most conventions against discrimination, have consistently referred to both Covenants. Although it would scarcely be possible to integrate these Covenants into a single document, it is essential to view their implementation processes together, as a networked system.

The second observation related to the nature of human rights obligations is that numerous nation-states underline the distinction between international and national norms. According to this distinction, an international treaty does not form part of national law as such, but to come into effect, the treaty has to be implemented by national legislative measures. In principle, Finland follows the so-called dualistic system of implementation. Some other countries follow the monistic model instead, in which international law and national law are considered parts of a single integrated judicial system. As the system of international treaties expands, international development is likely to move in the direction of the monistic model.

Notes

1. This comment was written by Jean-Paul Costa specifically for this book and is published, unedited, with his permission. It has not been previously published.
2. This comment was written by Matti Pellonpää specifically for this book and is published, unedited, with his permission. It has not been previously published.
3. The Grand Chamber judgment in the *Delfi* case was given on 16 June 2015. The Grand Chamber confirmed the Chamber's holding that the applicant company, the owner of the internet news portal in question, could in the circumstances of the case be held liable for comments posted by its readers.
4. Endnote: "I have dealt with some of the issues discussed above in more detail in Dr. Matti Pellonpää, 'Some thoughts of the principle of subsidiarity and margin of appreciation in the context of freedom of expression', in *Freedom of Expression: essays in Honour of Nicolas Bratza*, Wolf Legal Publishers 2012, 519–540."
5. Available at http://www.cilvektiesibugids.lv/en/themes/freedom-of-expression-media/media-freedom/duties-responsibilities/resources/4448, accessed 5 September 2016.
6. See https://books.google.fi/books?id=rDe4iQInmywC&pg=PA33&lpg=PA33&dq=%22with+satisfaction+that+Austria+has+introduced+legislation+to+ensure+the+fulfilment+of+its+international+obligations%22&source=bl&ots=yzJbF-rmph&sig=gI9TEX8_PsCHuhWKuQjV6xXjulo&hl=fi&sa=X&ved=0ahUKEwi46Y-ig_nOAhXDAJoKHR-uBwwQ6AEIGTAA#v=onepage&q=%22with%20satisfaction%20that%20Austria%20has%20introduced%20legislation%20to%20ensure%20the%20fulfilment%20of%20its%20international%20obligations%22&f=false, accessed 5 September 2016).

7. See https://books.google.fi/books?id=rDe4iQInmywC&pg=PA49&lpg =PA49&dq=%E2%80%9Ca+fair+balance+was+accordingly+not+struck+be tween,+on+the+one+hand,+the+public+interest+requiring+the+preventio n+of+disorder+and+the+upholding+of+territorial+integrity+and,+on+the +other,+%5Bthe+applicant%E2%80%99s%5D+freedom+of+expression%E2 %80%9D+piermont&source=bl&ots=yzJbF-sdpo&sig=fMBxD_SBYiXTD n5y9YFemySJXNA&hl=fi&sa=X&ved=0ahUKEwjBl5XVg_nOAhUMSJo KHVOODAwQ6AEIGTAA#v=onepage&q=%E2%80%9Ca%20fair%20 balance%20was%20accordingly%20not%20struck%20between%2C%20 on%20the%20one%20hand%2C%20the%20public%20interest%20requiring%20the%20prevention%20of%20disorder%20and%20the%20upholding%20of%20territorial%20integrity%20and%2C%20on%20the%20 other%2C%20%5Bthe%20applicant%E2%80%99s%5D%20freedom%20 of%20expression%E2%80%9D%20piermont&f=false, accessed 5 September 2016.)
8. The European Union homepage at http://europa.eu.int/comm/ enlargement/intro/ag2000_opinions.htm, last accessed June 2015.
9. This comment was written by *Niilo Jääskinen* specifically for this book and is published, unedited with his permission. It has not been previously published.
10. See: http://www.article19.org/resources.php/resource/3001/en/iccpr-anniversary:-opportunity-for-protection-of-freedom-of-speech#sthash. MEG9FFGe.dpuf.
11. See O'Flaherty, M., Freedom of Expression: Article 19 of the International Covenant on Civil and Political Rights and the Human Rights Committee's General Comment No 34, *Human Rights and Law Review* 12 (4) (2012), p. 627–54.
12. See http://www.mmtimes.com/index.php/opinion/15579-blasphemy-statutes-deny-human-rights.html, accessed 5 September 2016.

CHAPTER 7

Violations and Threat Scenarios

Extremes—Terrorism and Oppression of Media

There are Many Different Ways to Put Pressure on the Media Let us recall two events that demonstrated how different entities continuously try to put pressure on the media and tamper with content. The methods can be brutal but may also be subtle and polished. Media actors all over the world must work with all their might to preserve their integrity in the eyes and ears of society—the readers, viewers and listeners. In the digital era there is now a larger audience than ever, even though traditional print media is in trouble with falling sales.

Terrorist Attacks in Paris Our first example is the cruel and bloody terrorist attack on the office of the French magazine *Charlie Hebdo*—known for its satirical and critical attitude towards rulers, political systems and religions—on 7 January 2015. The left-wing magazine takes its right to free speech to the extreme, even to the extent where in most countries—although not in France—it would have crossed legal boundaries. The traditional Roman, all-encompassing, mocking satire lives on in France, granted an exceptional status in comparison to other nations. The following piece is an overview of that tradition, written by Professor Paavo Hohti,[1] who has a specific research interest in the ancient culture.

"It is difficult not to write satire", said Juvenalis, the most notable satirist of the ancient Rome (*Decimus Iunius Iuvenalis* c. 60Aquinum—c. 135²).

Satire written in hexameter verses is an authentic Roman genre. The three most notable poets of the genre, Horatius, Persius and Juvenalis, all lived during the first century. Each had his own personal style; Juvenalis had the most cutting style. The reputation of this disappointed pessimist was defined by his cutting mockery and offensive contempt.

Satirical poetry was forgotten in the Middle Ages. It bloomed again only as late as during the Renaissance, when these ancient poets were rediscovered. Satire was revived in the form of poetry and prose in those countries where Renaissance had influence and it had the most influence in France. The best known satirists were Rabelais and Voltaire. Alongside the prosaic satire, satirical pictures were drawn. In writing poetry, simplified, short phrasing was sought. These features lead to the satire of our time. Its roots are deep and it is tied to the developments of cultural history.

The terrorists hit the editorial office in Paris and killed eleven staff members and a police officer in cold blood. Later on four Jewish hostages also lost their lives in a nearby kosher shop, where the third aggressor was shot dead by the police. The terrorists, French Islamists, were killed by the police trying to free the hostages. The journalists of *Charlie Hebdo* lost their lives upholding Western freedom of speech as it exists in its purest and most critical form. They became martyrs for free speech.

The attempt by Islamist terrorists to scare media actors into self-censorship when reporting on Islam and Islamic countries clearly represents a threat to freedom of speech, media and consumers. These individuals want to refuse the right to critically analyse—including with the instruments of mockery and satire—political systems based on Islam. To submit to this pressure would be to embark on a dangerous type of self-censorship that should not be practised. The same freedom of critical journalism naturally also concerns other political and economic systems. That every media institution must define its own relationship with different religions as well as the tone in which they are discussed is a separate question.

"I disapprove of what you say, but will defend to death your right to say it."[3] This phrase has often been attributed to Voltaire, the French Enlightenment philosopher, although in reality the author is Englishwoman Evelyn Beatrice Hall, writing under the pen name S.G. Tallentyre, in her book *Friends of Voltaire*. The fact that the phrase is not Voltaire's does not lessen its strength; the meaning of traditional freedom of speech could not be any more eloquently and compactly expressed (see also Chap. 2).

The Paris terrorist attacks and later attacks in Brussels remind us that we have arrived in an era where difficult controversies are more and more often cultural in nature. Are we now closer to Samuel Huntington's "clash of civilizations" (1996) than we could ever have imagined? We are indeed moving towards a moment in time when we must solve a difficult dilemma: If controversies are genuinely cultural in nature, then who decides which values are valid? Culture in our time is something collective and shared, not only something people believe in. We must simply learn to live in a multicultural society and tolerate diversity. In reality it is not really possible anywhere in the world to go back to being a society of a single race or national philosophy. That was just a short passing stage in the history of humanity.

The *Charlie Hebdo* terrorist attack was a shocking event that is difficult to understand. Why kill those who aspire to mock those in power, in politics just as much as religions? Laughter cannot be stopped by murder. Nor should it be forgotten that Islamists and Muslims have not been the only subjects of *Charlie Hebdo*'s satire. One of the strikes targeted a kosher store and the Jewish community during a time when anti-Semitism is again rearing its head in Europe, where just over 70 years have passed since the mass murder of Jews during the Holocaust. The Copenhagen attacks of February 2015 are a reminder of the fact that there are also problems in the Nordic countries, which have generally been considered peaceful.

As has been established in this book, the right to free speech is the privilege of less than a billion people in the world. The Paris terrorist attack struck at the very core of freedom. The right to free speech is a fundamental right in a democratic society, just as the right to know is a fundamental right of the citizen of a democratic society. If we yield in regard to this cause, an irreplaceable foundational pillar of the rule of law will be lost.

Luckily, this appalling terror attack has consolidated people's faith in freedom of speech, and woken up those who had not previously considered it to a new thought that everyone should "be Charlie" at times. The comical—if one dares to use this word—side is that heads of states from countries where the freedom of speech situation is extremely unsatisfactory also marched in Paris alongside other people. What were, for example, Hungary's Prime Minister Viktor Orbán, Turkey's Prime Minister Ahmet Davutoglu or Mali's President Ibrahim Keita doing there? They were simply polishing the crumbling reputation of their own countries when the opportunity arose to march for freedom in front of international TV cameras.

Censorship in Hong Kong Our second example comes from Asia. The events in Hong Kong at the beginning of July 2014 remind us of the tough everyday life of media in another, maybe more traditional way. Hong Kong has been under Chinese rule since 1997, when the British gave up the region. As Hong Kong was transferred, the Chinese vowed to preserve social order in the region. In June democracy protests started.

In spite of the Communist Party's objections, the independent media regularly monitored and reported the protests; that was until, on the evening of 1 July, the *Ming Pao* newspaper—known for its editorial independence—stopped its printing presses, and management changed the bold headlines into common everyday news that no longer commented on the demonstrators' demands for democracy. The circle had once again been completed and the officials of the autocratic Communist Party had shown its power. *Ming Pao Daily News* had been normalised.

Charlie Hebdo and *Ming Pao* are two extremes of one phenomenon. The purpose of terrorists and despotic governments is to silence free speech and intimidate journalists into silence. If self-censorship does not work, the autocratic political system will use its own methods; terrorists, on the other hand, accelerate the violence. Recent developments, from the images of Mohammed in Denmark's *Jyllands Posten*, to Paris and *Charlie Hebdo*, indicate the absurd acceleration of this violence. Hopefully, however, the question is also about the violence coming to an end, although it certainly does not look like it for now.

The murders in Paris and censorship in Hong Kong are a part of everyday life in many countries. The forces of evil are persecuting free media while it is fulfilling its most important duty: to tell readers and audiences what kind of a world they live in, what is wrong and right and what could be done to change things for the better. High-quality media always works for the benefit of the consumer in the search for a better world by any means necessary—sometimes, luckily, by means of satire and irony.

Different ways of putting pressure on media are unfortunately common not just in authoritarian countries but also in long-established democracies. Weakened by this pressure, media surrenders to ever more sophisticated methods of influencing its substance.

Change of Environment The unhealthy state of the media is tied to its changing environment. The progressive digitalisation of societies is drastically changing traditional business models. Traditional print media is weakened as sales decrease and adverts force editorial offices to cut expenses and staff. Commercial television is also under pressure from changing technology and the changing consumer behaviour tied to it.

Smartphones and tablets are tools that have altered the operating environment of media and consumers faster than we could have imagined. The fact that there were only around 200 million smartphones in the world in 2008 is an indication of the power of this change. In 2013 there were two billion smartphones, and according to estimates the number will rise to four billion in 2020. This change was predicted; its speed, however, was not. Over the next few years over half of the world's population will connect to the web using a smartphone. It is a powerful force shaping consumer behaviour in the media sector. It is no wonder that instead of traditional media, media houses lean more and more towards providing digital content.

On the other hand, technological change has led to people having better opportunities than ever to be well informed on different sides of the world. There is more information available than ever before if one knows how to navigate the world of the internet. The weakening of the gatekeeper role of journalists has lowered the threshold for publishing. With the help of the internet everyone has the chance to publish information, but all are equally able to publish hearsay and inaccuracies. The internet also makes it possible to spread government propaganda without the risk of getting caught. Sometimes the risk of getting caught is irrelevant, as we have seen in the activities of Russia during the Ukrainian crisis. The internet age also needs high-quality media content that is independent of government power and must be guaranteed by high-class, quality media brands.

It has turned out to be difficult for governments to completely block access to social media, but there are already examples of governments closing down the internet. The worst restrictors of the internet are, in order: North Korea, Burma, Cuba, Saudi Arabia, Iran, China, Tunisia, Vietnam and Turkmenistan.

Different Ways to Restrict Media

Case Categories of Threat Scenarios This section uses the categorisation of the most important threats to freedom of the press and expression set out by the International Press Institute (IPI), where Janne Virkkunen has served as President.

1. Targeted **murders and violence** against journalists by state or non-state actors with the aim of silencing their reporting

In 2014, according to IPI, 100 reporters died while fulfilling their journalistic duty to report from conflict zones. Since 2009, 100 reporters have lost their lives either while reporting on conflicts or just due to the fact they were journalists.

Those who died in the line of duty were not only war reporters. Drug and criminal organisations attempt to influence reporters by threats, to prevent them from carrying out investigations. Mexico is an excellent example of this. In August 2014 Octavio Rojas Hernandez was shot in front of his home after he had carried out investigations for his newspaper, *El Buen Tono*, on the local police corruption in Cordoba, Vera Cruz.

2. Use of **state security** and **anti-sedition laws** beyond their legitimate purpose to prosecute journalists or impose restrictions on the publication of information

A large proportion of journalists who are arrested are sentenced for compromising national security or inciting revolt. One of the best-known journalists charged with the breaking of these laws is Turkish Nedim Sener, who is still facing years in a Turkish prison.

Sener is well known around the world for his book on murdered journalist Hrant Dinkista, in which he conclusively proved the connection between security officials and the murder of Dinkista.

Nedim Sener has been awarded many journalistic prizes. He is the IPI Press Freedom Hero, and the Committee to Protect Journalists (CPJ) has awarded him a freedom of press award. When Sener accepted the CPJ award in New York, he ended his response speech with the following words:

> There is a red line now that journalists in Turkey know not to cross. The ones who do cross it pay a steep price, and we owe them a great debt.
>
> Enemies of free expression more than anything want to hear the sound of silence. They want to scare us, incarcerate us, and eliminate us so we cannot speak the truths we have uncovered.
>
> And so we must speak at every opportunity. This is what Hrant Dink would have wanted.[4]

3. Use of criminal **defamation** laws and *lèse-majesté* laws to prosecute journalists

Penalties for destroying someone's reputation are very common in countries where the justice system has not evolved. Freedom of speech organisations know of numerous cases where the revelations of journalists and media about questionable and corrupt activities have led to unjustifiable sentences.

This matter is not one-sided. Even in those countries where freedom of speech is at an advanced level, and where the principles of the rule of law operate, there are paragraphs of law that criminalise defamation. There are no objections to this. A citizen should have their right to privacy and their own dignity and the right to stand up for that dignity; the ECtHR has even upheld this. In countries where these laws are used to protect those in power, however, it is a completely different matter.

Lèse-majesté legislation protects royal houses by prohibiting criticism of them. The royal house of Thailand is possibly the most active user of this type of legislation to protect its own reputation.

In November 2014, Nut Rungwong, a journalist on a Thai e-news web page, was sentenced to four and a half years in prison for publishing an article in 2009 that offended King Bhumibolia. Professor Giles Ungpakorn, who faced a lèse majesté charge, wrote the article. Ungpakorn lives in Great Britain and is safe from charges. Paragraph 112 of the *lèse-majesté* law states that criticism of the king is an act punishable by up to 15 years' imprisonment.

4. Arbitrary **detention** of journalists in violation of the rule of law

This is a very powerful way to pressurise reporters into self-censorship, and has been used particularly in Turkey, which ranks top for number of reporters in detention. Other countries that use these methods include China, Iran, Vietnam and Ethiopia. Detention without any hint of a trial is an effective way to stir up insecurity in the journalistic community. This threat also works well as an initiator of self-censorship when the reporter does not enjoy the right of a trial.

A CPJ delegation visited Turkey's capital, Ankara, in October 2014. In February 2015 CPJ wrote a letter to the Prime Minister of Turkey, Ahmed Davutoglulle, expressing its disappointment in the Turkish officials who had promised to secure the work of journalists during the visit. The letter concludes:

These recent violations against press freedom and freedom of expression obscure the positive steps taken by your government, including the stark reduction of the number of journalists imprisoned in relation to their work in Turkey.

Mr. Prime Minister, Turkey's leaders have said that they support a free press, at least in principle, but the same leaders—including yourself—have also publicly criticized journalists and disparaged their work. This official attitude facilitates the actions of police, prosecutors, courts and regulators against the media, and contributes to an environment in which hostile elements of society may feel free to threaten or even physically attack journalists.

We ask that you use the authority of your high office to speak up in defense of press freedom and against attacks on journalists, creating a more tolerant atmosphere for the media.[5]

5. Legal frameworks that grant only **limited access to information** (lack of freedom of information Act and presence of secrecy laws)

Access to information is often the greatest problem for reporters. The essence of a transparent society is that it is as transparent as possible when it comes to access to information. Work must be done to accomplish this objective, because transparency is not always a virtue of even the most transparent of societies. The work of journalists as well as independent NGOs is impossible if information is not accessible to all. The transparency of a society is an important indicator of freedom of speech.

6. **State control** of the broadcasting sector through direct influence on the bodies in charge of regulating its functioning (lack of independence in decisions related to allocation of frequencies, governance, editorial policies)

In many countries where freedom of speech is restricted, print media are allowed broader freedoms than e-media. In Russia print media can even be critical whereas e-media are always in the tight grip of Moscow and the regional administrations.

The immunity of public service broadcasters is a very sensitive matter in those countries that have a long tradition as defenders of free speech. In Western democracies a lot of effort has been devoted to creating administrative systems that aim to guarantee operational freedom of public service broadcasters from the owner. The BBC has been used as a model example. The BBC Trust is the highest operational organ, followed by an Executive

Board which operates separately from the Trust. The Trust controls general policy while the Executive Board directs operational matters.

The independence of the BBC: The BBC shall be independent in all matters concerning the content of its output, the times and manner in which this is supplied, and in the management of its affairs. Paragraph 1 is subject to any provision made by or under this Charter or any Framework Agreement or otherwise by law.

In Finland the public service broadcaster, the Finnish Broadcasting Company, is funded by a special tax paid by all taxpayers regardless of whether they use its services or not. It has an administrative board that consists of members of parliament and a separate governing body of independent members. The objective is to ensure the operational independence of the company.

The distress of commercial media has shifted the focus of the conversation on public broadcasting onto how a public service company fulfils its obligations in the digital era. In general there is a danger that the company benefits disproportionately from its position as society guarantees its funding, while commercial media have to make money in the market in order to fund their operation.

It might be a good thing that the duties of public broadcasting are adapting to the digital age. Otherwise there is a danger that the public service company becomes too powerful and may be a threat to its own activity.

7. Undue **economic pressure** on media content as a consequence of the control of the advertising market by an oligarchy

In many countries oligarchs and management of big enterprises can easily influence different media by threatening to direct funding elsewhere. It is very likely that all chief editors have some experience of this. Financial troubles expose individual media actors to greater dependency on advertisers. This type of pressure can easily lead to a media actor being intimidated into refraining from raising issues for fear of losing advertising revenue. In time this will lead to dangerous self-censorship that will reduce trust in the media actor in the eyes of its audience. The self-censorship of Japanese media was noticeable during the Fukushima nuclear accident.

In February 2015 the London-based *Guardian* reported events at *The Daily Telegraph*, its competitor, in an interesting manner. The *Guardian* is generally regarded as to the left of centre politically, while the *Telegraph* on the other hand supports the Conservative Party and is popularly known as the "Torygraph".

The political commentator of the *Telegraph*, Peter Oborne, resigned, voicing his suspicions that the owners of the newspaper, Frederick and David Barclay, were withholding from publication articles about irregularities in the operation of the major bank HSBC. HSBC is involved in a complicated scheme enabling tax evasion for its customers and now faces a large fine. According to Oborne the style of the *Telegraph* changed a couple of years ago when the Barclay brothers received a loan of about £250 million from HSBC that saved their distribution company.

The heaviest of Oborne's accusations is that the loan the company received from the bank affected its editorial policy. The *Telegraph* has of course denied all accusations but the suspicion lives on. In the world of journalism this type of revelation or even the suspicion alone is the worst thing that can happen to a media company.

8. Use of perceived or real **cultural or religious sensitivities** to stifle journalism and free expression

Many political systems that question the universality of human rights also question freedom of the press; the idea that press freedom is not fulfilled in a society does not apply to authoritarian countries only. In many Western countries denial or downplaying of the number of victims of the Holocaust is an act punishable under the law. Meanwhile, in the UN there is an desire to restrain, for example, the insulting of religions.

The question of offending, mocking or ridiculing someone's religion or other conviction is a complicated dilemma in everyday journalism. To publish or not to publish is a question that eventually comes down to the chief editor.

In January 2015 the German newspaper *Der Spiegel* interviewed the *New York Times* chief editor Dean Baquet and asked him about the decision not to publish the Muhammad caricatures of *Charlie Hebdo*. While Baquet explained his initial reaction was to show solidarity with his murdered colleagues in France, "that particular brand of humour didn't meet the standards" they had established for the *New York Times*, and he pointed out there are ways to defend the freedom to publish while maintaining their standards and not offending their readership. He reminded the interviewer that these readers are not the Islamic State (IS) organisation, but Islamic New Yorkers going about their everyday lives, who would also find the drawing insulting.[6] Banquet concisely summarises the responsibility of the chief editor in a crisis situation. It is safe to assume that behind his decision in this case was a desire to secure the safety of his own newspaper and reporters.

The unresolved question remains as to what lengths solidarity must be taken to if you do not approve of the journalism practised by others in the name of their freedom of speech; in other words, when you find it distasteful.

9. Lack of media **professional ethics** that undermines media credibility and weakens the value of press freedom as a fundamental right

The question of professional ethics is also a tricky one. From the point of view of the press, publishing the information received from Edward Snowden was an exercise in freedom of speech, particularly so as they were careful not to publish the parts that threatened the security of private citizens. From the point of view of officials the information leak is, of course, criminal activity.

Freedom of speech allows for the publishing of quality information as well as bad journalism. The media has to believe and trust that the audience can tell the difference between quality journalism and questionable journalism. The question is complicated and there are no simple answers. The media industry can address the problem by creating systems of self-regulation that aspire to guard the survival of ethically high-class journalism. The challenge of self-regulation is how it can be implemented in the electronic news media and journals or social media.

10. **State censorship** of internet content for political purposes

Luckily it has proved difficult for states to block internet access, so the internet has enabled the flow of information even in those societies where freedom of speech is otherwise a target of oppression. However, we can start from the premise that, especially in authoritarian countries, the aspiration to block the internet is by no means decreasing. Prosecutions of bloggers alone are an indication of this.

The Conflict Between Security Interests and Privacy of Free Information

By Sanna Leisti, Rule of Law Finland—ROLFI

The Snowden Case "Laura, at this stage I can offer nothing more than my word. I am a senior government employee in the intelligence community ... For now, know that every border you cross, every purchase you make, every call you dial, every cell-phone tower you pass, friend you keep ... is in the hands of a system whose reach is unlimited ..." (*Citizenfour*, Laura Poitras, USA/Germany 2014).

In January 2013, reporters Laura Poitras and Glenn Greenwald received encrypted messages from the internet alias "Citizen Four", Edward Snowden—an IT professional, former CIA employee and contractor working for the United States National Security Agency (NSA), who had become uneasy during his work on the systemic surveillance system the government had set up. He wanted to blow the whistle.

This chain of events quickly escalated into something of a thriller and the Snowden case became a byword for the tensions between information leaks, security interests and privacy of free information.

In June 2013 newspapers started publishing Snowden's disclosures, reporting that the United States government obtained phone records of citizens and tracked user data from large internet sites without court warrants. After the revelations the IT companies apparently involved in NSA's surveillance programme (PRISM)—including Facebook, Apple, Microsoft, Google and Yahoo—were strictly forbidden to disclose information the government had classified as top secret. Google was then reported to have requested the Foreign Intelligence Surveillance Court (FISA) to ease these "gagging orders", arguing that the company had a constitutional right to talk about information that it had been forced to give the government. The legal filing invoked the First Amendment's guarantee of freedom of speech. These companies have been pressing the government for greater transparency in the wake of the revelations, and continued to push for more oversight and clear limits on the information US authorities are allowed to collect. The US government has since allowed the companies to publicly disclose the national security letters (NSLs) they had received asking for information about their subscribers.

Richard Salgado, Google's legal director of law enforcement and information security, wrote in a blog post:

"... our number of users has grown throughout the time period. We're also seeing more and more governments start to exercise their authority to make requests. We consistently push back against overly broad requests for your personal information, but it's also important for laws to explicitly protect you from government overreach. That's why we're working alongside eight other companies to push for surveillance reform, including more transparency."[7]

However, the documents that Snowden disclosed to the *Guardian*, *Washington Post* and other outlets showed that the NSA also siphons communications and associated data from information in transit across the global communications infrastructure—without court orders.

Security Interests Step In Surveillance became topical also in Europe after the NSA disclosures. Analysis of the documents released by Snowden revealed that the UK intelligence agency GCHQ's bulk surveillance of electronic communications scooped up emails to and from journalists working for some of the USA's and UK's largest media organisations.

Senior editors and lawyers called for the urgent introduction of a freedom of expression law amid growing concern over the police use of surveillance powers linked to the Regulation of Investigatory Powers Act 2000 (RIPA), used to access journalists' communications without warrants.

Emails from the BBC, Reuters, the *Guardian*, the *New York Times*, *Le Monde*, *The Sun*, NBC and the *Washington Post* had been saved by GCHQ and shared on the agency's intranet. The journalists' communications were among 70,000 emails harvested in the space of less than 10 minutes on a single day in November 2008 by one of GCHQ's many taps on the fibre-optic cables that make up the backbone of the internet.

The communications, which included correspondence between reporters and editors discussing stories, were retained by GCHQ and were available to all cleared staff on the agency intranet. New evidence from other UK intelligence documents also showed that a GCHQ information security assessment listed "investigative journalists" as a threat in a hierarchy alongside terrorists and hackers.[8]

The revelations have stirred worldwide interest in the dangers of large-scale surveillance and privacy in the digital era. The United States, among other countries, has in its policy emphasised security, and the general and political mood in the country has turned ever more patriotic. In this atmosphere abuse of power becomes easier as many new things can be presented as necessary to protect national security.

For instance, in the wake of the Paris terror attacks on *Charlie Hebdo*, British Prime Minister David Cameron stated that there should be no "safe spaces for terrorists to communicate"[9] that British authorities could not access. Cameron urged the USA to apply more pressure to tech giants such as Apple, Google and Facebook which have, since the revelations, been expanding encrypted messaging for their millions of users in order to promote their privacy.

Cameron stated that the companies "need to work with us. They need also to demonstrate … that they have a social responsibility to fight the battle against terrorism."[10]

The *New York Times* (*NYT*) has also felt the pressure. In his *Spiegel* interview, editor-in-chief Dean Banquet agreed that *NYT* had been too careful about publishing sensitive stories on, for example, the initial research on the NSA's bulk collection in 2004. The story was only published almost a year later. In retrospect Banquet says he now realises how much the country changed through the War on Terror.[11]

Does the Constitution Matter? The debate around the Snowden case has raised complex questions on the substance of the Constitution and the interpretation of its paragraphs. Are governments committing a crime by authorising surveillance; and what is their legal responsibility?

These programmes are problematic in a state that declares itself democratic, where people are under the impression that the separation of powers functions according to the Constitution, and where the legislative, executive and judicial powers have been separated in order for them to supervise each other as they are supposed to. A government that operates arbitrarily, in secret and without authorisation, endangers that careful balance.

Much of the American public did buy into the government's pursuit of Snowden, according to polls.[12] His media trial may have been entertainment for some and useful to others, but debating whether or not Snowden is a traitor may easily lead us off track. A useful debate would also be to find out whether or not citizens accept the fact that they are now under constant surveillance by their government.

> The greatest fear that I have regarding the outcome for America of these disclosures is that nothing will change. … They'll know the lengths the government is going to grant themselves powers unilaterally to create greater control over American society and global society but they will not be willing to take the risks necessary to stand up and fight to change things, to force their representatives to actually take a stand in their interests.

These things need to be determined by the public, not by somebody who is simply hired by the government. NSA is focused on getting intelligence wherever it can by any means possible. It believes on the grounds of self-certification that they serve the national interest. Any analyst at any time can target anyone. They can wiretap anyone, from any citizen to a federal judge to the President.

Even if you are not doing anything wrong, you are being watched and recorded. The storage capabilities of these systems increase every year consistently to where it's getting to the point you don't have to have done anything wrong. You simply have to eventually fall under suspicion from somebody, even by a wrong call. Then they can use this system to go back in time and scrutinize every decision you have ever made. Every friend you've ever discussed something with and attack you on that basis to sort of derive suspicion and paint anyone in the context of a wrongdoer. (Edward Snowden, 6 June 2013, Hong Kong)[13]

As Glenn Greenwald states in his book (*No Place to Hide* 2014), turning the internet into a surveillance system is destroying its most important potential. In other words, the original promise of the democratising influence on, for example, political debate has come to nothing. Moreover, people do not really have a choice any more—as they did during the early stages of the internet—of whether or not they will be a part of this system.

Greenwald calls our time a historic crossroads where we will decide whether the era of digital change will lead to greater individual and political freedom, or to a surveillance system that reaches everywhere.

Concern for the Rule of Law and Transparency Who is entitled to the private information governments collect and store? Should all our online communication have an equivalent privacy status to that of, for example, our criminal or medical records—gathered, stored and accessible to relevant officials when necessary? In days gone by we would know if our letters had been opened. In the modern era, we are oblivious to the spying eyes that record our every move in the virtual mazes we roam through on a daily basis.

Can a journalist or their source trust that their privacy and security is ensured? Can a company trust that the principle of commercial confidentiality endures? Can a citizen trust that the delicate personal information they have entrusted to the hands of IT companies remains intact in the future? Can a company, bank, newspaper or law firm ensure that the IT companies will be capable of keeping their and their clients' private information safe?

Surveillance of the information flow is in all its subtlety unnoticeable, efficient, relatively easy and, at present, large scale. The consequence is that nothing uploaded onto the web can be assumed to stay private.

The pace of technological development suggests that in the near future all information concerning a citizen will exist in electronic form and be connected to the World Wide Web (WWW). Therefore, in addition to the citizen becoming ever more dependent on digital services such as medical records, associations, affiliations, political organisations, and so on, it is not even possible to stop the flow of that evolution now that the administration of our society already operates online, making everyday errands easier and giving us unlimited possibilities, while at the same time compromising our security and the confidentiality of our personal data.

In the age of endless innovation we are excited and passionate about the fascinating possibilities that the internet offers us, but is the rapid progress under anyone's control? While we have become dependent on the services the internet provides us, we as users are rarely interested in the intricacies of how it actually works, or how or by whom exactly our messages are processed.

While we now know there is a good chance that every letter we, our companies or our business associates type, every piece of information we upload, our virtual footprints, wherever we go, can be traced and stored, we keep on treading on the same path. We still use Googlemail after learning it has been compromised, and everything we post via the service could be collected and stored by third parties.

But What are the Options? Can we ever again be sure that no-one is listening in? To what extent can national security agencies be allowed to work in the dark? How will we know that our letters have remained unopened on their way? It seems we are no longer capable of either pulling the plug or wanting to. Nor should it be necessary to do so.

Greenwald (2014) describes how, especially for the younger generation, the internet is no longer a separate domain but a place where practically all everyday errands are managed: from organising political activity to creating and storing the most private data. Allowing for the surveillance of internet data would mean that the state would be able to watch over all people's interactions, plans and even thoughts.

In a society where such extensive webs of information exist, citizens should have complete trust in the transparency and functionality of the governing administration. Where power is not carefully balanced, this new communication system could be turned into a tightening web that ties its subjects down with suspicion and fear, capable of supervising and controlling their every move, preventing in the worst case the forming of new opinions, movements or organisations.

Dissidents and idealists are motors of social change. "The abolition of" slavery, universal suffrage and the insistence on and eventual fulfilment of the rights of minorities all started from brave protests by small groups, while those in power, along with the rest of society, ferociously objected to the change. In a surveillance state where public power does not answer to the people or to a court of law, dissidents are usually the first victims and controversial thoughts and issues are suffocated by fear before they see the light of day.

"As I said (when I offered my amendment in 2009), 'someday the cloak will be lifted and future generations will ask whether our actions today meet the test of a democratic society—transparency, accountability and fidelity to the rule of law and our Constitution.' Today that cloak has been lifted and this important debate must begin again." (Assistant Senate Majority Leader Dick Durbin, June 2013).[14]

CORRUPTION DESTROYS TRUST AND FREE SPEECH

The Fight Against Corruption There is no single, comprehensive or universally accepted definition of corruption. Attempts to develop such a definition invariably encounter legal, criminological and in many countries political problems.

In the academic literature on corruption a distinction is often made between classic and modern concepts of corruption. The classical conception of corruption dates back to the times of Aristotle and Plato and has a moral meaning: it refers to the moral decadence of humans and society that is caused by an excessive concentration of power. The modern meaning of corruption is narrower, more value free, and is based on the characteristic of a modern state: the separation of public and private. It is understood as a twisted relationship between state and society.

Transparency International (TI) defines corruption as the abuse of entrusted power for private or political gain.[15] This definition of corruption represents a broader phenomenon where private agents also share responsibility with public servants. Corruption represents a challenge to the private as well as the public sector (Fig. 7.1).

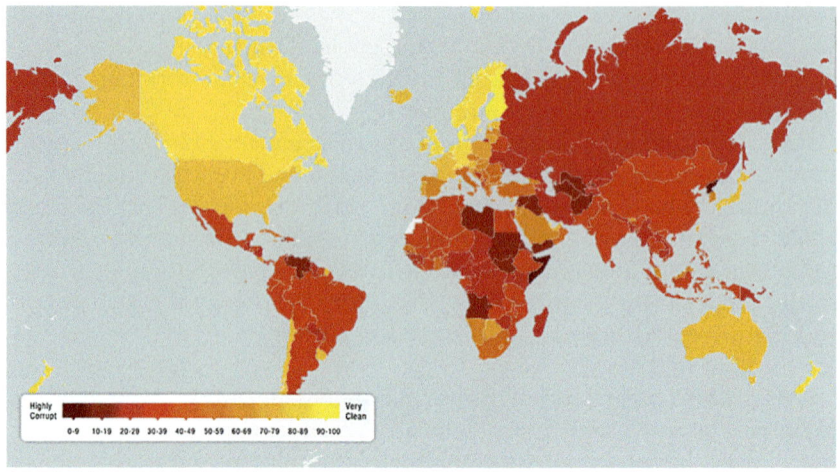

Fig. 7.1 Transparency International Corruption Perceptions Index 2015 (*Source*: Corruption Perceptions Index © 2015 by Transparency International. Licensed under CC-BY-ND 4.0, https://www.transparency.org/cpi2015/)

Corruption is an obstacle to development. Corruption distorts economic growth and threatens democracy, the rule of law and human rights. It is a concern for individuals, societies, the private sector and international organisations. The seriousness of corruption as a phenomenon is widely recognised.

World Bank research estimates that at least US$1000 billion changes hands annually in the cycle of corruption. Developing countries are often a very convenient breeding ground for corruption, to the extent that 20–40 per cent of development aid is lost in bribery in transitional economies and developing countries. Thus corruption hinders development, especially in the poorest regions of the world.

In Europe, corruption is part of the Euro-crisis. Of all EU member states political corruption has flourished most in Greece, Ireland and Italy. It has been estimated that in Italy Mafia business output forms as much as 10 per cent of GDP. Annually, 100 billion euros of tax revenue is lost to the underground economy.

Transparency International has a wide range of corruption index tools, both at global and local levels. TI led the global measurement of corruption by launching the Corruption Perceptions Index (CPI) in 1995.

The other main indices measuring corruption globally are the Global Corruption Barometer (GCB) and the Bribe Payers Index (BPI). CPI is the best-known corruption survey, measuring corruption in the public sector and determined by experts, while GCB takes into account the general public voice and studies public attitudes and experiences of corruption. BPI focuses on the supply side of corruption and the likelihood of firms from the world's industrialised countries engaging in bribery abroad.

The CPI ranks almost 200 countries around the world by the degree to which corruption is perceived to exist among public officials and politicians. This is determined by expert assessments and opinion surveys. Finland has been ranked from first to sixth; recently it shared first place with Denmark and New Zealand as the least corrupt country in the world. No country can, however, declare itself a model when it comes to these matters.

The Country Policy and Institutional Assessment (CPIA) examines policies and institutions, not development outcomes, which can depend on forces outside a country's control. The CPIA looks at sixteen distinct areas grouped into four clusters. For each criterion, very detailed guidelines are provided to help World Bank staff score individual countries along an absolute 1–6 scale. Table 7.1 shows the CPI's four clusters and 16 criteria.

Corrupt practices take place at all levels of society. The practices range from everyday petty corruption such as illegal school payments to outrageous state captures. Corruption can be divided into three main types: bureaucratic, political and state capture. Corruption is susceptible to variations across time and space. The main forms of corruption are bribery, extortion, favouritism, embezzlement, conflict of interest and fraud.

The United Nations Convention Against Corruption (UNCAC) does not define corruption as such. It rather defines specific acts of corruption that should be considered in every jurisdiction to be covered by UNCAC. These specific acts are described in the *Handbook* under the title "Understanding the Phenomenon of Corruption". UNCAC has eight chapters with a total of 71 Articles. The chapters are: General Provisions, Preventive Measures, Criminalization and Law Enforcement, International Cooperation, Asset Recovery, Technical Assistance and Information Exchange, Mechanisms for Implementation and Final Provisions.

UNCAC is unique not only in its worldwide coverage but also in the extent of its provisions, recognising the importance of both preventive and punitive measures. Many preventive measures stipulated by UNCAC—for

Table 7.1 Corruption perceptions index criteria

A. Economic management cluster	B. Cluster on structural policies	C. Cluster on policies for social inclusion/equity	D. Public sector management and institutions cluster
1. Macroeconomic management	4. Trade	7. Gender equality	12. Property rights and rule-based governance
2. Fiscal policy	5. Financial sector	8. Equity of public resource use	13. Quality of budgetary and financial management
3. Debt policy	6. Business regulatory environment	9. Building human resources	14. Efficiency of revenue mobilisation
		10. Social protection and labour	15. Quality of public administration
		11. Policies and institutions for environmental sustainability	16. Transparency, accountability, and corruption in the public sector

Source: Corruption perceptions index 2012 by Transparency International

example the building of sound financial management systems and effective access to public information—are extremely important for the success of development co-operation.

The question is: what connection is there between anti-corruption, good governance and the principles of the rule of law? The thesis is that the fundamental principles of the legal system—including participation in administration, proper management of public affairs and public property, integrity, transparency and accountability—play a key role in preventing corruption.

In Finland, good governance has been adopted as one of the key elements in the activities of public authorities. In accordance with the principle of the rule of law, the exercise of official authority must be based on law. Keeping public administration as transparent as possible is one of the fundamental principles of Finnish public administration. Decisions must be public so that citizens, NGOs and the media can comment on them where necessary. Everyone has the right to be heard in their matter, the right to receive a reasoned decision and the right of appeal. In practice, transparency and publicity are the most important anti-corruption tools.

The publication of documents guarantees that the actions of the authorities can be followed and monitored. Principally, citizens have the right to receive information about any documents of any civil service department.

As we saw in Chap. 3, the fourth corner of the rule-of-law house is the functionality of the system: acts should be comprehensible, bureaucracy reduced, decisions taken promptly and access to justice kept simple. In other words, public authority is the servant and the citizens are the masters.

According to modern information theory, public power should be responsible for making sure accurate information is available in order to guarantee a functional justice system. This is a cornerstone of the principle of publicity, which is an integral part of freedom of speech.

New Dark Clouds Rising

Venezuela's Information Hegemony Betrays Collapse While Hugo Chávez, President of Venezuela (1999–2013), was determined to implant "socialism of the twenty-first century" in his country through increasing domination of all pillars of state power, consolidating the government's hegemonic control over information, he was careful to give an impression of free speech to the outside world.

The channelling of all media communication into the hands of the government is a reminder of Francis Bacon's (1561–1626) well-known statement in the book *De Hesibus* (circa 1626): "Knowledge is power". The struggle for power has always also been a struggle for communication. Our guide to the tensions of recent years in Venezuela will be Mikko Pyhälä,[16] Finland's ambassador to Venezuela (2006–2013). His story is based on years of experience in Venezuela and its neighbouring region:

> While Hugo Chávez, President of Venezuela (1999–2013), was determined to implant his "Socialism of the XXI Century" by undermining the independence of his country's democratic institutions and pushing forward his avowed aim of consolidating the government's information hegemony, he was careful to give to the outside world the impression that free speech continued to be respected in Venezuela.
>
> The first radical limitation to freedom of expression was in 2007, when Chávez refused to renew the license of RCTV, the most popular TV station, and also the one with the most extended, nationwide, coverage. Chávez had

accused RCTV and several other TV channels, of having supported a *coup d'état* against him in 2002. All RCTV assets were confiscated, but it succeeded later to re-emerge as a cable channel. In September 2015, the Inter-American Court of Human Rights sentenced the government to return the concession to the owners, which the government has not done.

One major limitation to freedom of expression has been the use of "*cadenas*", compulsory rebroadcasting of government messages, most often *live*, by all non-cable TV and radio stations. In 1999, there had been annually about 70 hours of such *cadenas*, and in 2011 there were over 200 hours. In 2014, President Nicolás Maduro decreed that the media was obliged to broadcast two daily *cadenas*, and he used over 500 hours. In the first months of 2016 alone, Maduro has used 500 hours for *cadenas*.

The *cadenas* were established by the Law RESORTE (Social Responsibility in Radio and Television) with the intention of focusing on issues of national social importance. However, Chávez and Maduro have used them abusively for political propaganda, especially during electoral campaigns, with the National Electoral Commission turning a blind eye. Simultaneously, heavy restrictions were imposed on time allotted to competing candidates, and on the opposition in general. Civil society informational video clips were banned, official media were instructed not to broadcast live any statements by the opposition presidential candidate, and fines were imposed on a number of dissident newspapers, periodicals, reporters and humorists. Many topics were eventually declared illegal to be reported by the media, such as violent deaths, shortages, demonstrations, repression by the Armed Forces, etc. The editor of the independent journal *6to Poder* was imprisoned in 2011 and again in 2015, and after hunger strikes was allowed to serve his sentences at home. The editor of the internet page *Noticias24* had his car burned by unknown assailants.

A serious limitation to free speech is that the government has not been publishing macroeconomic data, periodic reports of public institutions, budgets, availability or shortage of food and medicines, balance sheets of the main development funds, as observed by the Inter-American Human Rights Commission in October 2015. For years, specific information on epidemics and violence has not been published.

The Chavista regime has imposed censorship, legally banning news that might cause *zozobra* (anxiety) within the population, thus really imposing self-censorship on the media. Gradually, all non-submissive TV channels have been eliminated. Diverse pressure from the government obliged the owners of Globovision to sell the channel to groups close to Chavism in 2014, and some 700 radio stations were subjected to official propaganda, with very few independent TV and radio stations remaining. The daily paper with the largest circulation, *Ultimas Noticias*, which had a pro-Chavista editorial line but fairly balanced reporting, was purchased in 2013 by a Chavista front-man and made almost totally compliant. In February 2014 when the Government launched violent repression of student protests, the only independently reporting cable TV channel, NTN24 of Colombia, was banned. In 2015, the largest newspaper *El Universal* was purchased by a Chavista front, and 20 journalists critical to the Government were dismissed. However, Venezuela's most accomplished investigative journalist, Nelson Bocaranda, has been allowed to continue with his column and website runrun.es "because even many Chavistas and military rank find it the only really truthful source".

Free speech in the National Assembly was supressed. While the opposition received 52 per cent of votes in parliamentary elections of 2010, they obtained less than half of the deputies. The National Assembly was off-limits to independent media. Several opposition members were expelled and opposition parliamentary speeches were often interrupted. María Corina Machado, a particularly courageous and determined independent member, was once thrown on the floor and kicked in the face by a Chavista member. After she addressed the OAS Council in March, 2014, she was expelled from the Assembly without due process. She has been constantly threatened with imprisonment. When the United Democracy Movement obtained a super-majority of twothirds in the National Assembly in December 2015, the withdrawing Chavista regime scrapped the Assembly's TV channel and studios, and took over the frequency.

Venezuela has had less killings of journalists than many other Latin American countries. According to the NGO IPYS, from 2005 to mid-2014, seven journalists were killed. In some cases, the motive may have been robbery, or was made to look like robbery. Some were evidently the result of general violence, Venezuela today being one of the most dangerous countries in the world. Some of these assassinations have raised suspicions of extrajudicial killings.

The NGO Espacio Público reports that in 2002 there were 141 violations of freedom of expression, and in 2015 these had grown to 287. In 2014, there had been detentions and beatings of journalists (also foreigners), and confiscation of their cameras and computers. CNN was thrown out and banned, and the government intervened in Twitter and Facebook. The worsening of the situation in 2014 was explained by wide protests by students and their supporters which were assuming aspects of insurgency. Venezuela arrested a number of Twitter users in 2014 and blocked more than 1000 internet sites. A number of media have had their internet use intervened in the last few years. Internet in Venezuela is the second slowest in the world, after Paraguay.

Since Maduro assumed the presidency in 2013, there has been a constant erosion of the legitimacy of the president and of his government, evidence of massive corruption, a growing shortage of basic foodstuffs, medicine, toiletry and spare parts; education and health services are in ruin, and the prevalence of poverty shot up to 75 %. Persons and media who question, denounce or seek information are seen as public enemies and slandered in official media broadcasts. The Chavista regime is using the Supreme Court of Justice to undermine legislation by the new majority in the National Assembly.

The Venezuelan regime has continued to tighten the screws on the free press by not allowing, or severely delaying, the import of newsprint to critical newspapers. This has forced some 10 smaller papers to close down in 2014, and the remaining few critical papers have had to decimate their number of pages. The Inter-American Press Society reported in February, 2016, that 86 regional newspapers might disappear for lack of paper.

In recent days the situation has grown tenser. International pressure towards Venezuela has increased. Already around twenty presidents from different parties in Latin American countries have promised to support the campaign to release Venezuela's political prisoners. The former Prime Minister of Spain Felipe González—whom government officials have severely attacked, accusing him of corruption and using death patrols against his political opponents—is the lead figure of the campaign. González is going to be a defence witness in the trial of Leopoldo López. Venezuelan officials have stated that González may do this only if he applies for a work permit and is granted one. The former President of Brazil Fernando Cardoso has announced he plans to accompany González.

The former nuncio of the Pope in Venezuela, the Cardinal Secretary of State Pietro Parolin, will participate in the OAS General Assembly in Panama. Parolin was a mediator in the normalisation process of Cuba and the USA. He now has the opportunity to talk with Maduro about the crisis in Venezuela. The shortage of food, medicine and replacement parts is growing worse, Mikko Pyhälä writes in his most recent report.[17]

Freedom of Speech's Growing Distress in Hungary Throughout 2010, Prime Minister Viktor Orbán's Fidesz party used its parliamentary supermajority to pass numerous mutually reinforcing legislative changes, tightening government control over broadcast media and extending regulation to print and online media. In July, the government amended the constitution, removing a passage on the government's obligation to prevent media monopolies. It then consolidated media regulation under the supervision of a single authority, the National Media and Info Communications Authority (NMHH), whose members are elected by a two-thirds majority in parliament and whose leader also chairs a five-person Media Council charged with content regulation.

The new Hungarian Constitution, adopted in April 2011 and effective 1 January 2012, created a new National Agency for Data Protection, prematurely ending the six-year term of the existing Data Protection Commissioner with no interim measures put in place. The head of the new authority is appointed by Orbán and can be dismissed by the prime minister or president on arbitrary grounds.

Another controversial component of the media law is the system of co-regulation. In July 2011, the NMHH concluded public administration agreements on media co-regulation with the four Hungarian self-regulatory media bodies: the Association of Hungarian Content Providers (MTE), the Advertising Self-regulatory Body (ÖRT), the Association of Hungarian Publishers (MLE), and the Association of Hungarian Electronic Broadcasters (MEME). These formerly independent bodies are now responsible for ensuring compliance with NMHH media content rules and risk becoming instruments of censorship.

Articles VII, VIII, IX, and X of the Fundamental Law of Hungary establish the rights of freedom of expression, speech, press, thought, conscience, religion, artistic creation, scientific research and assembly. Some of these rights are limited by the penal code. Section 269—Incitement against a Community—states: "A person who incites to hatred before the general public against: (a) the Hungarian nation, (b) any national, ethnic, racial group or certain groups of the population, shall be punishable for a felony offense with imprisonment up to three years". This list has been updated to include: "people with disabilities, various sexual identity and sexual orientation", effective from July 2013. It is also illegal under Section 269/C of the penal code and punishable with three years' imprisonment, to publicly "deny, question, mark as insignificant, attempt to justify the genocides carried out by the National Socialist and Communist regimes, as well as the facts of other crimes against humanity".

The media law, adopted in 2010 and in effect from 2011, has stirred up a lot of criticism in the EU and the international press. It has been seen as a return to the time of Kádár, when the country was ruled by one party and one truth. The law includes the establishment of a new Media Council. People associated with Fidesz were nominated as some of the lead actors. However, Hungary did make some changes to the law based on the concerns presented by the Commission.

The objective of the new law is "balanced communication", and someone who violates this may be fined hundreds of thousands of euros, which is expected to lead to self-censorship by leading media actors. Meanwhile the ownership of domestic media has been centralised further.

While foreign ownership of Hungarian media is extensive, domestic ownership is highly concentrated in the hands of Fidesz allies. The government is the country's largest advertiser and has withdrawn most of its advertising from independent media since the 2010 elections. There is anecdotal evidence that private companies withhold advertising from independent media to avoid losing government contracts. In 2011, Jobbik party co-founder Dániel Papp was named editor in chief of the news office at the MTVA media fund, which is responsible for the management of all public media.

The media law is being widely applied to traditional press, radio and television, as well as internet-based media including, among others, internet blogs. Protection of journalistic sources has also been abolished by the new law—journalists are obliged to reveal their sources if the supervising council so decides. The National Media and Communications Authority (NMHH) established alongside this new law supervises and regulates press sanctions and fines. All four members of the new body have been nominated by the right-wing Fidesz party for a period of nine years, putting a single party in control of the entire Hungarian media sector.

Journalists, media actors and students have demonstrated against the new media law in many ways: several newspapers, for example, published an empty front page as a protest when the law came into effect. Similarly opposition parliamentarians who objected to the law taped their mouths shut with orange tape before the vote.

The so-called media law is seen by many in the EU as an affront to European core values. The OSCE has also voiced its concern, stating that the new law gives the supervisory body an unforeseen level of authority to restrict the media. Great concern has arisen about rule of law development in general, as in Hungary the power of judges and constitutional justice had been weakened even before these new actions, as we saw in Chap. 5. New uproar arose when the face of the now retired President of the Supreme Court Zoltan Lomnici was obscured in news reports on the government's orders. This is an extreme indication of one of the EU's structural problems: during membership negotiations, the rule-of-law situation in a candidate country is evaluated in close detail, but after it has become a member, development in this area is not monitored at all.

The events in Hungary have provoked a conversation in the member states as to whether the EU should have more powerful ways to intervene in the politics of those countries that break the core values acknowledged by the Union.

Free Speech under Pressure in Turkey Turkey ranks 154th among 180 countries in the World Press Freedom Index. Translators, editors, publishers, poets and writers face criminal proceedings and even imprisonment for legitimate expression under a variety of legal restraints, including the country's draconian anti-terror law, the law on meetings and demonstrations and the Turkish penal code's articles on defamation (article 125), religious defamation (article 216), obscenity (article 226), insulting the Turkish people, state or its organs, and promoting conscientious objection to military service (article 318).

Freedom of speech has been curtailed in recent years during the authoritarian rule of the ex-prime minister, now President, Recep Tayyip Erdoğan. Nominally, freedom of speech is secured by the constitution in Turkey. Article 26 of the Constitution of Turkey guarantees the right to "freedom of expression and dissemination of thought". Moreover, the Republic of Turkey is a signatory to the European Convention on Human Rights and submits to the judgements of the European Court of Human Rights. Be that as it may, freedom of expression may be limited by provision in other laws, such as Article 301 of the Turkish Penal Code, which outlaws denigration of the Turkish nation while also providing that "expression of thought intended to criticize shall not constitute a crime".

The Turkish government has attempted in different ways to intervene in communication channels and close down Twitter and Facebook, suggesting a desire by President Recep Tayyip Erdoğan's government and the AKP party, which is in power, to prevent a conversation on social media that is troublesome to their power game.

In February 2013, the Turkish parliament passed a bill, which the then President , Abdullah Gül, later signed into law, giving the government broad control over the internet, including the ability to block sites without a court order and to collect and retain user histories. Among the forbidden pages was the video service, Youtube.[18]

Things came to a head in May 2013, when the government announced plans to redevelop Istanbul's Taksim Gezi Park into a shopping mall designed to look like an Ottoman-era military barracks. Locals were angry with a move that would have not only destroyed one of the most prominent green spaces in Istanbul's city centre, but would also replace it with a monument to the twin themes of Erdoğan's time as leader: capitalism and Islamist nationalism. Thousands of people descended on Gezi Park for huge anti-government protests. Police responded with a heavy-handed crackdown, and at least eight people died.

The Gezi Park protests were a huge challenge to Prime Minister Erdoğan's authority and Twitter clearly played a role in spreading discontent. Protesters used #geziparkı to share scenes from the protest, and the controversial death of a 15-year-old boy reportedly hit by a police tear-gas canister was announced on the service. But these protests alone might not have prompted such a drastic response from the Turkish government; Erdoğan's Twitter clampdown seems to be specifically targeting a more insidious threat that comes closer to his own base.

According to the Electronic Frontier Foundation, 14 per cent of Turkey's eighty million people use Twitter—a relatively high figure for a country where only 45 per cent of the population uses the internet. The blocking of Twitter backfired on the government, with people opposing it aggressively. When the news about the blocking spread shortly after news outlets reported the ban, articles about how to circumvent it began to circulate widely, and the hashtags #twitterisblockedinturkey and #turkeyblockedtwitter were among Twitter's trending keywords worldwide. According to the *Guardian*, Turkish users collectively tweeted 2.5 million times after the ban went into effect, potentially "setting new records for Twitter use in the country".[19]

Even the President Abdullah Gül stood out against Prime Minister Erdoğan's actions, and he took to Twitter to express his disapproval, saying that he hoped the ban would not last long. The spectacular failure of Turkey's Twitter ban shows it's a little more complicated than that, however. Astute internet users in the country soon realised they could still tweet via text by changing their DNS settings or by using a VPN. Many of Turkey's elite have broken the ban.

The blanket ban on Twitter and YouTube (Report, 27 March) comes in the aftermath of a regressive new internet law and is an unacceptable violation of the right to freedom of speech. With over 36 million internet users, Turkey should be proud to be home to Europe's youngest internet audience, placing it among the most globally connected countries in the Muslim world. By connecting people from a range of backgrounds and making it possible for them to express their thoughts, the internet is a valuable network that supports and strengthens democracy. Twitter and YouTube are vehicles of expression that give a voice to each and every user, regardless of class, religion, ethnicity or political stature. There are more than 12 million Twitter users in Turkey, which shows the vibrancy of civil society. Turkey is a state party to the European Convention on Human Rights and the International Covenant on Civil and Political Rights, both of which protect the right to legitimate freedom of expression.

Meanwhile, the Turkish lawyers' association asked the courts to overturn the ban. Turkey's main opposition party has also said that they are seeking to end the ban. Banning social media is nothing new to the country but the latest move has outraged the citizens of Turkey and the protests are happening online as well as offline. Users have been spreading their knowledge using hashtag #DirenTwitter online. Offline, residents have spray-painted graffiti on balconies and government portraits with the public DNS addresses to spread the word. The government stated that there are hundreds of court rulings in Turkey ordering Twitter to remove content. Meanwhile a Turkish court ruled that the government's blocking of access did not originate from a court ruling, but was rather a direct executive order. The administrative court in Ankara suspended the ban ahead of a full judgement. Eventually it turned out that blocking Twitter and Facebook was not possible, and President Erdoğan finally had to relent and give up his attempts to close down these internet channels. The struggle, however, will surely go on.

The political psychology of Turkey's ruling Justice and Development Party (AKP) is encapsulated in one of its most recent pieces of propaganda—a three-minute, professionally made video with imagery worthy of a Hollywood blockbuster. The video succinctly summarises the current grand narrative being promoted by Turkey's ruling party: the Turkish nation is under attack, and Erdoğan is calling on compatriots to unite and resist. The message is obvious: Erdoğan's political opponents are not only attacking him, they are attacking the nation itself. Turkish patriots must unite against these most wicked of enemies.[20]

The grip of the central government in Turkey has now tightened, with the attempted coup of July 2016 crushed forcefully. Arrests and clean-ups have been directed mainly at the army and the judiciary (3000 judges have been fired) as well as schools and universities. In all over 60,000 people have been arrested. The outlook for freedom of speech and access to information in Turkey seems dark.

Notes

1. This comment was written by Paavo Hohti specifically for this book and is published, unedited, with his permission. It has not been previously published.
2. See also https://books.google.fi/books?id=ldk9AAAAcAAJ&pg=PA15&lpg=PA15&dq=Decimus+Iunius+Iuvenalis+it+is+difficult+not+to+write+satire&source=bl&ots=4YEXHlK0f9&sig=yGDJEgqybTV5c-pjqIJorShH0pY&hl=fi&sa=X&ved=0ahUKEwjez677h_nOAhWCApoKHUBrAWkQ6AEISzAH#v=onepage&q=Decimus%20Iunius%20Iuvenalis%20it%20is%20difficult%20not%20to%20write%20satire&f=false, accessed 5 September 2016.
3. See also Quote Investigator at http://quoteinvestigator.com/2015/06/01/defend-say/, accessed 5 September 2016.
4. Available at https://cpj.org/awards/2013/nedim-sener-acceptance-speech.php, accessed 8 September 2016.
5. See https://cpj.org/2015/02/cpj-calls-on-turkish-government-to-reverse-anti-pr.php, accessed 5 September 2016.
6. *Der Spiegel*, 23 January 2015: http://www.spiegel.de/international/business/spiegel-interview-with-chief-new-york-times-editor-dean-baquet-a-1014704.html, last accessed 27 May 2016.
7. Available at https://www.theguardian.com/technology/2014/mar/27/us-government-requests-google-user-data, accessed 5 September 2016.
8. *The Guardian* at http://www.theguardian.com/uk-news/2015/jan/19/gchq-intercepted-emails-journalists-ny-times-bbc-guardian-le-monde-reuters-nbc-washington-post, last accessed June 2015.
9. See http://www.theguardian.com/politics/2015/jan/14/theresa-may-no-safe-spaces-terrorists-communicate, accessed 5 September 2016.
10. See https://www.theguardian.com/world/2015/jan/16/cameron-interrupt-terrorists-cybersecurity-cyberattack-threat, accessed 5 September 2016.
11. *Der Spiegel* at http://www.spiegel.de/international/business/spiegel-interview-with-chief-new-york-times-editor-dean-baquet-a-1014704.html, last accessed June 2015.
12. *Huffington Post* at http://www.huffingtonpost.com/daniel-raphael/why-edward-snowden-is-a-h_b_4227605.html, last accessed June 2015.
13. The *Guardian* at http://www.theguardian.com/film/2014/oct/11/citizenfour-review-snowden-vindicated-poitras-nsa-journalism, last accessed June 2015.
14. Available at Senator Durbin's homepage at:www.durbin.senate.gov/public/index.cfm/pressreleases?ID=23b8bfde-c0cc-4ec0-85d0-4ecf660486bc, last accessed 27 May 2016.

15. See https://www.transparency.org/what-is-corruption, accessed 5 September 2016.
16. This comment was written by Mikko Pyhälä specifically for this book and is published, unedited, with his permission. It has not been previously published.
17. Runrunes at http://runrun.es/internacional/195972/una-cumbre-de-ex-presidentes-a-favor-de-la-libertad-por-milos-alcalay.html, last accessed 27 May 2016. See also http://elpais.com/elpais/2016/07/17/opinion/1468783976_290662.html. Los desafíos a los que se enfrenta Venezuela son de tal magnitud que no admiten espera. La división entre Gobierno y oposición no facilita que se aborden medidas para resolver una triple crisis: institucional, social y económica, de seguridad.
18. The Next Web homepage at http://thenextweb.com/twitter/2014/03/22/turkey-blocks-google-dns-attempt-censor-twitter/#!A7BTT, last accessed 27 May 2016.
19. See https://www.theguardian.com/world/2014/mar/21/turkey-twitter-users-flout-ban-erdogan, accessed 5 September 2016.
20. Al Monitor at http://www.al-monitor.com/pulse/originals/2014/03/erdogan-nationalist-propaganda-video.html#, last accessed June 2015.

CHAPTER 8

Freedom of Speech in the Turbulence of the Changing World

Globalisation

Different Aspects of Globalisation Globalisation and above all the internet era have radically changed the culture of information and the operational environment of freedom of speech. Broadly speaking, the process of globalisation has two aspects. The first refers to those factors—such as trade, investment, technology, cross-border production systems, and flows of information and communication—that bring societies and citizens closer together.

The second refers to policies such as market liberalisation, international standards for labour, the environment, corporate behaviour and other issues, agreements on intellectual property rights, and other policies pursued at both national and international levels that support the integration of economies and countries. In terms of the latter aspect, the existing pattern of globalisation is not an inevitable trend—it is at least in part the product of policy choices. While technological change is irreversible, policies can be changed. Technological advances have also widened the policy choices available (see World Commission on the Social Dimension of Globalisation 2004).

Even though globalisation can be studied as a business-level process, it also affects the internal functioning and capacities of states and the status of citizens. This approach lies somewhere between the so-called

© The Author(s) 2017
P. Hallberg, J. Virkkunen, *Freedom of Speech and Information in Global Perspective*, DOI 10.1057/978-1-349-94990-8_8

maximalist and minimalist positions. The changes are primarily of domestic origin and only indirectly result from international factors.

Status of Nation-States Some scholars have written of the erosion of nation-states. This refers to (1) a decline in the state's capacities to control the effects brought about by actors beyond its borders; (2) democratic deficits resulting from the facts that decisions are made at levels beyond the reach of the democratic process, and that decisions in general affect people not involved in the decision-making process; and (3) restrictions on the state's capacity to implement social policies due to the freedom of capital (Habermas 1999, 49–50). It is argued that as a consequence of globalisation, the international system is no longer a system of states. The changes brought about by globalisation are such that they seriously impede the state's capacity to realise the common good as a genuine civil association (Cerny 1995, 595 ff).

If this is the situation then where does salvation lie for freedom of speech? This is the challenge of globalisation: the democratic, constitutional and social aspirations of people are still formed at the nation-state level, although the possibilities of collective action within this framework are decreasing. Even if opportunities for collective action also emerge in multilateral arrangements, these will always work farther away from the reach of democratic control. In this setting, the state will preserve its important role in the international political-economic system, but its holistic role as a "civil association" may be vanishing (Cerny 1995, 619).

However, states themselves are usually behind the actions that have changed the relation between states and markets, which is manifest in market liberalisation, human rights treaties and security arrangements. Even the international economic system depends on the power of states. If competition and market pressures shrank states into mere local authorities, this system would become extremely prone to political and social threats, such as terrorism, crime and protest movements. Thus, the triumph of economic liberalism would at the same time be the fall of the system.

For a more systematic vision of the role of the nation-state, we may argue that the national state is actually the only agent that can deliver on negotiations about matters of common interest; as Thompson (1999, 149–150) points out, it is also the nation-state "that regulates international legal provisions as the negotiated outcomes of common agreements are rendered into a legal framework for the conduct of both domestic and international economic activity. Thus, the state cannot be ignored in this process."

Essentially, the analysis of the relation between the state and globalisation may focus either on the structural factors on the one hand, or on the agents or actors on the other. Structural approaches emphasise the forces of globalisation with respect to the state, whereas agent-centric approaches underline the role of agents, or states, vis-à-vis globalisation. In the former approaches, the global market is a structure to which states have to adapt, and the latter still view the states as central actors. Neither is sufficient to account for the complex relationship. The state is an agent which both shapes the global system and at the same time is shaped by that system. Global structure represents not only a constraint, but also an opportunity for the state.

A middle way between agent-centric and structural approaches could be found by arguing that the powers of the state as such do not vanish but their contexts change. National governments are no longer automatically the location of effective political power, and the political community of fate cannot be regarded as lying within the borders of nation-states. Many processes operate outside the reach of national institutions, and if this is not acknowledged these processes will by-pass the democratic system.

Though states still hold substantial power, this can be seen more in international contexts than in domestic politics. The new forms of power are not territorially restricted power, but this does not result in the end of the state. In fact, the new strategies of governance require a more active role for the government. This also means that the centre of gravity for guarantees of freedom of speech will remain on the national level. National rule-of-law development is still in the key position. We have previously noted that there are not enough guarantees on the international level to secure freedom of speech, not to mention instruments to intervene in violations of free speech. It is another question altogether that in the digitalising world, also, rule-of-law development faces new demands on all levels (Hallberg 2004, 186).

Thus we arrive at the relevant questions. How does globalisation present itself in terms of the functionality of the rule of law? At the heart of the issue are the effects of globalisation on the foundations of the rule of law: (1) What is the law of the future? Are there new sources for norm giving besides the state, and will the nature of legislation move towards the international treaty system and soft-law types of norms? (2) How will the internal power structures of the state change with the possible strengthening of the economic nature of legislation and the process of integration? (3) How will fundamental and human rights, including freedom of speech, develop—will globalisation and regional inequality lead to cultural and economic-political relativism? (4) What are the practical effects of globalisation on the functioning of public authorities, especially on the structure of administration and on the conditions for a functioning court system? (see Hallberg 2004, 189).

In examining the evolution of the rule of law, it is also essential to stress a distinction: law is the means, not an end. Justice is the objective. This means neither a return to the tradition of natural law nor an emphasis on legal positivism. Understanding the principle of legality as a commitment to common, democratically chosen rules helps overcome this division. The inability to distinguish between law and the use of force has been a problem of legal positivism.

However, the nature of the law deliberated within democracies may itself be changing. The increase of laws of a private nature along with changes in the internal power structures of the state leads to the strengthening of the economic nature of national legislation.

From a functional point of view, the principle of legality could be understood somewhat more practically, as a commitment to norms that are general, clear, public, predictable and stable. This is a minimum requirement for the state-oriented rule of law, under pressure from globalisation and the competition between states to attract investments to their territories.

The effect of globalisation on the fourth cornerstone of our rule-of-law concept—the functioning of the system—deserves attention. As globalisation considerably changes the role of the state in society, this is inevitably also reflected in the structures and practices of administration and the functioning of the court system. The activities of the state are faced with increasing international competition, and the state is increasingly conceived of as a determinant of competitiveness. This leads not only to changes in regulatory policy and to the consideration of requirements for competition, but also to changes in administrative practices, for example cost–benefit analyses (Aman 1998, 791ff.).

A critical practical issue relating to the legitimacy of the state is the privatisation of state functions. Privatisation aims at cost savings, as in the light of experience it has seemed that the private sector has been more efficient than the public sector. However, the privatisation of services results in negative attitudes and democratic deficit if the principles of good governance and protection by law are not followed in the process. This development of privatisation also reflects on access to information. If officers are obliged to provide citizens with access to information, it loses its significance with privatisation. There are even instances where privatisation has extended to the core functions of the state, for example in the United States.

The "globalising state" does not have a monopoly on policy making, but it must co-operate with other states and private actors. This is mainly due to global processes, which do not recognise the powers of the state. When public obligations are passed to the private sector, the dimensions of citizenship and democratic participation can easily disappear in the process by which public values are translated into the language of markets. The danger is that the privatised activity will be based on economic values which, in turn, serve as a basis for the assessment of the activity, and thus non-economic values may vanish (see Hallberg 2004, 196).

Globalisation and Democracy The references to different views not only mean that there are differences in emphasis, but also that there are difficulties in the creation of a general description of the evolution of the relation between the state and globalisation. However, there seems to be a general opinion that the importance of national borders and nation-states will not vanish. This is partly due to the simple fact that the global economy eventually materialises in national territories, and the institutions influencing internationalisation are thus located within certain national borders. Several global arrangements influencing national territories actually strengthen certain components of nation-states. For example, the status of ministries of finance has strengthened along with the increasing importance of international banking systems. Does this indicate that the power of money may have a bigger role in the value foundation of the state? Let us see how researchers in the field have evaluated these developments.

Cerny's argument on the formation of the state as a mixture of civil society and enterprise society leads us to examine the competition state, a concept that has been widely used in recent times. The main direct objective of the state of this kind is, on the one hand, to promote the international competitiveness of the commercial activities taking place in its territory and, on the other hand, that the state should find ways to preserve the balance of its "civil association" and "enterprise association" activities. Therefore, the balance affected by concerns relating to international competitiveness and by the need to create infrastructure benefiting this economic competitiveness should be more broadly defined on the basis of the rule-of-law principles (World Bank, *World Development Report 1997*, 3).

In conclusion, there is a growing consensus that the maintenance of a global economic system is among the duties states have to undertake. In essence, deregulation is not solely loss of control, but also negotiation between states on the way in which globalisation is pursued. Development cannot result in the disappearance of the state, but its role will indeed change because of the integrating economy. An important way of both emphasising the new, more market-oriented, aspects of the global economy without giving up the rhetoric and concept of a strong state is to conceptualise its role in leading the fight for prosperity in the global economy.

The development of democracy and its relation to globalisation is an essential issue in the field of political science. Globalisation affects the conditions for participation and the development of democracy through several channels. Many regard globalisation as a wholly positive phenomenon, and interpret it primarily as economic development. On the one hand, economic welfare generates social welfare and furthers the strengthening of the core elements of humanity. On the other hand, economic power concentrates and accumulates in already wealthy places. This, in turn, has social consequences that affect the global balance and set requirements for systems of governance. Yet it is difficult to see prospects for global governments or cosmopolitan models.

When examining the development of democracy, we must start with the rights to and the actual opportunities for participation: from the political culture. Democracy should be analysed not only at the level of the political regime, but also in relation to the state—especially the state as a legal system—and to certain aspects of the overall social context. Hence, democracy should be analysed as a system that concerns the activities of the whole of society. This was the starting point in earlier times when the classic liberal rule of law, the democratic rule of law and the social dimensions of the rule of law were distinguished as the different developmental stages of the rule of law.

Cross-border conflicts and problems necessitate co-operation between states, and arrangements based on inter-state agreements are needed. Inter-governmental organisations differ from the coalitions of interest groups and NGOs which mainly aim at affecting the behaviour of states or inter-governmental organisations. On the one hand, international treaty arrangements establishing international organisations lead to the commitment of states to the general principles and political objectives of the organisation. The UN is a leading "normative realm" of this type (De Senarclens 2001, 511). On the other hand, international organisations are used by governments to promote their viewpoints and legitimate their policies (Hallberg 2004, 201).

Democratic deficits can be divided into structural and institutional ones (Scholte 2002, 281–304). Structural deficits are due to the disjunction between supraterritorial spaces and territorial self-determination, and to the changing contours of the demos under contemporary globalisation. Individuals identify their "people" in multiple fashions in addition to the nation-state, whereas the theories and mechanisms of democracy tend to only define "the people" in territorial-nation-state terms. Institutional deficiencies, in turn, refer to deficits that are caused by structural problems and are present in all institutional sites of the governance of supraterritorial space. At the state level, even governments with high democratic credentials have generally given limited publicity, in relation to both their public and elected representatives, to their activities in respect of global governance. At the inter-governmental level, technocrats (those of the G8, for example) have operated almost completely outside the public eye and democratic scrutiny.

Participation in the Information Society It is often argued that globalisation underscores technocratic criteria at the expense of democratic principles. Also, it seems that political commitment in the new technological-economic network is rather more issue and interest specific than general participation in social decision making. The danger is that the general interest of society is left in the background (see Castells 1996). The decrease in common deliberation on values and in an active role for citizens is also peculiar to this kind of development of democracy. Further, it may result in a growing emphasis on efficiency at the expense of democracy.

The legitimacy of decision making is measured by trust. This is characteristic of the democratic system of decision making. Scholars talk about representative democracy, interest-group democracy, direct democracy and participatory democracy. In addition, network democracy and teledemocracy are distinguished, but these expressions actually describe the technical aspects of participation (Hallberg 2004, 207).

According to some studies, the interest in internet participation is bigger when the issues in question concern close and concrete matters. In addition, independent initiatives are clearly more attractive than participation projects conducted by administrative agencies. However, the minutes and agendas of authorities appear to be very popular. Thus, there could be room for more dialogue and participation before decision making. Yet one should remember the ageing of the population, varying social conditions and migration. People are not equal with regard to opportunity for new forms of participation.

What do digital technologies teach us about the nature of freedom of speech, asks Jack M. Balkin in his essay (*New York University Law Review* 2004): "The Internet and digital technologies help us look at freedom of speech from a different perspective. That is not because digital technologies fundamentally change what freedom of speech is. Rather, it is because digital technologies change the social conditions in which people speak, and by changing the social conditions of speech, they bring to light features of freedom of speech that have always existed in the background but now become foregrounded."

The free speech principle is the battleground for many of these conflicts. For example, media companies have interpreted the free speech principle both broadly to combat regulation of digital networks and narrowly in order to protect and extend their intellectual property rights. The digital age greatly expands the opportunity for individual participation in the growth and spread of culture, and thus greatly expands the possibilities for the realisation of a truly democratic culture. But the same technologies also produce new methods of control that can limit democratic cultural participation.

Therefore, free-speech values—interactivity, mass participation, and the ability to modify and transform culture—must be protected through technological design and through administrative and legislative regulation of technology, as well as through the more traditional methods of judicial creation and recognition of constitutional rights. Increasingly, freedom of speech will depend on the design of the technological infrastructure.

There is a further principal aspect of internet participation to be considered. Although discussion on the web is influential, somebody always has to make and confirm the final decision and bear the responsibility for it. This is true for all issues, from urban planning and social security to the distribution of public support. So the question about future development is: How can the willpower that has gathered on the streets and squares be channelled into permanent reforms? Hence, an accountable parliament, government, city council, city executive board, municipal board or body of civil servants is always needed to enact common policies and to make decisions (Hallberg 2004, 207).

Today, we also have a complex network of indirect democracy, or an indirect electoral system, organised by interest representation. Scholars often talk about the reorganisation of civil society and the reappearance of non-governmental organisations. On the one hand, the formation of NGOs into public opinion formers may, as a side-effect, promote the development of local democracy and the democratisation of regions. On the other hand, NGOs are no panacea to diminish the democratic deficit of globalisation. They can help to overcome democratic deficits but also make them worse.

Nevertheless, there are several ways in which civil society can potentially contribute to the governance of globalisation: (1) NGOs can give a political voice to stakeholders who aren't heard through other channels; (2) they may raise public awareness of international issues, including legislation and institutions; (3) they can also enrich the debate on global governance issues by providing innovative proposals and constructive criticism; and (4) they can improve the transparency and accountability of transnational decision making by disseminating information and monitoring the implementation of policies.

Generally, these contributions make global governance more legitimate (Scholte 2002, 281 ff). In contrast, however, some of these movements are of an anti-democratic nature and may work against majority principles and pluralistic societal development. Therefore, there is a need to analytically examine the impact of NGOs and other movements on democratic development.

Associations can also be developed as a method of welfare provision and governance at national and local levels. The strength of associationalism lies in its ability to take account of changes in democratic participation, especially in growing interest specificity and the obscuring of the general interest. Associations give consumers more direct control over the services they are offered, accommodating plural communities with differing values and standards.

Hirst analyses four aspects of the crisis of democratic governance today. They are: (1) widespread decline of political participation; (2) states' lost governance capacity, both because of globalisation and because of the shift from public to market provision of services; (3) modern life does not facilitate traditional collective action; and (4) that the scope of both formal democracy and voluntary association is limited in advanced countries because they are organisational democracies that require strengthening of the association at the national and local levels rather than at the international level. Hirst also promotes associations as a nationally focused solution to the problems of democracy, as an alternative to global governance arrangements (see *Hirst* 2002, 410–412).

Cosmopolitan Models? Many scholars who focus on the gap between politics and the economy, and the power of neo-liberal thinking related to it, end up outlining cosmopolitan models that could be used to restore the broken link. This would be done by replacing states as individuals as the subjects of international law (see more Hallberg 2004, 210).

It is important to discuss the cosmopolitan models in rule-of-law development. This is especially significant considering that legal guarantees of freedom of speech mainly rely on national institutions. In essence, the cosmopolitan approach is from the top down, as the transformation of the nation-state is taken as read, and new systems are evolved above it. In contrast, from the perspective of the rule of law, the approach to globalisation must be from the bottom up: we have to examine the sustainability of the principles developed in the context of the nation-state in global markets, and particularly the rule of law as a strategy in globalisation. As this is one of the central points of our book, let us study the dialogue of researchers in this field.

In the cosmopolitan outline of Held (2002), the following institutional arrangements are needed to guarantee the legitimacy of power in an era where the state can no longer be the only centre of that power. Legal cosmopolitanism necessitates cosmopolitan democratic law, which strictly defines rights and duties with respect to political, social and economic power, the interconnected global legal system, commitment to the International Criminal Court (ICC) and the International Court of Justice, and creation of new human rights instruments.

Political cosmopolitanism requires multi-level governance, decentralised authority, a network of democratic forums from local to global level, enhanced political regionalisation, and the creation of an international army for the defence of the cosmopolitan law in extreme situations. Economic cosmopolitanism necessitates the reform of market mechanisms and economic powers, global taxation systems, and the transfer of resources to the poor. Cultural cosmopolitanism necessitates the appreciation of diversity, the understanding of the common fate of humanity, and the recognition of the linkages between political communities.

The rule-of-law theme forces us to examine the grassroots level, and seek solutions to govern the effects of globalisation: in other words, global governance. Darian-Smith (2000, 809) writes on state versus global law and grassroots globalisation. Cochran (2002, 517–548) criticises the excessively top-down approach of the cosmopolitan blueprint, and argues for the examination of governance issues from a bottom-up perspective. In her view, it remains doubtful that cosmopolitan democracy will spread in practice. For example, existing democratic states do not necessarily promote the adoption of common democratic values, but in fact are often opposed to them, as in the case of the ICC.

Are the contents of rule-of-law thinking and cosmopolitism inherently different, or is the difference rather in their standpoints? When looking for answers, it should be borne in mind that even though the relation between states and the market changes, it does not necessarily happen at the expense of states—and it definitely should not happen at the expense of citizens and their information! Various activities related to globalisation take place within states, and states themselves are behind many of them.

It is a question of adapting to the change. International law will be law between states in the future too, and not between the residents of the states, or world citizens. The implementation of norms and principles formed in international co-operation is dependent on decision making at the national level and the functioning of national systems. It is to be expected that in the implementation of international norms, the so-called dualistic principle, the demand for national legislation, will gradually vanish. The emphasis will be on the monistic principle, the direct adoption of international norms. Thus, the strengthening of the rule of law in the immediate environment does at the same time work towards adopting shared principles internationally. There are therefore reasons to stick to the bottom-up approach, instead of a cosmopolitan approach in which common principles are, in a way, taken as read.

To conclude, from the perspective of the individual, there are problems in those countries and regions where there are unstable conditions, or where democracy does not function well—in other words, where the rule of law is lacking and freedom of speech restricted. Without going into a detailed analysis, it may be generally noted that the problems are often due to the weak status of the authorities and the courts, deficient knowledge of human rights obligations and obstacles to the development of a legal culture.

Digital Era and Social Media Shaping the World
By Sanna Leisti, Rule of Law Finland—ROLFI

The Changing Environment Change defines generations and separates them from one another. What was yesterday considered the pointless folly of youth may change the human condition tomorrow. This section is a brief account of social media and its effects on society for those who may not yet have managed to familiarise themselves with it, those who discard it as one of the dull vanities of the next generation or those who like to reflect on the potential of modern information technology (IT) from a social perspective.

Scientist and author Carl Sagan has said:

> Writing is perhaps the greatest of human inventions, binding together people who never knew each other, citizens of distant epochs. Books break the shackles of time. A book is proof that humans are capable of working magic.[1]

The drive to link with others, to understand and communicate with each other, is built into human nature. The ability to store information on the walls of caves, in books or online has gradually changed our understanding of the world as well as our own capabilities and set us apart from other animals. We have linked up through ever-faster communication tools, until now, as historian David Christian phrased it, through mass communication, we form as if a "single, global brain of 7 billion people, learning at warp speed".[2]

Social media builds on the ancient invention of writing, and takes the craft of storing information to a new level. One might say that it is a virtual copy of the physical world. The user can visit any country, corporation or institution and connect with anyone with access to the internet. All levels of actors are "users": governments, corporations, communities, politicians as well as private citizens. The users create their own content and tell their own truth to the rest of the collective. As the world of social media develops and opens new, ever-faster ways of communicating and exploring the outside world, people become more "literate" and aware of the potential of these tools every day. The web society has continued to grow in population as well as become faster, more convenient and more practical.

Modern Communication Social media is a communication tool of the more advanced era. It is designed to enable a user-friendly experience, a simple way of harnessing the full potential of the web for everyone. The social media of today goes beyond traditional emailing or text messaging. Facebook has up till now been the flagship of the more sophisticated tools of online communication. It started off as Mark Zuckerberg and his college peers' dorm project in 2004, and grew into a global commercial trendsetter. Facebook now connects over 1.39 billion people around the world, and creates significant economic impact. According to a study by Deloitte (2015), Facebook had a global economic impact of US$227 billion in 2014.

Although many social media companies have arisen alongside it, its users still represent the largest audience reachable on a single social media platform in the world. As of June 2014 more than 30 million small and medium-sized businesses have established a Facebook page. As a result, Facebook has also become a hub that democratises marketing: it facilitates economic activity for businesses of all sizes in that it allows them to reach customers locally, nationally and globally. It also reduces barriers to marketing by helping businesses rise, and contributing to the increasing demand for mobile devices and internet services.

In addition, there is a wide variety of other tools designed to harness the vast amount of data the internet holds: Twitter, YouTube, Linkedin and Instagram, to mention only a few. Linkedin is a tool for professionals to connect with each other; YouTube is for sharing video content; Instagram specialises in covenient picture sharing and Twitter is a simple platform for politicians, journalists, researchers, companies and citizens alike to "tweet" short comments and opinions on, for example, daily events in real time.

The pivotal idea behind all social media is the instant, effortless connection to the rest of the world in the form of articles, pieces of news, protests, video clips and personal commentaries. Thoughts and ideas flow in real time, around the clock. People are no longer dependent on the occasional conference, where one person speaks at a time, that lasts only a few hours. Social media facilitates an endless multilateral inter-city or inter-continental conversation. It can at best lead to an environment of unrestrained innovation. A company or an individual can effortlessly find the actors in their field. Social media is a newborn tool for promoting economic, political and social change. "Six degrees of separation" will no longer begin to cover it.

Social Media and Revolution Social media is not the change, but it is a part of the change. It is a driver of social change and it changes the field of information media. In the political arena, it can help a loosely coordinated public to assemble and demand change together.

When foreign journalists were banned from reporting during the Arab Spring, the dozens of Facebook pages that sprang up as well as the activists' daily Twitter feeds became vital sources of information that provided a glimpse of the conditions for users in the country.

In Egypt, shortly after President Hosni Mubarak stepped down, activist Wael Ghonim, a marketing manager for Google, spoke with CNN's Wolf Blitzer and credited Facebook with the success of the Egyptian people's uprising. From the interview:

> This revolution started online. This revolution started on Facebook. This revolution started [...] when hundreds of thousands of Egyptians started collaborating content. We would post a video on Facebook that would be shared by 60,000 people on their walls within a few hours.[3]

In Syria, a young revolutionary behind the internet pseudonym Malath Aumran joined the growing ranks of internet activists playing a big role in the Arab uprising. They organised protests via Twitter and Facebook and used YouTube to post videos and photos documenting government abuses.

Aumran established a web magazine called Syria News, which included an open forum for civil rights issues, and launched a campaign against the Syrian mobile-phone network Syriatel, owned by *Rami Makhlouf*, a cousin of President Assad, who controls much of the Syrian economy and is regarded by many Syrians as the personification of the endemic corruption in the country. The tech-savvy revolutionary used so-called proxy servers to avoid detection and to access banned websites, set up Facebook pages and launched an e-mail campaign calling for mobile phone boycotts.

Turkey's "Twitter-gate" is another good example of how trying to block social media activity can backfire on the rulers. After Twitter was blocked, users realised they could still tweet via text, by changing their DNS (domain name server settings) or by using a VPN (virtual private network). This may already sound like a foreign language to many, but it serves to show how IT-literate, resourceful citizens do stand a chance against censorship. Services that monitor Twitter usage in Turkey reported no visible drop at the time. Not only was the government unable to block social media channels, the fact that it tried and failed boosted morale.

There are ways for the public to resist internet censorship if it has technological know-how. The IT specialist and whistleblower Edward Snowden thinks we might think of it in terms of literacy: IT is a new system of communication, a new set of symbols that people have to intuitively understand in the same way children learn to write in school. Technical literacy, as he calls it, in our society is a rare and precious resource that today has to be explained and interpreted to most in the same way as a foreign language.

Social media will not liberate a society or fix a distorted rule-of-law system, but it may be a building block. Just as freedom of speech depends on a functional rule of law, and a functional rule of law needs freedom of speech, social media, too, is a part of the bigger picture. It can function as a source of inspiration and information and as a meeting place. The awareness and consensus it sows may lead to a gradual decay of the carefully polished coulisses of authoritarian governments and a weakening of their credibility among citizens. On the other hand, if the balance of power fails to gain a footing after a revolution, followed by a change of power or even a free election, if the next government is again able to arbitrarily force its own agenda through, a revolution will have no future other than to fall in the stampedes of the next one.

Life in the Collective While social media can be a tool for citizens to oppose an autocratic government, it will also work against them in the form of government surveillance. We have already witnessed the unveiling of the magnificent surveillance systems of the Western world and pondered and debated over what this type of activity might mean for our societies in this time of relative peace and balance. The examples of the Arab world and Ukraine give us some indication of what it might mean for a society when it is suddenly thrown into chaos and disorder. In a surveillance state, contrarians of the present condition, the opposition, may easily be brought down with accusations of treason or terrorism, or by labelling them threats to national security.

When it comes to social media, a balance between freedom and responsibility is difficult to achieve, as the messages, whether truthful or untruthful, insulting or hate speech, often come about randomly and unexpectedly.

The chances are that in a decade or two we will have surrounded ourselves with technology that connects everything and everyone instantly. Meanwhile, if we haven't solved the surveillance dilemma by then, we may also find ourselves in George Orwell's Oceania. Citizens may be free to communicate but will think twice before doing so, not because of embarrassing personal secrets, but because privacy is a necessity in certain fields of a functioning society.

To conclude the topic, we might point out that in times of deceit, telling the truth becomes a revolutionary act, as the old anecdote states. However, in a country full of well-informed citizens, the government must eventually feel the pressure to loosen its grip; this pressure is less strong in a society where it is still possible to hide facts from the public. The free flow of information and autocratic governments do not go well together.

Social Media in Numbers Already 89 per cent of the developing world has a mobile device, and the assumption is that these users will soon transition to smartphones. Smartphone sales now eclipse traditional mobile phone sales, and according to the International Telecommunication Union "mobile broadband" subscriptions grew from 278 million in 2007—when the iPhone was first introduced—to 2.1 billion in 2013. Researchers say the trend is already making a big difference when it comes to global poverty and is enabling and promoting entrepreneurship.[4]

Inexpensive smartphones are opening up new opportunities for marketing and commerce in emerging markets where many consumers previously had no access to internet; meanwhile in mature, established markets, smartphones are quickly shifting the paradigm for consumer media usage and creating the need for marketers to become more mobile-centric.

By 2018 it's estimated more than 2.56 billion people—over one-third of consumers worldwide will use smartphones. By 2018, nearly half the world's population—3.6 billion people—will access the internet at least once each month.[5]

Table 8.1 shows the top 25 countries ranked by smartphone users in 2014, according to eMarketer estimates.[6]

As Brian Hall notes, and as we may conclude from the numbers, "fewer and fewer people … will be denied always-on, any-place connectivity to the global Web".[7]

Table 8.1 Top 25 countries ranked by smartphone users, 2013–2018 (Millions)

	2013	2014	2015	2016	2017	2018
1. China[a]	436.1	519.7	574.2	624.7	672.1	704.1
2. USA[b]	143.9	165.3	184.2	198.5	211.5	220.0
3. India	76.0	123.3	167.9	204.1	243.8	279.2
4. Japan	40.5	50.8	57.4	61.2	63.9	65.5
5. Russia	35.8	49.0	58.2	65.1	71.9	76.4
6. Brazil	27.1	38.8	48.6	58.5	66.6	71.9
7. Indonesia	27.4	38.3	52.2	69.4	86.6	103.0
8. Germany	29.6	36.4	44.5	50.8	56.1	59.2
9. UK	33.2	36.4	39.4	42.4	44.9	46.4
10. South Korea	29.3	32.8	33.9	34.5	35.1	35.6
11. Mexico	22.9	28.7	34.2	39.4	44.7	49.9
12. France	21.0	26.7	32.9	37.8	41.5	43.7
13. Italy	19.5	24.1	28.6	32.2	33.7	37.0
14. Turkey	15.3	22.6	27.8	32.4	37.2	40.7
15. Spain	18.9	22.0	25.0	26.9	28.4	29.5
16. Philippines	14.8	20.0	24.8	29.7	34.8	39.4
17. Nigeria	15.9	19.5	23.1	26.8	30.5	34.0
18. Canada	15.2	17.8	20.0	21.7	23.0	23.9
19. Thailand	14.4	17.5	20.4	22.8	25.0	26.8
20. Vietnam	12.4	16.6	20.7	24.6	28.6	32.0
21. Egypt	12.6	15.5	18.2	21.0	23.6	25.8
22. Colombia	11.7	14.4	16.3	18.2	19.7	20.9
23. Australia	11.4	13.2	13.8	14.3	14.7	15.1
24. Poland	9.4	12.7	15.4	17.4	19.4	20.8
25. Argentina	8.8	10.8	12.6	14.1	15.6	17.0
Worldwide	**1311.2**	**1639.0**	**1914.6**	**2155.0**	**2380.2**	**2561.8**

Source: eMarketer, Dec 2014

Note: Individuals of any age who own at least one smartphone and use it/them at least once per month; [a]excludes Hong Kong; [b]forecast from Aug 2014

What books were to the previous generation, social media is to the next: a stepping-stone towards reform. They are already here. They are tech-savvy and resourceful and will build on what we leave them with, just as we did. The two-year-old at your feet, who already knows how to operate a smartphone and will be fluent in a language foreign to us, may possibly know a world where the flow of information is practical in ways we cannot yet imagine, available to those that it does not yet reach and, above all, free.

The Arab Spring—Disruption or Development in Egypt?

Starting Point of Old Power In Egypt the 1971 Constitution set the presidential term of office at six years and, as originally drafted, allowed the President to be re-elected once for a total of two terms of office (article 77). In 1980, this article was amended to remove the term limit, allowing presidents to serve an unlimited number of successive terms. Following Anwar Sadat's assassination in 1981, Hosni Mubarak stepped from the vice-presidency to the presidency and immediately introduced a state of emergency under article 148 of the 1971 Constitution (amended in 2007). Mubarak was serving his fifth successive term when he was ousted in 2011.

There has not been a vice-president since Mubarak took office in 1981, but as we know, Mubarak as a last hope appointed his intelligence chief and confidant, Omar Suleiman, as a vice-president in 2011. The past few years have seen more presidents, Mohammed Morsi and Abdul Fattaf al-Sisi, and further constitutional reforms.

The Arab Spring The events occurred so quickly that it is difficult for an outside observer to compile a solid picture from conflicting news reports. We begin with an overview of the chain of events, based on internet material.[8] Next, some hands-on observations are presented (based on Pekka Hallberg's visit from 28 November to 4 December 2014) about the development of freedom of speech today.

- The revolutionary wave starts to spread to Egypt in mid-January 2011.
- 25 January: protesters call for resignation of Hosni Mubarak. The government blocks Twitter and shuts down mobile and internet networks. Cairo turns into a war zone. Hundreds are arrested including foreign journalists. An anonymous group of hackers threatens cyber-attacks if the Egyptian government fails to stop censoring media.
- 28 January: President Mubarak makes his first TV appearance after four days of protests, refusing to step down. The West toughens stance against Mubarak. Tens of thousands of people take part in protests in Cairo, Suez, Alexandria and other cities.

- Saudi Arabian reaction: King Abdullah backs Mubarak according to the official Saudi Press Agency and Saudi Arabia stands with the government of Egypt and its people.
- Reaction from the United States: US senator John Kerry says Mubarak's dismissal of his government failed to address the Egyptian people's concerns and called on the President to go further to deal with their frustrations. The *Washington Post* calls on Obama to break ties with Mubarak.
- The events rumble on: 29 January, Ahmed Shafiq, the former air force commander and civil aviation minister, is appointed prime minister.
- 30 January: Mohamed El Baradei, a well-known dissident and a critic of the Egyptian government, calls for the President to step down.
- 31 January: Egypt's army makes its first explicit statement in favour of the protesters, assuring them they would not use force against them.
- 1 February: Mubarak pledges to step down at the next election. Tony Blair warns against rushed elections that could bring the Muslim Brotherhood to power.
- 4 February: Cairo's biggest demonstration yet with hundreds of thousands of people demands Mubarak's immediate departure.
- 10 February: President Mubarak appears on state television to say he is handing over powers to his vice-president, but will remain president. The following day Vice-President Omar Suleiman makes an announcement about Mr Mubarak stepping down and the military's supreme council running the country.[9]
- Follow-up events take a new turn: By 24 May 2011, judicial officials announce that Mr. Mubarak, along with his two sons—Alaa and Gamal—are to stand trial over the deaths of anti-government protesters.
- 2 June 2012: Mubarak is found guilty of complicity in the murder of some of the demonstrators who took part in the wave of protests that began on 25 January 2011.
- January 2013: Egypt's Court of Cassation allows an appeal against Mr Mubarak's and Mr al-Adly's convictions and orders a retrial. Mr Mubarak and his sons are due to be retried on corruption charges.

- May 2013: The new trial over the killings starts but is adjourned several times because of the political violence that sweeps the country following the military's removal of Islamist leader Mohammed Morsi on 3 July.
- 19 August: Mr Mubarak is acquitted of one corruption charge related to embezzlement of public funds. Two days later, a Cairo court orders his release from prison and Egypt's prime minister is placed under house arrest.

Winds of Change In the midst of these events, a national referendum on constitutional reform was arranged; the parliament, the legislative chambers, as well as the new President were all elected. Turnout in the election was quite low. The following compilation of the votes indicates the direction of democratic development:

- First vote: Constitutional referendum of March 2011. The Brotherhood campaigned for amendment rather than abolition, an argument which won with 77 per cent of votes as opposed to 23 per cent against. Turnout was 41 per cent of the electorate.
- Second vote: Elections to People's Assembly, November 2011– January 2012. The Brotherhood's FJP was one of dozens of competing parties. It won 43 per cent of the seats in the People's Assembly, the lower house of parliament, with 37.5 per cent of the votes cast, and turnout was 52 per cent of the electorate.
- Third vote: Elections to Shura Council, January–February 2012. Again, the FJP is the single best performing party, winning 58 per cent of the contested seats from 45 per cent of the cast votes. Turnout was a meagre 10 per cent of registered voters.
- Fourth vote: Presidential election, June 2012. Mohammed Morsi, representing the FJP and Muslim Brotherhood, won less than a quarter of the votes in the first round. Yet in the second round he achieved the group's best ever electoral performance—51.7 per cent of the vote from a turnout of 52 per cent.
- Fifth vote: Constitutional referendum of December 2012. This referendum was far more controversial than the first, and far more a vote on the Brotherhood's popularity. Several liberal and Christian groups had withdrawn from the assembly tasked with writing Egypt's new constitution, complaining that Islamists were dominating the process.

The document was put to a public vote, and the opposition called on their supporters to boycott the referendum. The Brotherhood, and other Islamist groups, urged their supporters to vote. The constitution was approved, 64 per cent in favour and 35 per cent against, but the turnout was only 33 per cent of the electorate.

Significant public opposition to President Morsi and the Ikhwan began building in November 2012. Wishing to ensure that the constituent assembly could finish drafting the new constitution, President Morsi issued an interim constitutional declaration granting him far-reaching powers. As opposition mounted, Morsi issued a decree authorising the armed forces to protect national institutions and polling stations until a referendum on the draft constitution was held in December 2012, which critics said amounted to a form of martial law.

Eventually, the Military Assumed Power The army returned to their barracks after the charter was approved. At the end of January 2013, the military warned that the political crisis might lead to a collapse of the state. When President Mohammed Morsi was ousted by the military, senior leaders and thousands of members of his organisation were detained, and the Muslim Brotherhood's headquarters was ransacked and burned.

The unrest and rising death toll prompted the military to warn Mr Morsi on 1 July that it would intervene and impose its own "roadmap" if he did not satisfy the public's demands within 48 hours and end the political crisis. On 3 July, the military deployed troops and armoured vehicles in the streets. It declared that the constitution had been suspended and that the chief justice of the SCC would assume presidential powers, overthrowing Mr Morsi.

After weeks of deadlock, hopes rose that the protests would remain peaceful. However, on 14 August security forces swept into the camps and the authorities imposed a state of national emergency.[10]

Abdul Fattah al-Sisi was elected as president on May 2014, almost a year after he removed his predecessor from office. On 27 October 2014 the BBC reported that al-Sisi had authorised the military to protect state facilities after jihadists killed more than 30 soldiers the week before.

Sisi had already cracked down on the Muslim Brotherhood. Thousands of its members were detained, many being sentenced to death in mass trials that have drawn criticism from Western governments and rights groups. Parliamentary elections are the final step in the roadmap set out by Sisi after ousting Morsi, but without a date set they could miss the plan's self-imposed deadline. They were due to take place within six months of the presidential vote in May. Egypt's military, which has long played a key role in the economy, is taking a leading role in a multi-billion dollar project to expand the Suez Canal.

The 2012 Egyptian Constitution, which limited the President's power and strengthened parliamentarianism, was suspended on 8 July 2013.. The experienced former diplomat and foreign minister, Amr Moussa, was appointed to lead reform. A ten-member technical committee proposed changes to the 2012 Constitution, which were published on 20 August 2013. On 1 September 2013 a presidential decree called for the establishment of a 50-member committee to prepare a complete draft constitution. The proposed new constitution was the subject of a national referendum 14–15 January 2014, when it was approved by 98.1 per cent of the votes, although turnout was relatively low at 38.6 per cent.

The 2014 Constitution is detailed and has been divided into six parts consisting of a total of 247 articles. The structure is descriptive: The Arab Republic of Egypt is a sovereign, united, indivisible State, where no part may be given up, having a democratic republican system that is based on citizenship and rule of law (article 1). The titles of the following chapters depict these starting points. Components of Society (Part II) are Social Components, Economic Components and Cultural Components. Presenting the components in a comprehensive manner (Articles 7–50) in the Constitution creates a great challenge in implementing them in practice so that the Constitution preserves its nature as a realistic fundamental norm.

The principles of Public Rights, Freedoms and Duties (Part III) and Rule of Law (Part IV) are especially significant, and have been thus been placed in the very beginning of the Constitution. Although constitutional rights are set out in detail, there are options when it comes to general legislation and the Supreme Constitutional Court has to interpret legislative provisions (Art. 192). How binding are the constitutional rights in practice and how can the contradictions concerning fundamental rights be solved?

We may predict that the new unicameral parliament, the legislature, will have a stronger status than before. Similarly, the government as the supreme executive and administrative body will probably play a more significant role in the future, and the judiciary will be more independent than in the past. The Supreme Constitutional Court holds a key position in many ways, and it has a great responsibility when it comes to rule-of-law development. Additionally, the State Council plays an important role in questions of public power and access to justice, and its operation also encompasses a consultative role rather like that of the Conseil d'Etat in France. Pekka Hallberg commented that the President of the Supreme Constitutional Court and former interim President of Egypt, Counsellor Adly Mansour, displayed some optimism in conversations on 3rd December 2014.The Constitution of 2014 has meant further steps on the path to parliamentary reform, at least in principle, but implementation will come up against many hurdles. Disbelief still occasionally bursts out as demonstrations that are then smothered by force. Tanks appear on the streets every now and then.

Latest Developments In 2013, Egypt (158th) rose eight places in the index, two years after Hosni Mubarak's departure. This was a slight improvement on 2011 when violence against media personnel caused the country to plummet 39 places from 127th. Journalists and netizens continued to be targets of physical attacks, arrests and trials. Shortly after winning the elections, the Muslim Brotherhood appointed new executives and editors to run the state newspapers, which had a major impact on their editorial policies. News media could still be closed or seized on the orders of a judge.

Is the situation now changing? The new Constitution of 2014 includes detailed regulations on freedom of speech (articles 64–72). It guarantees freedom of thought and opinion, scientific research, artistic and literary creativity and press, printing and paper, visual, audio and electronic publication. Similarly, according to the Constitution, information, data, statistics and official documents are the property of the people. Censorship of the press is also forbidden, and the state must ensure the independence of all state-owned press institutions and media outlets.

These regulations on freedom of speech awoke optimism towards freedom of speech development in Egypt; however, other hopes may also have faded. Realistically, the stabilisation process and change of judicial culture takes more time. It is a question of how the new principles are adopted and how the relevant sub-regulations and practices evolve.

Trouble on the Path to Freedom of Speech Even journalists who had done nothing more than report on the Brotherhood have ended up in jail, frequently without charge, or on trumped-up charges of "spreading false news".

The trial of three Al-Jazeera journalists accused of aiding terrorists, doctoring footage and endangering Egypt's national security began in Cairo on 23 June 2014. The court alleged they had ties with Islamists and said that "the devil guided" the group to spread false news defaming the country. Canadian-Egyptian bureau chief of Al-Jazeera English Mohamed Fahmy and local producer Baher Mohamed both faced fifteen years in jail if found guilty, while Australian ex-BBC reporter Peter Greste faced seven years. They had already been held in jail for nearly six months, after being arrested from their homes and hotel rooms in December 2013. After heavy pressure from the international community the military leadership had to agree to release them. Egypt's president Abdel Fatah al-Sisi acknowledged for the first time that the heavy sentences handed down to the three Al-Jazeera journalists had a "very negative" impact on his country's reputation, saying he wished they had never been put on trial (theguardian.com).

The aftershow continued with Egypt's Supreme Court overruling the decisions of the lower courts and ordering the case to be tried again on the last day of 2014. As the first outcome, Peter Greste has now been deported. The most recent news from September 2015 states they were all sentenced to three years in prison. The functional freedom of media is narrow and reporters are forced to tiptoe around events.

With the collapse of tourism and the deteriorating economic situation, problems were brewing although here was some hope that the situation would stabilise with the parliamentary election in 2015 even though the incompleteness of electoral legislation had caused problems in arranging the election. The new unicameral parliament is now in a key position when it comes to implementing the promises of the Constitution.

Challenges of Rule of Law in the Digital Era

We have already established that the safeguard of freedom of speech is a functioning rule of law, and that free speech in itself is a fundamental precondition for the development of a democratic rule of law. How does this correlation work at a time when WikiLeaks is challenging the Pentagon, when Facebook and Twitter can mobilise huge crowds instantly and when information operations and use of information technology are to the fore?

Is the situation still under control? Are the familiar principles of good governance and, if necessary, the search for justice through the courts enough to guarantee freedom of speech? Are new instruments needed?

What if limitations on freedom of speech are a follow-up to the continuing struggle for power, the aspiration of government powers to restrict the flow of information? Or are the powers of the market behind the manipulation of information? In these situations an individual citizen is quite powerless. Information that the US and British intelligence services had stolen "keys" from the biggest manufacturer of sim cards, Gemalto, was a shocking example of our digital era. At worst, this may have led to around 450 big operators and 1.5 billion people's mobile phones coming under official surveillance.

This is just a part of the new threats to freedom of speech. Our modern high-tech society is vulnerable in other ways as well, for example through malfunctions and risks of accidents concerning data traffic, urban technologies and food supply. Even though major strategic decisions are based on modern risk analysis, preparing for violations and malfunctions is difficult. Therefore we should be asking "how" rather than "what" to prepare for. Can a citizen in any way prepare for these types of threat, when the government crosses the line? These questions also concern rule-of-law development.

In order to preserve societal trust, the rules of the game must be followed. Democracy and freedom of speech are to be respected. To grow the capital of trust, normal relations of authority must be adhered to. Exceptional circumstances only apply when the situation cannot be controlled by normal authority. Access to accurate information and credible assessment of the situation create preconditions for controlling it and making decisions, which will involve officials from all levels including the highest authority.

How adequate are these principles as guarantee in the digitalised society of the modern era? The world of the internet is filled with new solutions and possibilities for innovation. It opens up enormous possibilities for a skilled person, as we pointed out at the beginning, like a "customer at a bazaar". The unlimited web makes it possible to create an unprecedented network of contacts that can mobilise people, just as we saw during the Arab Spring. Here we stand at the new crossroads of freedom of speech and access to justice.

As we observe freedom of speech and access to information as the constitutional right of an individual over the course of several years, the centre of gravity of course comes down to questions of freedom of information, accessibility of public documents and access to justice guaranteed by independent courts. Will this change when it comes to the functioning of internet connections, protection of e-mails or limitations concerning data traffic technology? Jack M. Balkin reflects on these questions in his article.[11]

In the modern digital world, freedom of speech is not only about individual rights to express oneself or access information; the question is, more widely, about the state of society as a whole, communication technology and people's ability to use it. The status of an individual in society and their relation to public power appears in an altogether new light. A passive role for public administration is not enough. Service should be active in the sense of ensuring information is even-handedly available, as well as opportunities for participation. We may describe the new service principle as a leap from strategy for publicity into strategy of information.

In the public sector, therefore, good governance and accountability play key roles. In international contexts, there are two competing approaches to good governance. First, there is a tradition of democratic governance, according to which good governance is mainly defined as being a method of governance that serves democracy and equality. The other approach has been to characterise good governance as meaning efficient governance, in which governance is interpreted more narrowly on the basis of neo-liberal economic policy, as principles underlining the productivity and efficiency of public administration. The democratic governance tradition attempts to give politics a central role. The question is about participatory governance, which it is easier for the people to commit to.

One important recommendation concerns the improvement of administrative structures. Above all, the law on disputes with the authorities, how to take legal action, how hearings are organised and reasoned decisions made, and how to proceed if the decision is not satisfactory, should be clearly established in law. Behind these laws on general administrative procedure, the general principles of administrative justice are often to be found, such as:

- equality, hence the authority has the duty to treat every customer of the administration in an equal manner;
- purposefulness, hence the duty to exercise the power of the authority solely for the justified purposes;

- objectivity, according to which the actions of the authorities must be impartial;
- relativity, according to which the actions of the authority must be in correct proportion to the identified goal;
- protection of trust, according to which the actions of the authority must be legitimate and protect expectations based on the legal order. Achieving a general administrative law and at the same time emphasising the service principle and the administrative authorities´ duty of guidance is an important goal. This new information strategy is the driving force of the four-cornered structure that symbolises rule-of-law development. A fourfold analysis identifies the building blocks of a democratic and free society: (1) preconditions for common rules of the game, uncomplicated legislation and better legislative policy; (2) relationships of government bodies and the balance of power as well as the independence of the courts; (3) status of the people and their opportunities to participate, as well as respect for their rights and obligations; and (4) the functionality of the system on an everyday basis, people's access to power, hearing and participation.

The conditions and limitations of freedom of speech must be observed as part of rule-of-law development, otherwise we drift into a narrow account that will list the problems but fail to show how to solve them. Caring about one another and the reality of doing so are an integral part of societal ideals. If the reality of everyday life disappears and the functionality of the system becomes the most important thing, the people who the system is created for can easily fade into the background. In a state that abides by the principles of the rule of law the pursuit of balance, justice and fairness is expected from those in power. Once again it is appropriate here to bear in mind that the role of an independent judiciary is to adhere to the values confirmed by legislation and the principles of a participatory government system.

This brings to mind John Rawls and his theory of justice (*A Theory of Justice* 1971). The message of the book, a critique of mediocrity and plea to improve the status of the unfortunate, ignites resistance to the increase in general negligence. The human rights champion Martin Luther King appropriately stated that society's "ultimate tragedy is not the oppression and cruelty by the bad people but the silence over that by the good people". He himself, however, died at the hands of bad people in 1968.

The Role of Media in a Radically Changing Environment

Without going into the background, we can conclude that in many countries class divisions have been broken down, the number of interest groups has increased, and faith in politicians and achieving change through the electoral system has faded. Common guidelines are as difficult to politicise as before, as people are now making more and more choices individually. There are other directions for development towards an ever more compartmentalised society and a shattered image of development.

The trend is clear: writer and reporter Fareed Zakaria described the new democracy movements as allowing easily marginalised groups to take advantage of the passiveness of the majority (see *The Future of Freedom* 2003). Blogs and Facebook have also gained ground; the market is the competitor of the political arena. In general we are witnessing weakening democratic decision making and the emergence of the cult of personality. Is the big picture of building a society fading out into "short tales" – entertainment offered by professional actors? What are the real interests behind the scenes that also affect the preconditions of freedom of speech?

When the Gatekeeper Became Obsolete According to the US Center for Democracy and Governance, the media serves two primary functions. First, the media has an "informing function". It is responsible for the spread of information and enables citizens to make informed decisions. Secondly, the media performs a 'checking function' by ensuring that elected representatives uphold their oaths of office and carry out the wishes of those who elected them.

> For the newspaper is in all literalness the bible of democracy, the book out of which a people determines its conduct. It is the only serious book most people read. It is the only book they read every day. Now the power to determine each day what shall seem important and what shall be neglected is a power unlike any that has been exercised since the Pope lost hold on the secular mind. (Walter Lippmann 1920)

John Keane refers to Thomas Jefferson's quote (1787), in *The Media and Democracy* (1991): "Were it left to me to decide whether we should have a government without newspaper, or newspaper without a government, I should not hesitate a moment to prefer the latter." According to Thomas

Jefferson's quote, the media or the 'Fourth Estate' is an important component to building a state's democracy.

> The power struggle that occurs between the press and governing institutions comes into particularly sharp relief over the issue of access to documents generated by governmental decision-making—the so-called 'freedom of information' issue. Community concern about governmental secrecy has led to freedom of information legislation being passed in a number of liberal democracies. (Economou & Tanner 2008)

The previous quotes tell us about the world gone by where newspapers, radio and television defined publicity, and reporters were in the position of the doorman. In the editorial offices it was possible to decide what the viewers, listeners and readers should know about the surrounding world.

It has often been wondered how newspapers survived first the invention of the radio, and after that the television, and managed to retain their position as a central and popular creator of content and communicator of news. Newspapers were for a long time a part of people's everyday life and celebration; to some extent they are still just that.

The answer about survival is quite simple: as tools of media all three—the newspaper, radio and television—are similar because they are based on one-way communication. The editorial offices tell their own viewers, listeners and readers what is important in the world. The media had an important role as the doorman and watchdog associated with democracy.

However, the world started to radically change in the 1990s with the internet and growing digitalisation. Reporters lost their monopoly as producers of information. Everyone had the possibility to produce content into the limitless internet; and this is exactly what happened. Along with social media a whole new multi-channelled reality was born. A piece of news information could first spread on social media and only after that end up in the traditional media.

Alan Rushbridger, the chief editor of the *Guardian* newspaper, stated that the future of every newspaper is digital as early as the previous decade. He was right, although for many it took too long to understand that in the future of information service the digital side holds key position. A modern media house does everything through all channels. The multi-channel way is already the world of today, and even more so of the future.

Traditional commercial media is going through a big change. Only national broadcasting companies seem to be safe—for now—but they too have their own challenges as the behaviour of consumers change. People's way of watching television, for example, is no longer tied to schedules. Television is watched when it suits everyone best. Programmes are also watched on smartphones and tablets.

The core of the great change is that the printed newspaper is doomed to decreasing sales numbers while, along with new digital technology, advertisement is also going through a radical change. We are still far from the time where income from digital advertisement could replace the loss suffered by printed newspapers from traditional advertising. The most cost-effective part—in other words, classified advertising—has already taken a digital form. This has happened because the digital form is much handier for the user than the old model.

The decreasing sales and advertisement incomes have led to a weakening in profits, and the need to pick up the pace has naturally followed. Staffing has been cut in editorial offices all over the Western world. In the United States alone thousands of jobs from different offices have been lost. The editorial offices are smaller than before, while advertisement offices and other lobbyist organisations grow. The editorial offices face more and more pressure from outside as well as from the publisher. "Do more but do better" is the guideline in many media houses today. Social media has a controlling influence over media reporters, which is both a good and a bad thing.

Journalism is still able to fulfil its function, which has remained unchanged throughout the past few decades. The reporters' duty is to tell of the kind of world people live in, and what is important and relevant in that world. It is the constitutional right of a citizen of a democratic country to be informed. It is also important for reporters to fulfill their role as a watchdog in the new media circumstances. It is the reporter's duty to make sure that societies remain open and that decision makers publicly answer for the policies they practise. Publicity must also go beyond politics into the trade and industry sector.

Journalism is not in crisis today, but the business model of media has drifted into one, requiring new methods and innovations to improve the quality of media content. Much commercial media sits today on a quivering swamp, not knowing whether or not they will again find solid ground under their feet.

However, as the dark clouds of the economy gather around media houses, it must be pointed out that new technology also helps and makes it easier for them to survive. Along with these developments, new better ways and possibilities of reporting events make an account of the world and its complicated causal connections available to everyone. Media has ever better content. Editorial offices have better maps, and data journalism gives access to information that was impossible to transmit to audiences before. It is possible to create good journalism even with a depleted staff.

The traditional duties of journalism have not gone anywhere, even though technological development has changed the picture. Reporters must still know how to tell stories in the new circumstances. They must be able to keep watch on the government and institutions that try to elude publicity, to bring defects out into the daylight and give voice to the marginalised and oppressed. One lasting duty of journalists is to build a better world for people to live in.

As the world grows more complicated, people's urge to know is not disappearing. There is room and a real demand for journalism. When it comes to international quality journalism, cynicism is replaced by realism, scale and hierarchy. When it comes down to good journalism, societal meaning directs journalistic choices. Good journalism is the perquisite of a democratic society, completely regardless of the medium used to present it.

From the democratic point of view the weakening of the media sector is concerning. Media is just as dependent on democracy and rule of law as they in turn depend on reliable and quality media. What is to become of society if there is no quality media?

Social media has already showed its power during many conflicts. Through social media the oppressed may keep in touch with each other without the secret police tracing them. Social media is also a way to market good media substance for everyone's use. When considered from this perspective, social media is a part of today's freedom of speech, even where speech is not otherwise free.

Of course there is also another side to social media. It is a forum to practise hate speech, insults, spread inaccurate information and made up rumours. Trolling is ever more common. Cyber war is also a part of today's world.

No-one can claim that people do not have the opportunity to be better informed today than they ever had before. There is so much information in this world if one knows how to access it, and that is just a matter of skill. A basic condition for successful quality journalism is, however, that even in the digital world means will be found to finance the making of quality journalism. Quality still costs, regardless of the digital change.

Notes

1. See http://www.tor.com/2013/01/25/exploring-carl-sagans-cosmos-episode-11-qthe-persistence-of-memoryq/, accessed 5 September 2016.
2. TED organization at http://www.ted.com/talks/david_christian_big_history?source=faceb ook#t-911375, last accessed 27 May 2016.
3. The *Huffington Post* at http://www.huffingtonpost.com/2011/02/11/egypt-facebook-revolution-wael-ghonim_n_822078.html, last accessed June 2015.
4. See more at ReadWrite homepage: http://readwrite.com/2013/05/17/smartphones-have-bridged-the-digital-divide, last accessed 27 May 2016.
5. See more at E Marketer homepage at: http://www.emarketer.com/Article/2-Billion-Consumers-Worldwide-Smartphones-by-2016/1011694#sthash.68etydhF.dpuf, last accessed June 2015.
6. E Marketer: http://www.emarketer.com/Article/2-Billion-Consumers-Worldwide-Smartphones-by-2016/1011694#sthash.68etydhF.dpuf, last accessed June 2015.
7. The ReadWrite homepage at http://readwrite.com/2013/05/17/smartphones-have-bridged-the-digital-divide, last accessed June 2015.
8. See http://www.theguardian.com/world/2011/jan/18/mohamed-elbaradei-tunisia-egypt.
9. http://www.bbc.com/news/world-middle-east-12301713
10. See http://www.bbc.com/news/world-middle-east-12313405, accessed 8 September 2016.
11. See Jack M. Balkin (2005), "Protecting freedom of speech in the digital age means promoting a core set of values in legislation, administrative regulation, and the design of technology. What are those values? They are interactivity, broad popular participation, equality of access to information and communications technology, promotion of democratic control in technological design, and the practical ability of ordinary people to route around, glom on, and transform. Free speech values include those aspects of liberty of expression that the digital age makes most salient: popular participation, interactivity, and the encouragement and protection of cultural creativity and cultural transformation".

CHAPTER 9

Final Chords

ON A PATH TOWARDS FREEDOM OR RESTRICTIONS?

The Play of Light and Shadow The path of freedom of speech from the ancient to the modern information society was lit in the beginning by the torches of the right to speak; then, after the birth of the free press, the burning piles of books; with the modern age came the enormous possibilities of free information and its control in the digital world. The traveller on the path sees a ceaseless contest between light and shadow and may observe the reality of societal development in some perplexity.

One of the best-known philosophers of liberalism as well as freedom of speech, John Stuart Mill, pondered that the essence of freedom should not be merely freedom from but it must also be freedom to (*On Liberty*, 1859). Free speech has over the centuries struggled to be freed from the shackles of censorship in order to achieve the fundamental right for everyone to express and participate in the decision-making process when it comes to matters that affect us all. The goal of participation has also been to enhance democracy, which in turn has provoked the old rulers to counterstrike to defend their positions.

The environment of free speech is constantly changing. In the digitalised world, new types of problem await. It is essential for an individual to know how to access information and participate in determining the common rules of the power game, to know where they stand, their rights and obligations, and to be able to trust the operation of society's institutions. The question of free speech is also closely associated with the rule of law and its development.

The flow of information, especially in the media, must constantly struggle in a new type of environment in the modern digital age. The power of the mass media is often characterised by its ability to influence the audience's opinions, attitudes and, in the end, behaviour. On the other hand, the power of the media may turn out to be somewhat illusory. Communication consists of so many layers: reporting and commenting on events, as well as tying them into a context; the construction of values; and taking a stand on the state of affairs. Journalism is also tied to values because of the human factor, and requires an ever more comprehensive grasp of affairs. The essential element is the information, whether accurate or inaccurate, that is accessible at any given time. The question of influence is directed back to the receivers of information and to their behaviour.

In this way communication is beginning to look more and more like competition in the information market. The possibilities for both freedom and surveillance, brought about by new technology, also raise questions not only about the infrastructure of communication, but also about the spirit of the age in society as a whole.[1]

Different Development Trends There are significant differences when it comes to the practical fulfilment of the right to free speech. The communications environment and its associated market have been restricted in many different ways. Different indicators have been created to measure development trends. Ranking matters of social development is difficult. The assessments we have, however, point in the direction of ever-tightening restrictions of free speech in many countries in recent years. Therefore, "freedom from something" is once again relevant—this time from the tightening shackles around free speech.

Power struggles are frequently the underlying reason for free speech violations, threats and restraints. A well-known Finnish diplomat, Max Jakobson—originally a journalist—stated in his book *Vallanvaihto* [*Changeover of power*] (1992) that "history offers an abundance of examples of how cynical political leaders are mistaken in their calculations when evaluating the power which faith, principle and sentiment give to a people". Revolutions like the Arab Spring and gatherings of people in market squares, objecting to the shackles of power, always seem to come as a surprise.

On the international great-powers stage, as well as in the war against terrorism, the principles of international law are often subverted when it comes to the information war, the surveillance of information flow and espionage systems. These dark clouds should be carefully monitored.

Globalisation has also brought increasing economic implications. We can see the relevant historical image in the words of Juvenalis, who as long ago as ancient Rome reflected on how "everyone wants to know and yet no one is ready to pay the bill" (see comments about the satires of Decimus Junius Juvenalis in Chap. 7). The comparisons with the internet are not far-fetched.

Communication has become a large-scale business, reflected in the concentration of media ownership. A dominant position curbs competition. The building of a favourable public image has become an essential part of politics as well as business in the global market. Public as well as private actors have an ever-growing number of media outlets providing their own information that serves their own purposes. This can be seen in the increasing difficulty of differentiating between right and wrong information.

"If only one-sided arguments see the light of day, then the high-level associates in these cases will get to remain in the shadows,"[2] stated Anders Chydenius, arguing for freedom of the press in the Nordic countries at a parliamentary session in 1766. In those days criticism of the political system was rare. Where do we stand nowadays? Are one-sided arguments on the frontlines again? Now is the time to outline the "big picture", the vision of the future!

For Freedom of Speech!

Taking Freedom of Speech onto the International Agenda It is time for the world to wake up and defend free speech; otherwise we will live as if in a state of "intellectual climate change". The essence of the Paris Declaration, signed at the UNESCO World Press Freedom Day International Conference 2014, is that freedom of expression across all media platforms is an enabler of human development, including a culture of peace.

It is often forgotten that freedom of speech is the right of only a small minority of the world's population. Of the 7.2 billion people in the world, less than a billion live in societies where the right to free speech is, at least to some extent, a reality. Things should now be shaken up everywhere.

It is important to place freedom of speech more firmly on the international agenda. The UN General Assembly decided in 1993 that International Press Freedom Day should be celebrated annually on 3 May. This is not just a matter of principle: the idea somehow needs to be put into action. The promotion of free speech and transparent governance are the basis of welfare and economic growth, as well as sustainable development more generally. Public long-term interests as well as private-sector economic interests are therefore combined in this context to promote social welfare and the optimal use of resources.

Sustainable Development The 2013 report by the World Bank and the OECD on integrating human rights with economic development also indicates the significance of freedom of speech as a component of sustainable economic development. The general conclusion of this report, which was compiled under the leadership of Ireland's former president Mary Robinson, was that since 2005 the added value of human rights has been taken into account in the economic projects of the World Bank and other actors.

The obligations necessitated by human rights have also been acknowledged in the Charter of the European Investment Bank and the activities of the European Central Bank. Similarly, the UN's development arm, the UNDP, has sought to establish good practice for human rights obligations, and the UN Millenium Report has also been renewed on this basis. Now it represents a programme for the future with a human face—real rule-of-law development.

It is now high time to shift our focus onto freedom of speech as a universal objective. In 2016, 250 years had passed since the world's first free press act was adopted in the Nordic region. UNESCO is to arrange a world conference on free speech which will provide both a historical perspective and an opportunity to focus on the essential relevance of freedom of speech in the modern world. Hopefully it will also be a step that brings freedom of speech as a universal value in a wider sense into the operations of the UN and its specialised agencies.

Images and Imaginings

Where Are We Going? What is the future for freedom of speech? How can the balance between freedom, responsibility and surveillance be found in our constantly changing environment? Can we outline options for development in the information flood of the modern era?

The ancients will help us here. In his posthumous book *Laws* (published around 350 CE), Plato offers a model of an ideal state in a story about the conversation of the three wise men as they are walking on the hillsides of Mount Ida. One of them is Plato and the other two are Klenias of Crete and Megillos of Sparta.

An Ideal The three go about pondering on the best state and society in the following manner: "When laws are made for the common welfare of the people should be persuaded to observe them voluntarily and consciously even when the hopes and benefits of one might conflict with them. Therefore ethical grounds must be presented as introductions to each law (…) In a society, consensus, friendship and trust as wide as possible must be attained between different interest groups (…) Citizen must, with education and constant argumentation be convinced about the necessity of institutions of a well-established society, and relevance of its laws. Citizens must not be forced or betrayed; they must be made to understand what is truly in their interest."[3]

This is one of the first published stories about the meaning of trust and social capital. The wisdom of the story is simple as well: citizens do understand the importance of law and institutions if it is carefully explained. The question is how to do it.

This historical story teaches us that social trust—social capital—is essential. This, however, cannot be commanded to grow. A society based on trust can only be built by citizens themselves. Social capital means community and the building and strengthening of a common value base. The justification, the legitimacy of public power, participatory and just governance and the experience of a common idea of justice can only be based on this type of foundation. One of the most important support structures of this interaction is freedom of speech.

Gloomy Option What would, then, the opposite image of the future look like; an image of a closed society? At the beginning and along the journey we have been contemplating the nature of the Big Brother described by Orwell in his book *Nineteen Eighty-Four* (1949). Is this Big Brother already in our midst without us even realising it? Does this Big Brother limit our freedom of speech, already shackled and violated in so many ways today?

The interests of centralised power and the power of money do not align with those of freedom of speech. The book bonfires of the Church and the many struggles of the Enlightenment period all affirm this statement. Changes in the external environment have complicated the traditional setting. Censorship and internet restrictions can no longer stop the flow of information.

The new society is an information society whose foundations are being continuously moulded by digital development. Information is easier to access but surveillance mechanisms are ever more efficient. The old wisdom *epistula enim non erubescit*—"a letter does not blush"—is no longer valid. Before, it was possible to express things privately in a letter that one could not otherwise express freely. This protection does not work in the changed environment of the digital era. We had lost an element of our privacy long before we realised it.

Predictions about technological development talk about the separation of people into three groups: the developers, the adopters and the marginalised. Refraining from the use of technology means giving up the chance to impact on the development of affairs, turning one's back on the future. Conscious withdrawal will not solve any problems.

Counteraction Will the "big picture" for the development of free speech be found in the interests of power and money, or does the solution lie elsewhere after all, possibly within us? Is there hope? We live somewhere in between two worlds. On the one side is democracy, the rule of law and freedom of speech, and on the other the virtual world where rules are vague. The atmosphere of freedom can be preserved even as technology advances if people keep up with and retain control of the new technology and take part in world affairs.

Is there still time to fight for free speech and against unfounded restrictions uncharacteristic of a democratic society? We have to try, as the French sociologist Pierre Bourdieu describes in *Counterfire* (1998), to combine technological development and humanity—to preserve the ideal of a free society in the digitalised world. We ought to strive for genuine understanding and unity, mutual trust and a balance between freedom and responsibility in order to promote sustainable development locally and globally.

NOTES

1. In the digital age, the technological and regulatory infrastructure that undergirds the system of free expression has become increasingly important. If we place too much emphasis on judicial doctrine at the expense of infrastructure, we will be left with formal guarantees of speech embedded in technologies of control that frustrate their practical exercise. (See the infrastructure of free expression written by Jack M. Balkin: From free speech rights to free speech values.)
2. See electronic book on the homepages of the Anders Chydenius Foundation: http://www.chydenius.net/pdf/words_first_fola.pdf, accessed 5 September 2016.
3. See *Laws*, first book, translated into Finnish 1999, Otava (pp. 7– and 385–).

Rule of Law Finland—Rolfi

Bibliography

In this book information compiled from the internet has been used to describe the development of freedom of speech, principles of democracy and the rule of law, constitutions and freedom of speech Acts from different countries and the application of international human rights treaties, as well as conversations on restrictions and violations of freedom of speech. The internet references have been placed within the relevant paragraphs in order to indicate the precise sources of information and enable the reader more easily to access additional information.

In the following bibliography there is a list of books used for background research for the writing of this book. To avoid bulky presentation, detailed footnotes have been avoided and the text includes only essential references.

Aman, A. C. (1998). The globalizing state: A future-oriented perspective on the public/private distinction, federalism, and democracy. *Vanderbilt Journal of Transnational Law, 31*(3), 769–870.

Aman, A. C. (2002). Globalization, democracy, and the need for a new administrative law. *UCLA Law Review, 49*, 1687–1716.

African Media Barometer (AMB) 2013. Media Institute of Southern Africa (MISA). Friedrich-Ebert-Stiftung (FES) fesmedia Africa Windhoek, Namibia.

Amnesty International. (2002). 2003 UN commission on human rights: A time for deep reflection, 1.12.2002. IOR 41/025/2002.

Annan, Kofi A. and United Nations. (2000). *'We the peoples': The role of the United Nations in the 21st century*. New York: United Nations, Department of Public Information.

Armstrong, D. (1999). Law, justice and the idea of a world society. *International affairs, 75*(3), 547–561.

Bacon, F. De Hesibus (c. 1626).

Balkin, J. (2005). *Digital speech and democratic culture in information ethics: Privacy, property, and power.* A. D. Moore (Ed.). University of Washington Press, p. 339.

Balkin, J. M. (2004a): *How rights change: Freedom of speech in the digital Era*, 26 Sydney Law Rev. 5.

Balkin, J. M. (2004b). *Commentary: Digital speech and democratic culture: A theory of freedom of expression for the information society.* Chapter IX: The infrastructure of free expression: From free speech rights to free speech values. New York University Law Review.

Barro, R. J. (1997). *Determinants of economic growth: A cross-country empirical study.* Cambridge, MA: The MIT Press, cop.

Barro, R. J. (2002). *Nothing is sacred: Economic ideas for the new millennium.* Cambridge, MA: MIT Press.

Barro, R. J. (2013). Democracy, law and order, and economic growth. In T. Miller, K. R. Holmes, E. J. Feulner, A. B. Kim, B. Riley, & J. M. Roberts (Eds.), *Index of economic freedom* (Chapter 3). Washington, DC: The Heritage Foundation and Dow Jones & Company, Inc.

Barton, A. H. (1986). *Scandinavia in the revolutionary era – 1760–1815.* Minneapolis: University of Minnesota Press.

Baxi, U. (2001). Globalisation: Human rights amidst risk and regression. *IDS Bulletin, 32*(1), 94–102.

Beck, U. (2000). *What is globalization?* (trans: Camiller, P.). Cambridge: Polity Press.

Benvenisti, E. (1999). Exit and voice in the age of globalization. *Michigan Law Review, 98*, 167–213.

Bonner, D. (2002). Managing terrorism while respecting human rights? European aspects of the anti-terrorism crime and security act 2001. *European Public Law, 8*(4), 497–524.

Bourdieu, P. (1998). *Acts of resistance: Against the new myths of our time* (trans: Nice, R.). Cambridge: Polity Press.

Bouwen, P. (2002). Corporate lobbying in the European Union: The logic of access. *Journal of European Public Policy, 9*(3), 365–390.

Boyle, E. M., & Gerhart, G. (2002). *The Russian context: The culture behind the language.* Bloomington: Slavica.

Brennan, G. (2003). What's new in globalisation: The American military predominance? In *2nd annual meeting of the Tampere club*, 18–20 Aug 2003.

Bulmer, S. J. (1994). The governance of the European Union: A new institutionalist approach. *Journal of Public Policy, 13*(4), 351–380.

Caldeira, G. A., & Gibson, J. L. (1997). Democracy in the European Union: The court of justice and its constituents. *International Social Science Journal, 49*(2), 207–224.

Castells, M. (1996). *The rise of the network society. The information age* (Vol. 1). Cambridge, MA: Blackwell.

Cerny, P. G. (1995). Globalization and the changing logic of collective action. *International Organization, 49*(4), 595–625.

Cochran, M. (2002). A democratic critique of cosmopolitan democracy: Pragmatism from the bottom-up. *European Journal of International Relations, 8*(4), 517–548.

Coglianese, C., & Nicolaidis, K. (2001). Securing subsidiarity: The institutional design of federalism in the United States and Europe. In K. Nicolaidis & R. Howse (Eds.), *The federal vision: Legitimacy and levels of governance in the United States and the European Union*. Oxford: Oxford University Press.

Coliver, S. (2000). Rule of law is crucial ingredient in democracy. *Elections Today, 8*(4), 14–15.

Commission on Human Rights. (2001). *Economic, social and cultural rights. Globalization and its impact on the full enjoyment of human rights.* Progress report by Oloka-Onyango and Udagama. E/CN.4/Sub.2/2001/10.

Costa, J.-P. (2013). *La Cour européenne des droits de l'homme Des juges pour la liberté*. Paris: Dalloz.

Darian-Smith, E. (2000). Structural Inequalities in the Global Legal System (Review Essay). *Law and Society Review, 34*(3), 809–828.

de Senarclens, P. (2001). International organisations and the challenges of globalization. *International Social Science Journal, 170*, 509–522.

Deloitte. (2015, January). Facebook's global economic impact, a report for Facebook.

Diogenes, Laertius (VI). 2007. *Classical rhetorics and rhetorians. The lives and opinions of eminent philosophers* (Literally trans: Br. Yonge, C.D.). London: MDCCCLIII.

Donahue, J. D., & Pollack, M. A. (2001). Centralization and its discontents: The rhytms of federalism in the United States and the European Union. In K. Nicolaidis & R. Howse (Eds.), *The federal vision: Legitimacy and levels of governance in the United States and the European Union*. Oxford: Oxford University Press.

Du, G., & Song, G. (1995). Relating human rights to Chinese culture: The four paths of the confucian analects and the four principles of a new theory of benevolence. In M. C. David (Ed.), *Human rights and Chinese values. Legal, philosophical, and political perspectives* (pp. 35–56). Hong Kong: Oxford University Press.

Economou, N., & TannerMedia, S. J. (2008). *Media, power and politics in Australia*. Frenchs Forest: Pearson Education Australia.

Eide, A. (1998). The historical 'significance of the universal declaration. *International Social Science Journal, 50*(4), 475–497.

Eisenstadt, E. (1992). *Traditional patrimonialism and modern neopatrimonialim*. London: SAGE Publications.

Elazar, D. J. (1995). From statism to federalism: A paradigm shift. *Publius: The Journal of Federalism, 25*(2), 5–18.

Elazar, D. J. (2001). Religious diversity and federalism. *International Social Science Journal, 53*(1), 61–65.
Ellis, J. J. (2000). *Founding brothers: The revolutionary generation.* New York: Alfred A. Knopf.
Evans, A. (2003). Regional dimensions to European governance. *International and Comparative Law Quarterly, 52,* 21–51.
Farber, D. A., & Frickey, P. P. (1991). *Law and public choice: A critical introduction.* Chicago: The University of Chicago Press.
Felice, W. F. (1999). The viability of the United Nations approach to economic and social human rights in a globalized economy. *International Affairs, 75*(3), 563–598.
Fink-Hafner, D. (1999). Dilemmas in managing the expanding EU: The EU and applicant states' point of view. *Journal of European Public Policy, 6*(5), 783–801.
Folsom, R. H., Minan, J. H., & Otto, L. A. (1992). *Law and politics in the people's republic of China.* St. Paul, Minn: West Pub. Co.
Foreign Ministry of Finland. (2003). *Preventing corruption: A handbook of anti-corruption techniques for use in international development cooperation.* Helsinki: Ministry for Foreign Affairs of Finland.
Freedom of the Press. World wide-index, see http://en.rsf.org/IMG/pdf/2013_wpfi_methodology.pdf
Frey, B. S. (2005). Flexible government for a globalized world. In R. Zimmerling (Ed.), *Globalisation and democracy,* Tampere Club Series Vol. I. Tampere: Tampere University Press.
Friedman, L. M. (1984). *American law.* New York: Norton.
Friedman, T. L. (2000). *The lexus and the olive tree.* New York: Farrar, Straus and Giroux.
Fukuyama, F. (1995). The primacy of culture. *Journal of Democracy, 6*(1), 7–14.
Fukuyama, F. (2001). Social capital, civil society and development. *Third World Quarterly, 22*(1), 7–20.
Galtung, J. (1973). *The European community: A superpower in the making.* London: Allen & Unwin.
Garcia-Sayan, D. (2002). Strengthening the rule of law in building democratic societies: Human rights in the administration of justice. *Presentation in the seminar on the interdependence between democracy and human rights* (pp. 25–26) November 2002. Geneva: Office of the High Commissioner for Human Rights.
Ghai, Y. (2001). *Human rights and social development. Towards democratization and social justice.* Geneva: United Nations Research Institute for Social Development.
Gosepath, S. (2001). The global scope of justice. *Metaphilosophy, 32*(1–2), 135–159.
Governance and Anti-corruption: Ways to enhance the World Bank's impact. Copyright IEG World Bank. July 2006, The World Bank, Washington, DC.
Grabbe, H. (2002). European Union conditionality and the Acquis communautaire. *International Political Science Review, 23*(3), 249–268.

Greenwald, G. (2014). *No place to hide: Edward snowden, The NSA and the U.S. Surveillance State*. New York: Metropolitan Books/Henry Holt.
Gunlicks, A. B. (1998). Land constitutions in Germany. *Publius: The Journal of Federalism, 28*(4), 105–125.
Habermas, J. (1998). On the internal relation between the rule of law and democracy. In *The inclusion of the other: Studies in political theory* (trans: Cronin, C.). Cambridge, MA: MIT Press.
Habermas, J. (1999). The European Nation-State and the pressures of globalization. *New Left Review, May–June 1999*, 46–59.
Habermas, J. (2001). Why Europe needs a constitution? *New Left Review, September–October 2001*, 5–26.
Hall, E. B. (1907). *Friends of voltaire*. New York: G. P. Putnam's Sons, GB.
Hallberg, P. (1998). *Fundamental rights in the constitution of Finland*. Helsinki: Publications of Ministry for Foreign Affairs.
Hallberg, P. (1999). *Perusoikeudet*. Helsinki: WSOY.
Hallberg, P. (2004). *The rule of law*. Helsinki: Edita Publishing Oy.
Hallberg, P. (2013). *Rule of law, prospects in central Asia, rural areas and human problems*. Helsinki: Edita Publishing.
Hallberg, P., & Pietarinen, P. (2001). *Yi fazhiguo ji qi jianshe* (trans: Arponen, A. and Helsinki, S.). Helsinki: Sitra.
Haller, G. (2002). *Die Grenzen der Solidarität. Europa und die USA im Umgang mit Staat, Nation und Religion*. Berlin: Aufbau-Verlag.
Harrington, J. (1656). *The commonwealth of oceana*. London: George Routledge.
Harris, P., & Reilly, B. (Eds.). (1998). *Democracy and deep-rooted conflict: options for negotiators*. Stockholm: International Institute for Democracy and Electoral Assistance.
Hart, H. L. A. (1961). *The concept of law*. Oxford: Clarendon Press.
Haubrich, D. (2003). September 11, anti-terror laws and civil liberties: Britain, France and Germany compared. *Government and Opposition, 38*(1), 3–28.
Held, D. (2000). Regulating globalization? The reinvention of politics. *International Sociology, 15*(2), 394–408.
Held, D. (2002). Law of states, law of peoples: Three models of sovereignty. *Legal Theory, 8*, 1–44.
Held, D., McGrew, A., Goldblatt, D., & Perraton, J. (1999). *Global transformations: Politics, economics and culture*. Cambridge: Polity Press.
Henderson, K. (2000). The challenges of EU eastward enlargement. *International Politics, 37*, 1–18.
Higgins, R. (2003). The ICJ, the ECJ, and the integrity of international law. *International and Comparative Law Quarterly, 52*, 1–20.
Hilson, C. (2002). New social movements: The role of legal opportunity. *Journal of European Public Policy, 9*(2), 238–255.
Hirst, P. (2002). Renewing democracy through associations. *The Political Quarterly, 73*(4), 409–421.

Hirst, P., & Thompson, G. (1999). *Globalization in question: The international economy and the possibilities of governance* (2nd ed.). Cambridge: Polity Press.

Hirst, P., & Thompson, G. (2002). The future of globalization. *Cooperation and Conflict, 37*(3), 247–266.

Hix, S. (1999). *The political system of the European Union.* Basingstoke: Macmillan.

Hobson, J. M., & Ramesh, M. (2002). Globalisation makes of states what states make of it: Between agency and structure in the state/globalisation debate. *New Political Economy, 7*(1), 5–22.

Howard, D. A. (2001a). *America after September 11.* Blacksburg: Pamplin Lecture, Virginia Tech.

Howard, D. A. (2001b). *The skewed path of the elightenment in central and Eastern Europe.* Conference on "America and the Enlightenment": Constitutionalism in the 21st Century, London.

Howard, D. A. (2002). *Another "springtime of nations"? Rights in central and Eastern Europe.* Conference on Thomas Jefferson, Rights, and the Contemporary World, Bellagio.

Howard, D. A. (1996). The indeterminacy of constitutions. *Wake Forest Law Review, 31,* 383.

Hugelier, S. Freedom of expression and transparency: Two sides of one coin. *Jura Falconis Jg. N. 47,* 2010–2011. Available at https://www.law.kuleuven.be/jura/art/47n1/hugelier.pdf

Human development report 1999. New York: Oxford University Press.

Human development report 2002: Deepening democracy in a fragmented world. New York: Oxford University Press.

International Institute for Democracy and Electoral Assistance. (2000). *Ideas for democracy 1999: Annual report.* Stockholm: International IDEA.

Israel, J. (2010). *A revolution in the mind.* Princeton: Princeton University Press.

Jacobsen, M., & Lawson, S. (1999). Between globalization and localization: A case study of human rights versus state sovereignty. *Global Governance, 5*(2), 203–219.

Jayasuriya, K. (2001). Globalization, sovereignty, and the rule of law: From political to Economic constitutionalism? *Constellations, 8*(4), 442–460.

Jellinek, G. (1905). *A general theory of the state.* St. Petersburg: O. Häring.

Jin-Guk Kim (Konyang University), Tae-Yun Kim (Hanyang University) and Junsok Yang (KIEP). *Regulatory transparency: What we learned in Korea.* Available at http://www.apeccp.org.tw/doc/APEC-OECD/2002-10/004%20paper.pdf

Joireman, S. (2001). Inherited legal systems and effective rule of law: Africa and the colonial legacy. *Journal of Modern African Studies, 39*(4), 571–596.

Jones, W. C. (2003). Trying to understand the current Chinese legal system. In S. C. Hsu (Ed.), *Understanding China's legal system. Essays in honour of Jerome A. Cohen* (pp. 7–45). New York: New York University Press.

Kagan, R. (2003). *Of paradise and power: America and Europe in the new world order.* New York: Alfred A. Knopf.

Karlekar, K. D., & Dunham, J. (2014). *Press freedom in 2013. Media freedom hits decade low*, available at https://freedomhouse.org/report/freedom-press-2014/overview-essay. Accessed 29 Aug 2016.
Kathrada, A. (2004). No Bread for Mandela: Memoirs of Ahmed Kathrada, Prisoner No. 468/64. University Press of Kentucky. Reprint edition (December 28, 2010).
Kavan, J. (1999). McCarthyism has a new name – Lustration: A personal recount of political events. In B. Wejnert (Ed.), *Transition to democracy in Eastern Europe and Russia*. Westport: Praeger.
Kelsen, H. (1960). *Reine Rechtslehre*. Wien: Deuticke.
Kelly, S., Truong, M., Earp, M., Reed, L., Shahbaz, A., & Greco-Stoner, A. (Eds.). (2013, October 3). *Freedom on the Net 2013: A global assessment of internet and digital media*. Freedom House.
Keohane, R. O. (2002). Ironies of sovereignty: The European Union and the United States. *Journal of common market studies*, 40(4), 743–765.
Kohn, M. (2002). Panacea of privilege? New approaches to democracy and association. Review Essay. *Political Theory*, 30(2), 289–298.
Krasner, S. D. (2001). Abiding sovereignty. *International Political Science Review*, 22(3), 229–251.
Krzeminski, S. (1895). *Zarysy Literackie* (published 1 May 2009). Kessinger Publishing.
Lamb, D. (2002). *The Arabs. Journeys beyond the mirage*. New York: Vintage Books.
Lichtenstein, N. G. (2003). Law in China's economic development: An essay from Afar. In S. C. Hsu (Ed.), *Understanding China's legal system. Essays in honour of Jerome A. Cohen* (pp. 274–295). New York: New York University Press.
Lippmann, W. (1920). *Liberty and the news*. New York: Hardcourt, Brace and Howe.
Loechel, J. Last updated 30 April 2013, Free speech and free press around the world, available at https://freespeechfreepress.wordpress.com/the-netherlands/, last accessed 30 Aug 2016.
Lombardini, M. (2001). The international Islamic court of justice: Towards an international Islamic legal system? *Leiden Journal of International law*, 14, 665–680.
Luck, E. C. (2002). Rediscovering the state. *Global Governance*, 8, 7–11.
Luo, H. (1997). *The core and theoretical models of administrative law* (trans: Yang Yin). Peking.
Luo, H. (2012). *Essays on human rights*.
Luo, H. (2013). *Soft law governance: Towards an integrated approach*. Buffalo: William S. Hein & Co., Inc.
MacCormick, N. (1984). Der Rechtsstaat und die rule of law. *Juristenzeitung*, 39(2), 65–70.
MacCormick, N. (1999). *Questioning sovereignty*. New York: Oxford University Press.
Mahoney, P. (2002). The charter of fundamental rights of the European Union and the European convention on human rights from the perspective of the European convention. *Human Rights Law Journal*, 23(8–12), 300–303.

Manners, I. (2002). Normative power Europe: A contradiction in terms? *Journal of Common Market Studies, 40*(2), 235–258.

Manninen, S. (2011). *Perusoikeudet.* 2. p. Toim. P. Hallberg, H. Karapuu, T. Ojanen, M. Scheinin, K. Tuori, ja V.-P. Viljanen. Helsinki.

Marcotte, R. (2003). How far have reforms gone in Islam. *Women's studies international forum, 26*(2), 153–166.

Mason, A. T., & Beaney, W. M. (1954). *American constitutional law. Introductory essays & selected cases.* New York: Prentice-Hall, Inc.

McCorquodale, Robert with Fairbrother, Richard. (1999). Globalization and human rights. *Human Rights Quarterly, 21*(3), 735–766.

McKenzie, A. B. *World press freedom review 2012–2013.* International Press Institute. Available at http://ipi.freemedia.at/fileadmin/resources/application/IPI_World_Press_Freedom_Review_2013_single_pages.pdf

Mercer, C. (2002). NGOs, civil society and democratization: A critical review of the literature. *Progress in Development Studies, 2*(1), 5–22.

Milton, John (1608–1674), first liberal opposing censorship

Miller, N. (2002). An international jurisprudence? The operation of "precedent" across international tribunals. *Leiden Journal of International law, 15,* 483–526.

Monk, L. R. (2003). *The words we live by. Your annotated guide to the constitution.* New York: Hyperion Press.

Moravcsik, A. (2001). Federalism in the European Union: Rhetoric and reality. In K. Nicolaidis & R. Howse (Eds.), *The federal vision: Legitimacy and levels of governance in the United States and the European Union.* Oxford: Oxford University Press.

Morris, J. (2003). *Africa's food crisis as a threat to peace and security.* 8 April 2003. Statement to the United Nations Security Council.

Naldi, G. (2001). Reparations in the practice of the African commission on human and peoples' rights. *Leiden Journal of International Law, 14*(3), 681–693.

Nardin, T. (2000). International pluralism and the rule of law. *Review of International Studies, 26,* 95–110.

NATO, Membership Action Plan (MAP). (1999, April 24). Press Release NAC-S(99)66. www.nato.int/docu/pr/1999/p99-066e.htm

Nicolaidis, K., & Howse, R. (2001). Introduction: The federal vision, levels of governance, and legitimacy. In K. Nicolaidis & R. Howse (Eds.), *The federal vision: Legitimacy and levels of governance in the United States and the European Union.* Oxford: Oxford University Press.

Norris, P. (2000). Global governance and cosmopolitan citizens. In J. S. Nye & J. D. Donahue (Eds.), *Governance in a globalizing world.* Washington, DC: Brookings.

Nowak, M. (1999). Human rights 'conditionality' in relation to entry to, and full participation in the EU. In P. Alston (Ed.), *The EU and human rights.* Oxford: Oxford University Press.

OECD. (1998). *Conflict, peace and development co-operation on the threshold of the 21st century*. Paris: Development Assistance Committee.
OECD. (2002). *Regulatory policies in OECD countries: From interventionism to regulatory governance*. Paris: OECD.
Oestreich, G. (1968). *Geschichte der Menschenrechte und Grundfreiheiten im Omriss*. Berlin: Duncker & Humblot.
O'Flaherty, M. (2012). Freedom of expression: Article 19 of the international covenant on civil and political rights and the human rights committee's general comment No 34. *Human Rights and Law Review, 12*(4), 627–654.
Orwell, G. (1949). *Nineteen eighty-four*. New York: Harcourt, Brace and Co.
Owens, J., Ph.D. (December 1998). *Socrates, freedom of Speech and hate crime* p. 3., available at http://www.solargeneral.org/wp-content/uploads/library/Free-Speech/socrates-freedom-of-speech-and-hate-crime.pdf. Accessed 27 May 2016.
Paine, T. (2005). *Keystones of democracy*. New York: Barnes and Noble.
Peaslee, A. J. (1956). *Constitutions of nations* (2nd ed., Vol. I–III). The Hague: Springer.
Peerenboom, R. (2002). *China's long march toward rule of law*. Cambridge: Cambridge University Press.
Peers, S. (2003). EU responses to terrorism. *International & Comparative Law Quarterly, 52*(1), 227–243.
Pellonpää, M. (2012). Some thoughts of the principle of subsidiarity and margin of appreciation in the context of freedom of expression. In *Freedom of Expression: Essays in Honour of Nicolas Bratza* (pp. 519–540). Oisterwijk: Wolf Legal Publishers.
Petersmann, E. U. (2002). Time for a United Nations 'Global Compact' for integrating human rights into the law of worldwide organizations: Lessons from European integration. *European Journal of International Law, 13*(3), 621–650.
Petrova, D. (2002). Strengthening the rule of law in building democratic societies: Human rights in the administration of justice. *Presentation in the seminar on the interdependence between democracy and human rights*, 25–26 Nov 2002. Geneva: Office of the High Commissioner for Human Rights.
Pharr, S. J., Putnam, R. D., & Dalton, R. J. (2000). Troble in the advanced democracies? A quarter-century of declining confidence. *Journal of Democracy, 11*.
Plato. *Laws* (VI, published around 350 a.d.), first book, translated in Finnish 1999, Otava. pp. 7– and 385–.
Plato. *Teokset VI*, published in Finnish 1999.
Preston, C. (1995). Obstacles to EU enlargement: The classical community method and the prospects for a Wider Europe. *Journal of Common Market Studies, 33*(3), 451–463.
Pridham, G., & Vanhanen, T. (Eds.). (1994). *Democratization in Eastern Europe: Domestic and international perspectives*. London: Routledge.

Pridham, G., Sanford, G., & Herring, E. (Eds.). (1994). *Building democracy: The international dimension of democratisation in Eastern Europe*. London: Leicester U.P.

Putnam, R. (1993). *Making democracy work. Civic traditions in bertmodern Italy*. Princeton: Princeton University Press.

Putnam, R. (1995). Bowling alone: America's declining social capital. *Journal of Democracy*, 6(1), 65–78.

Rawls, J. (1971). *A theory of justice*. Cambridge, MA: Belknap Press of Harvard University Press.

Rawls, J. (1999). *The law of peoples: With "The idea of public reason revisited"*. Cambridge, MA: Harvard University Press.

Reisinger, W. M. (1999). Legal orientations in post-soviet Russia. In S. J. Kenney, W. M. Reisinger, & J. C. Reitz (Eds.), *Constitutional dialogues in comparative perspective*. New York: St. Martin's Press.

Report of the International Law Commission on its 52. Session, UN. Doc. A/55/10.

Report of the Panel on United Nations Peace Operations (2000). United Nations, General Assembly – Security Council. A/55/305-S/2000/809.

Report of the World Summit on Sustainable Development (2002). Johannesburg, and Johannesburg Declaration on Sustainable Development. A/CONF.199/20.

Riker, W. H. (1987). *The development of American federalism*. Norwell, MA: Kluwer, cop.

Rodrigez, G., & Maria, J. (2001). Scientia Potestas Est – Knowledge in Power: Francis Bacon to Michel Foucoult. *J.M. Neohelicon*, 28, 109.

Romashkin, P. S. (Ed.). (1960). *Fundamentals of soviet law*. Moscow: Foreign Languages Pub. House.

Rose, R., & Haerpfer, C. (1995). Democracy and enlarging the European Union eastwards. *Journal of Common Market Studies*, 33(3), 427–450.

Rosen, L. (2000). *The justice of Islam: Comparative perspectives on Islamic Law and Society*. Oxford: Oxford University Press.

Ross, A. (1966). *Om ret og retfaerdighet. En indforelse i den analytiske retsfilosofi*. 2. oplag. Kobenhavn.

Roth, K. (2002). Misplaced priorities. Human rights and the campaign against terrorism. *Harvard International Review, Fall, 2002*, 14–19.

Sajo, A. (1995). On old and New battles: Obstacles to the rule of law in Eastern Europe. *Journal of Law and Society*, 22(1), 97–104.

Sanders, K. (2003). *Ethics and journalism*. Universidad de Navarra. London: Sage Publications.

Sassen, S. (2000). Territory and territoriality in the global economy. *International Sociology*, 15(2), 372–393.

Schabas, W. A. (2001). *An introduction to the International Criminal Court*. Cambridge: Cambridge U. P.

Scheuerman, W. E. (1999). Economic globalization and the rule of law. *Constellations*, 6(1), 3–25.

Schimmelfennig, F. (2002). Liberal community and enlargement: An event history analysis. *Journal of European Public Policy*, 9(4), 598–626.

Scholte, J. A. (2002). Civil society and democracy in global governance. *Global Governance*, 8(3), 281–304.

Schuhmann, J. Legal education and judicial reform in Central Asia – perspectives and reality. In *Law in transition 2011: Towards better courts*. European Bank for Reconstruction and Development.

Schultz, D. A. (2010). *Encyclopedia of the United States constitution*. New York: Infobase Publishing.

Schwellnus, G. (2001). "Much ado about nothing?" Minority protection and the EU charter of fundamental rights. *Constitutionalism Web-Papers*, ConWEB no. 5/2001. http://les1.man.ac.uk/conweb/

Sigler, J. A. (1970). *Courts and public policy. Cases and essays*. Homewood/Illinois: Dorsey Press.

Smith, J. M. (Ed.). (1995). *The republic of letters: The correspondence between Thomas Jefferson and James Madison, 1776–1826*. New York: Norton.

Smith, D. (2002). Europe's peacebuilding hour? Past failures, future challenges. *Journal of International Affairs*, 55(2), 441–460.

Spence, T. World association of newspapers and news publishers in November 2013.

Ståhlberg K. J. (1931). *Suomen hallinto-oikeus, Sisäasiain hallinto* (p. 180–). Finland: Otava.

Stuermer, M. (2008). *Putin and the rise of Russia*. New York: Pegasus Book.

Swaine, E. T. (2000). Subsidiarity and self-interest: Federalism at the European court of justice. *Harvard International Law Journal*, 41(1), 1–128.

Terriff, T., Croft, S., Krahmann, E., Webber, M., & Howorth, J. (2002). 'One in, all in?' NAT's next enlargement. *International affairs*, 78(4), 713–729.

Teubner, G. (2002). Breaking frames. Economic globalization and the emergence of Lex Mercatoria. *European Journal of Social Theory*, 5(2), 199–217.

The Commission on Global Governance. (1995). *Our global neighbourhood: The report of the commission on global governance*. Oxford: Oxford University Press.

The Dutch Advisory Council for Government Policy. (2002). The future of the national constitutional state. www.wrr.nl/en/frameset.htm

The Experiences of Local Actors in Peace-Building. (2002). *Reconstruction and the establishment of rule of law*, March 23–25, Singapore. Program Chair, Gareth Evans.

Thembu, E., & Majola, V. (2015). *Press freedom in post-apartheid South Africa*. Hamburg: Anchor Academic Publishing.

Therborn, G. (2000). Globalizations. dimensions, historical waves, regional effects, normative governance. *International Sociology*, 15(2), 151–179.

Thompson, G. (1999). Introduction: Situating globalization. *International Social Science Journal, 160,* 139–152.
Tuori, K. (1991). Four models of the Rechtsstaat. In *The finnish constitution in transition.* Helsinki: The Finnish Society of Constitutional Law.
Tuori, K. (2002). The 'Rechsstaat' in the conceptual field – adversaries, allies and neutrals. *Associations, 6*(2), 201–213.
United Nations – General Assembly. (2000). Globalization and its impact on the full enjoyment of all human rights. Preliminary report of the Secretary-General. A/55/342.
United Nations – General Assembly/Security Council. (2002). Report of the policy working group on the United Nations and terrorism. A/57/273-S/2002/875.
United Nations. (2003). Economic and Social Council, E/CN.4/2003/59, 27 January 2003. *Civil and political rights.* Continuing dialogue on measures to promote and consolidate democracy. Report of the High Commissioner for Human Rights submitted in accordance with Commission resolution 2001/41. Seminar on the interdependence between democracy and human rights, 25–26 Nov 2002. Chairperson's conclusions. Office of the High Commissioner for Human Rights, Geneva.
United Nations Peace-Building. Establishing rule of law: Recommendations from the field. The United Nations Association of the United States of America and the Project on Justice in Times of Transition of Harvard University. *A policy report of the partnership program on peace-building and rule of law* (2003). Harvard University.
University of Maryland. (2002). Polity IV, political regime characteristics and transitions, 1800–2000. http://www.cidcm.umd.edu/inscr/polity/
Vachudova, Milada A. (2001). The leverage of international institutions on democratizing states: Eastern Europe and the European Union. *European University Institute Working Papers,* RSC no 2001/33.
Vartiainen, E. (2007). Publishing Saima: J.V. Snellman and his influence on finnish nationalism between the years 1844–1846. Providence College.
Väyrynen, R. (2001). Sovereignty, globalization and transnational social movements. In *International relations of the Asia-Pacific* (Vol. 1/2001, pp. 227–246). Oxford: Oxford University Press.
Vermeersch, P. (2002). Ethnic mobilisation and the political conditionality of European Union accession: The case of the Roma in Slovakia. *Journal of Ethnic and Migration Studies, 28*(1), 83–101.
Vidal, G. (2003). *Inventing a nation: Washington, Adams, Jefferson.* New Haven: Yale University Press.
Vihavainen, T., & Ketola, K. (2014). *Changing Russia?: History, culture, business.* Helsinki: Finemor.
Villstrand, Nils Erik. (2009). *Riksdelen.* Helsingfors: Svenska Litteratursällskapet.
Von Wright, Georg Henrik. (1983). *Philosophical writings,* book-series, Part I: Practical Reason, and Part II: *Philosophical logic.*
Vyshinsky, A. Y. (1948). *The law of the soviet state.* New York: Macmillan.

Wade, H. W. R. (1967): Administrative law. 2nd nd. edition. Oxford.Oxford University Press.
Wallerstein, I. (2000). Globalization or the age of transition? A long-term view of the trajectory of the world-system. *International Sociology, 15*(2), 249–265.
Warleigh, A. (2000). The hustle: Citizenship practice, NGOs and 'policy coalitions' in the European Union – the cases of auto oil, drinking water and unit pricing. *Journal of European Public Policy, 7*(2), 229–243.
Weiler, J. H. H. (2000). Federalism and constitutionalism: Europe's Sonderweg. *The Jean Monnet Working Papers*, 10/00, NYU School of Law.
Weiler, J. H. H. (2001a). Human rights, constitutionalism and integration: Iconography and fetishism. *International Law FORUM, 3*(2001), 227–238.
Weiler, J. H. H. (2001b). The rule of lawyers and the ethos of diplomats: Reflections on the internal and external legitimacy of WTO dispute settlement. *Journal of World Trade, 35*(2), 191–207.
Weiler, J. H. H. (2001c). Federalism without constitutionalism: Europe's Sonderweg. In K. Nicolaidis & R. Howse (Eds.), *The federal vision*. Published in print November 2001, published online November 2003.
Weiler, J. H. H. (2002). A constitution for Europe? Some hard choices. *Journal of Common Market Studies, 40*(4), 563–580.
Wiener, A. (2002). Finality vs. Enlargement – Constitutive practices and opposing rationales in the reconstruction of Europe. *The Jean Monnet Working Papers*, 8/02, NYU School of Law.
Wohlin, S. S. (2001). Tocqueville between two worlds. Princeton: Princeton University Press.
Woodiwiss, A. (2002). Human rights and the challenge of cosmopolitanism. *Theory, Culture & Society, 19*(1–2), 139–155.
World Bank. (1997). *World development report 1997: The state in a changing world*. New York: Oxford University Press.
World Commission on the Social Dimension of Globalization. (2004). *A fair globalization: Creating opportunities for all*. Geneva: ILO.
World Public Sector Report. (2001). *Globalization and the State*. New York: United Nations, Department Of Economic And Social Affairs.
World Values Survey. (2000). Joseph S. Nye – John D. Donahue. *Governance in a globalizing world*. Washington: Brookings.
Young, E. A. (2002a). Protecting member state autonomy in the European Union: Some cautionary tales from American federalism. *New York University Law Review, 77*(6), 1612–1737.
Zakaria, F. (2003). *The future of freedom*. New York: W.W. Norton & Co.
Zepeda Paterson, J. (2015, March 4). *House of Cards' a la Mexicana, Los esfuerzos de Peña Nieto para hacer frente a la corrupción son tibios y desangelados*. Published in El País (Madrid).
Zimmenrling, R. (2003). Globalization and democracy: A framework for discussion. *2nd Annual Meeting of Tampere Club*, 18–20 Aug 2003.

450-year-old Judicial Instructions – "The good of the common man is the supreme law". Helsinki: Ministry of Justice.

Personalia

Abbott, Tony, Prime Minister of Australia
Alaniz, Rogelio, Argentinian researcher and columnist
Alexander VI, pope, ratified the 1501 law on unauthorised books
Aliev, President of Azerbaijan
al-Sisi, Abdul Fattah, President of Egypt 2014–
Aumran, Malath, young Syrian rebel
Aznar, José Maria, Spanish Prime Minister
Bach, Johann Sebastian, among the best-known composers in the world
Bachelet, President of Chile
Bacon, Francis (1561–1626), catchphrase for freedom of speech: "knowledge is power"
Baglay, Marat, former President of the Russian Counstitutional Court
Baheer, Mohamed, local producer of al Jazeera
Bakiyev, Kurmanbek, former President of Kyrgyzstan
Balbay, Mustafa, Turkish journalist
Balkin, Jack.M., analyst of digital development in the United States
Barclay, Frederick and David, owners of the *Daily Telegraph*
Baquet, Dean, Chief Editor of the *New York Times*
Beckerman, Michael, President of the Internet Association (Facebook, Google etc.)
Berlusconi, Silvio, former Italian Prime Minister and media mogul
Bettencourt, Liliane, reporter at the French *Le Monde*
Blackstone, Sir William, writer of famous *Commentaries on the Laws of England*
Blitzer, Wolf, a marketing manager for Google
Bonamour, Andrew, chief of South African media group
Bond, James, number one fiction hero
Bourdieu, Pierre, French sociologist
Bruno, Giordano, author of the Enlightenment period
Caesar, Julius, Emperor of Rome
Cameron, David, former UK Prime Minister
Caroline, Princess of Monaco
Castells, Manuel, a guru of the modern information society
Catherine the Great, ruler of Russia during the Enlightenment
Cháves, Hugo, President of Venezuela (1999–2013)
Chirac, Jacques, former President of France
Church, Frank, US senator

Chydenius, Anders, a Finnish representative of the Assembly of the Estates during the Enlightenment period, championed the first Freedom of the Press Act in 1766
Cicero, executed for his speeches in Rome during Caesar's reign
Davutoglu, Ahmet, Turkish Prime Minister
Descartes, René, artist of the Enlightenment period
De Tocqueville, Alexis, author of the famous *Democracy in America* (1835–1840)
Dicey, A.V., developer of the British rule of law doctrine
Diderot, Denis, Enlightenment philosopher
Douglass, Frederick, plantation slave in the United States in the 1800s
Durham, Jennifer, Freedom House reporter
El Baradei, Mohamed, the best-known opposition leader of Egypt
Elbegdorj, Tsakhiagiin, President of Mongolia
Ellis, Joseph, American historian of the revolutionary period
Enkhbold, Spokesman of the Parliament of Mongolia
Erbey, Muharrem, a Kurdish writer
Erdoğan, Recep Tayyip, Turkish President 2014-
Fahmy, Mohamed, reporter of al Jazeera
Forsskål, Peter, researcher of economic liberalism, *Thoughts on Civil Liberties* (1759)
Friedrich the Great, a ruler of the German empire
Galilei, Galileo, astronomer, physicist, engineer, philosopher and mathematician, who changed the view of the world, sentenced to death for heresy
Genghis Khan, founder of the Mongol state
Gorbachev, Mikhail, First Secretary of the Communist Party of the Soviet Union 1985–1991
Greenwald, Glenn, reporter of the Snowden case
Günersel, Tarik, president of PEN Turkey
Gutenberg, introduced printing to Europe 1436
Guül, Abdullah, former President of Turkey
Guülen, Fethullah, leader of Turkish Hizmet movement, lives in United States
Haller, Gret, OSCE Human Rights Ombudsperson for Bosnia and Herzegovina 1996–2000
Harrington, first presenters of separation of powers doctrine in the Oceana publication in 1656
Helvetius, Claude Adrian, Enlightenment philosopher
Hernandez, Octavio Rojas, Mexican reporter, murdered 2014
Hlebnikov, Paul, Russian reporter, murdered 2003
Hodorkovski, Mihail, Russian businessman, prosecuted in court
Hollande, François, President of France
Howard, Phillip, Professor of Communication, Washington University
Hughes, Charles Evans, former President of the US Supreme Court

Hume, David (1711–1776), Scottish philosopher, known for radical philosophical empiricism and scepticism.
Hume, Mick, English polemicist
Issoufou, Mahamadou, President of Niger
Ivan IV (1533–1584), commonly known as Ivan the Terrible in Russia
Jakobson, Max, Finnish diplomat and journalist
Jefferson, Thomas, American Founding Father, principal author of Declaration of Independence, President of the United States
Johnson-Sirleaf, Ellen, nobelist, signed the Declaration of Table Mountain
Kant, Immanuel, German philosopher and rule of law cultivator
Kathrada, Ahmed, cellmate of Nelson Mandela
Keita, Ibrahim, President of Mali
Kelsen, Hans, the best-known justice philosopher of Austria in 1800s
Kerry, John, US senator
Khrushchev, Nikita, First Secretary of the Communist Party of the Soviet Union
King Abdullah, former king of Saudi Arabia
King Charles XI, king of Sweden in 1600s
King John, signed Magna Carta in 1215
King, Martin Luther, human rights fighter
Kirchner, Christina, President of Argentina
Kirchner, Nestor, former President of Argentina
Krzeminski, Stanislaw, Polish thinker
Kungfutze, a great champion of Chinese ethics (500 BCE)
Kyi, Aung San Suu, President of Myanmar
Lenin, Iljits, Russian revolutionary leader, 1917
Lippman, Walter, American writer, reporter, political commentator, among the first to introduce the concept of Cold War
Loccatelli, Giovanna, freelance Italian journalist
Locke, John, first British Enlightenment philosopher (1632–1704)
Lord McGregor of Durris, Chair, Press Complaints' Commission
Lukashenko, Aleksandr, president of Belarus
Luo, Haocai, Chinese judge and researcher
Machado, Maria Carina, Member of Parliament in Venezuela
Maduro, Nicholás, President of Venezuela
Mandela, Nelson, consensus builder in South Africa and the President, imprisoned for 27 years, died in 2015
Mansour, Adly, former interim president of Egypt
McKenzie, Alison Bethel, IPI director until2014
Montesquieu (1669–1755), an introducer of the separation of powers doctrine
Morsi, Mohammed, former President of Egypt
Mousavi, Hossein, Iranian opposition politician
Mubarak, Hosni, former President of Egypt
Nakschot, Gregorius, cartoonist in Netherlands

Nemtsov, Boris, Russian opposition politician, murdered 2015
Nieto, Enrique Pena, President of Mexico
Nisman, Alberto, Argentinian prosecutor, died in suspicious circumstances 2015
Nordenskiöld, A. E., Finnish explorer in the 1800s
Obama, Barack, President of the United States 2008–2016
Oborne, Peter, reporter, *Daily Telegraph*
O'Connor, Sandra Day, first female member of the US Supreme Court
O'Flaherty, Michael, UN HRC member
Orban, Viktor, Prime Minister of Hungary
Orwell, George (Eric Blair 1903–1950), author of the prophetic *Nineteen Eighty-Four*
Özkan, Tuncay, Turkish journalist
Paine, Thomas (1737–1809), British author of the Enlightenment period
Pericles, statesman of Ancient Greece
Persson, Johan, Swedish reporter
Pillay, Navi, the UN High Commissioner for Human Rights
Plato, Ancient philosopher
Poitras, Laura, reporter, known for reporting the Snowden case
Politkovskaja, Anna, Russian reporter, murdered 2004
Pushkin, Alexander (1799–1837), Russian poet
Putin, Vladimir, President of Russia for the third time 2014–
Qu, Yan, famous Chinese poet
Ramstedt, G.J., Finnish linguist, diplomat and explorer
Robinson, Mary, former President of Ireland
Rousseau, Jean-Jacques (1712–1778), Enlightenment philosopher
Rousseff, Dilma, President of Brazil
Rushbridger, Alan, Chief editor of the *Guardian*
Rushdie, Salman, a persecuted author
Sagan, Carl, author, astronomer, cosmologist, astrophysicist, astrobiologist
Sarkozy, Nicolas, former President of France
Schibbye, Martin, Swedish reporter
Schuman, Robert, architect of European co-operation in the 1950s
Sener, Nedim, Turkish reporter, in prison
Shafiq, Ahmed, the former air force commander of Egypt
Smith, Adam, pioneer of economic liberalism in the 1700s
Smith, Hanna, Finnish researcher
Smith, Winston, protagonist of the Orwellian prophecy
Snellman, J.V., national philosopher of Finland in 1800s
Snowden, Edward, former NSA contractor
Socrates, Ancient Greek philosopher, executed 399 BCE
Solzhenitsyn, Aleksandr, Russian author
Spence, Timothy, senior press freedom advisor, IPI

Spinoza, Baruch, philosopher of the Enlightenment period
Ståhlberg, K.J., the first President of Finland 1919–1925
Stalin, Josef, long-term Russian dictator
Stuermer, Michael, German columnist
Sturenseen, Johann Friedrich, Prime Minister of Denmark-Norway in the 1770s
Survé, Igbal, chairman of Sekunjalo Holdings, a black peoples'consortium
Taubira, Christiane, former Minister of Justice of France
Thucydides, Ancient Greek author
Trionfi, Barbara, chair of IPI 2015–
Twyn, William, executed for opposing the English government in the eighteenth century
Underwood, Frank, President of the United States in the TV show, *House of Cards*
van der Graaf, Jolande, Dutch journalist
Vargas, Estado Novo, former dictator of Brazil
Voltaire, author and philosopher of the 1700s Enlightenment period
von Bismarck, Otto, Chancellor, primarily responsible for the unification of Germany
Wright, Georg Henrik, among the best known Finnish philosophers
Wulff, Christian, chairman of the German Bild
Xi, Jinping, President of China 2013–
Zapeda, Jorge, Argentinian columnist
Zuckerberg, Mark, chairman and chief executive of Facebook, Inc.
Zumra, Jacob, President of South Africa

Index[1]

A

access to information, viii, 2, 5, 10–12, 34, 40, 49, 54, 56, 59, 71, 81, 83, 92, 105, 119, 123, 125, 128, 129, 143, 170–1, 182, 198, 219, 226, 248, 253, 254n11

access to justice, 41, 44, 50, 53–6, 210, 245, 247, 248

accountable government, 55, 143

African Media Barometer (AMB), 127–9

Arab Spring, v, 6, 27, 28, 33, 126, 127, 139, 181, 236, 240–7, 256

Associated Press, 37

B

Big Brother, 13, 259

C

censorship, vii, 7, 10, 16, 29, 33, 34, 36, 65, 80, 82, 84, 86, 87, 89–91, 103, 104, 107, 113, 119–24, 130, 139, 142, 144, 146, 148, 149, 176, 192, 194, 197, 199, 201, 212, 215, 236, 237, 245, 255, 260

Charlie Hebdo, v, 6, 191–4, 200, 203

Charter of Fundamental Rights of the European Union (CFR), 173, 174

Committee to Protect Journalists (CPJ), 3, 16, 196, 197

Commonwealth Press Union (CPU), 3, 16

Confucianism, 137

constitution, 47, 69–73, 81–3, 85–9, 91–4, 96, 97, 100, 101, 104, 107, 110–12, 117, 118, 121–4, 127, 128, 132, 134, 137, 138, 140–50, 176, 204, 207, 214, 217, 240, 243–5

corruption, vi, viii, 11, 12, 23, 28, 32, 35, 48, 54, 56–8, 70, 71, 91, 94, 97, 98, 105, 120, 125, 130, 131, 133, 141–4, 172, 196, 207–11, 214, 236, 242

Corruption perceptions index (CPI), 57n15, 208, 209

[1] Note: Page numbers followed by "n" refers to notes.

D

database(s), 58, 139
Declaration of Table Mountain, 28–31
Declaration of the Rights of Man and of the Citizen, 72, 90, 153n16
de facto, 11, 98, 164, 178
defamation, 28–30, 32, 34–7, 67, 85, 89, 90, 94, 106, 110, 124, 128, 129, 134, 142, 146–9, 162, 164, 172, 181, 184, 196, 197, 217
de jure, 10, 164, 178
demonstration, v, vii, 6, 106, 108, 131, 138–40, 143, 146, 148, 177, 212, 216, 241, 245
digitalisation, vii, 12, 194, 251

E

ECHR. *See* European Convention on Human Rights (ECHR)
ECtHR. *See* European Court of Human Rights (ECtHR)
enlightenment, vi, 2, 9, 10, 14n1, 40, 45, 65–9, 76n9, 102, 192, 260
EU. *See* European Union (EU)
European Convention on Human Rights (ECHR), vi, 4, 54, 90, 96, 100, 159–71, 174, 175, 177, 217, 218
European Court of Human Rights (ECtHR), viii, ix, 4, 90, 91, 160–2, 165, 166, 171, 174, 182, 197, 217
European Court of Justice (ECJ), 45, 177
European Economic Community (EEC), 173
European Union (EU), viii, 4, 32, 34–6, 45, 47, 53, 84, 87, 90, 92, 101, 145, 172–8, 186, 208, 215, 216

F

Facebook, 7, 9, 13, 93, 98, 112, 116, 136, 202, 203, 213, 217, 219, 235, 236, 247, 250
Freedom House (FH), 3, 11, 15, 23, 24, 28, 37, 38, 41, 84, 92–4, 117, 119, 130, 132

G

Google, 116, 135, 136, 176, 202, 203, 206, 236
guarantee, v, ix, 1–5, 16, 28, 30, 33, 38, 45, 48, 64, 70–3, 81, 82, 90, 91, 93, 97, 98, 101, 110, 118, 123, 128, 133, 134, 137, 142, 144–7, 149, 160, 162–5, 169, 182, 195, 198, 199, 202, 210, 211, 217, 225, 232, 245, 247, 248, 261n1

H

Hague Institute for Innovation of Law (HiiL), 53

I

independent judiciary, 54, 56, 58, 109, 249
indicators, 2, 3, 11, 53, 55–8, 141, 143, 144, 182, 185, 198, 256
indices, 12, 15–18, 23–5, 27, 36, 37, 59, 70, 127, 134, 208
information war, v, 12, 102, 257
Inter American Press Association (IAPA), 3, 16
International Court of Justice (ICJ), 232
International Covenant on Civil and Political Rights (ICCPR), vi, 4, 159, 178–82, 190n11, 218

International Covenant on Economic, Social and Cultural Rights (ESC Covenant), 178, 188
International Criminal Court (ICC), 232, 233
International Institute for Democracy and Electoral Assistance (IDEA), 126, 127
International Press Institute (IPI), vi, 3, 7, 16, 31–8, 105, 106, 195, 196
internet, vii, ix, 9, 12, 13, 31, 33, 34, 41, 98, 100, 103, 106, 110–12, 115–17, 120, 129, 135, 136, 139, 140, 163, 176, 177, 181, 189n3, 195, 201–3, 205, 206, 212, 213, 216–19, 223, 229, 230, 234–8, 240, 247, 248, 251, 257, 260

J
Jenny and Antti Wihuri Foundation, ix

L
legislation, 5, 29, 33, 36, 37, 42–5, 59, 70, 73, 82, 84, 89, 95, 111, 119, 120, 123, 129, 135–7, 142–4, 150, 151, 164, 170, 172, 180, 197, 213, 225, 226, 231, 233, 244, 246, 249, 251, 254n11
lèse-majesté, 34, 149, 196, 197
libel, 34, 62, 67, 95, 96, 119, 124, 145, 148, 172

M
Magna Carta, 10, 72, 93
monitoring, vi, 4, 12, 18, 33, 53, 55, 88, 113, 127, 144, 159, 160, 162–9, 173, 181, 182, 231

N
National Security Agency (NSA), 11, 37, 151, 202–4
Nineteen Eighty-Four (Orwell), 13, 259
NSA. *See* National Security Agency (NSA)

O
Oceania, 13, 14, 46, 238

P
Palgrave MacMillan, ix, xn3
Press Freedom Index, vi, viii, 11, 19, 27, 45, 70, 87, 96, 110, 124, 134, 136, 216
protest, 65, 76, 86, 87, 99, 106, 115, 121, 126, 131, 147, 155n52, 194, 207, 212, 213, 216–19, 224, 235, 236, 240, 241, 243
publicity, 47, 69–71, 74, 79, 80, 82, 83, 119, 133, 210, 211, 229, 248, 251–3

R
Renaissance, 64, 65, 192
Reporters Without Borders (RSF), 3, 11, 15–27, 45, 84, 87, 96, 110, 124, 134, 137, 157n72
RSF. *See* Reporters Without Borders (RSF)
rule of law, vii, ix, 2, 3, 5–7, 15, 27, 28, 34, 38–45, 49–53, 55, 56, 58, 59, 60n19, 64, 72, 75, 82, 87, 88, 93, 97, 101, 104, 108, 109, 125, 135, 138, 141–5, 156n62, 160, 168, 172, 173, 185–7, 193, 197, 205, 207, 210, 216, 225–8, 232, 233, 237, 244–7, 249, 253, 256, 258, 260
Rule of Law Finland–ROLFI, ix

S

safeguard, 5, 12, 16, 45, 48, 59, 69, 72–4, 82, 83, 91, 93, 96, 148, 246
Sanoma Company, ix
security, 11, 17, 27, 32, 33, 36, 37, 39, 41, 45, 51, 56–8, 68, 82, 91, 108, 110, 111, 113–15, 122, 129, 131, 132, 134–7, 145–8, 150, 151, 157n69, 161, 170, 172, 181, 183–6, 196, 197, 201–7, 224, 230, 237, 243, 246
separation of powers, 3, 42, 45–8, 65, 68, 75, 89, 93, 104, 140, 204
smartphone, 135, 195, 238–40, 251
social capital, viii, 5, 51–3, 60n15, 97, 259
sources, vii, 4, 9, 23, 35, 37, 55–7, 74, 95, 106, 114, 119, 123, 124, 128, 144, 150, 153n21, 161, 171, 177, 216, 225, 236, 258
surveillance, vii, 7, 9, 11, 13, 31, 34, 37, 41, 94, 113, 135, 136, 177, 202–7, 237, 238, 247, 256–8, 260
Swedish Freedom of the Press Act of 1766, 5, 68, 69

T

terrorist, v, 6, 31, 57, 94, 96, 101, 110, 134, 191–4, 203, 246
transparency, 1, 6, 11, 12, 18, 35, 44, 51, 55, 57, 60n12, 71, 83, 103, 114, 141, 152, 172, 198, 202, 205–10, 231
Transparency International, 12, 57, 207–9
Twitter, 7, 9, 13, 93, 98, 213, 217–19, 235, 236, 240, 247

U

UN Convention Against Corruption (UNCAC), 210
UNESCO. *See* United Nations Educational, Scientific and Cultural Organization (UNESCO)
United Nations (UN), vi, 3, 11, 30, 32, 56, 109, 142, 145, 146, 151, 159, 178–85, 187, 188, 200, 210, 228, 258
United Nations Declaration of Human Rights (UNDHR), 3
United Nations Educational, Scientific and Cultural Organization (UNESCO), 11, 30, 179, 257, 258
United Nations Human Rights Committee (UNHRC), 151
United Nations Millennium Development Goals (UNMDG), 30
United Nations Universal Declaration of Human Rights, 159

W

WAN. *See* World Association of Newspapers (WAN)
whistleblower, 37, 237
Wikileaks, 115, 150, 246
World Association of Newspapers (WAN), 3, 16, 28, 30, 31, 59n6
World Bank, 12, 55, 57, 143, 144, 185, 186, 208, 209, 227, 258
World Bank Governance and Anti-corruption Strategy, 12
World Economic Forum, 56, 70
World Press Freedom Committee (WPFC), 3, 16